NO.6 #1

Story by: Atsuko Asano
Art by: Hinoki Kino

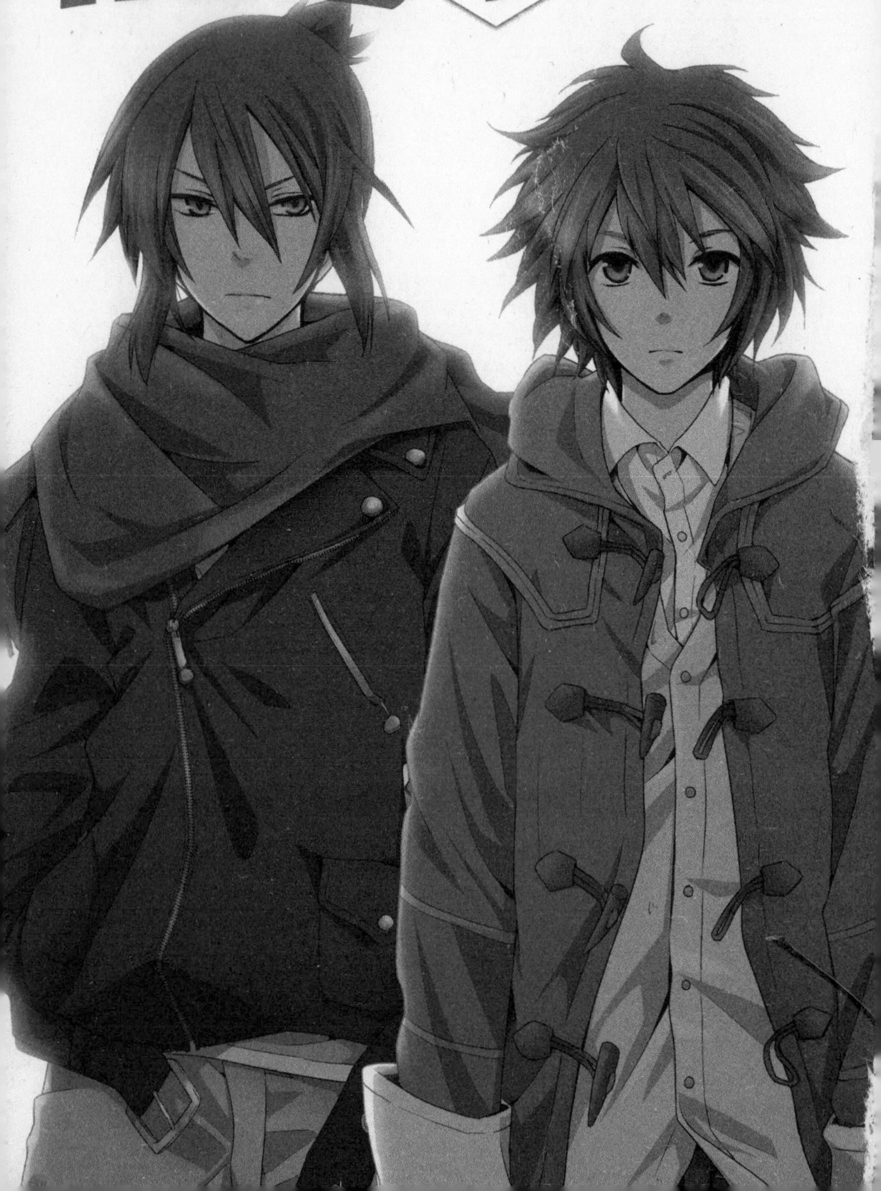

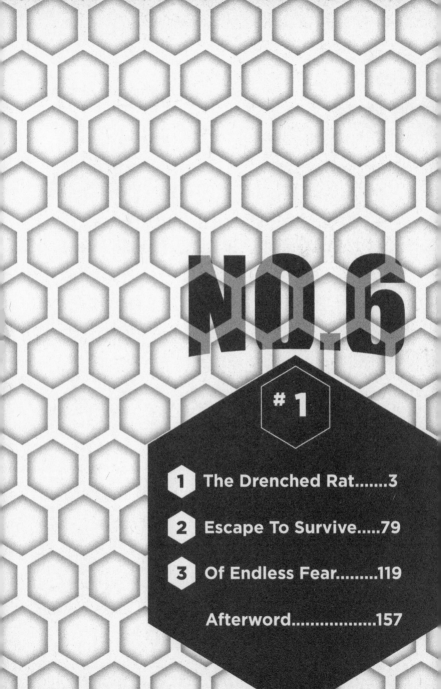

NO.6

1

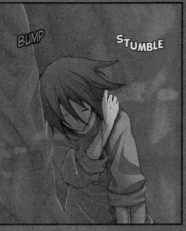

BUMP   S⊤UMBLE

DRIP

DRIP

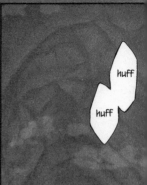

huff

huff

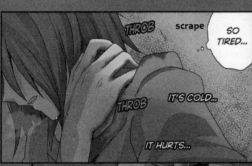

THROB   scrape

SO TIRED...

THROB   IT'S COLD...

IT HURTS...

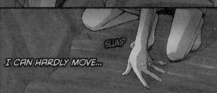

SLUMP

I CAN HARDLY MOVE...

huff

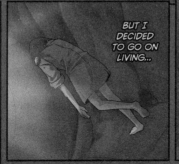

BUT I DECIDED TO GO ON LIVING...

SO I'VE GOT TO KEEP GOING.

NO.6

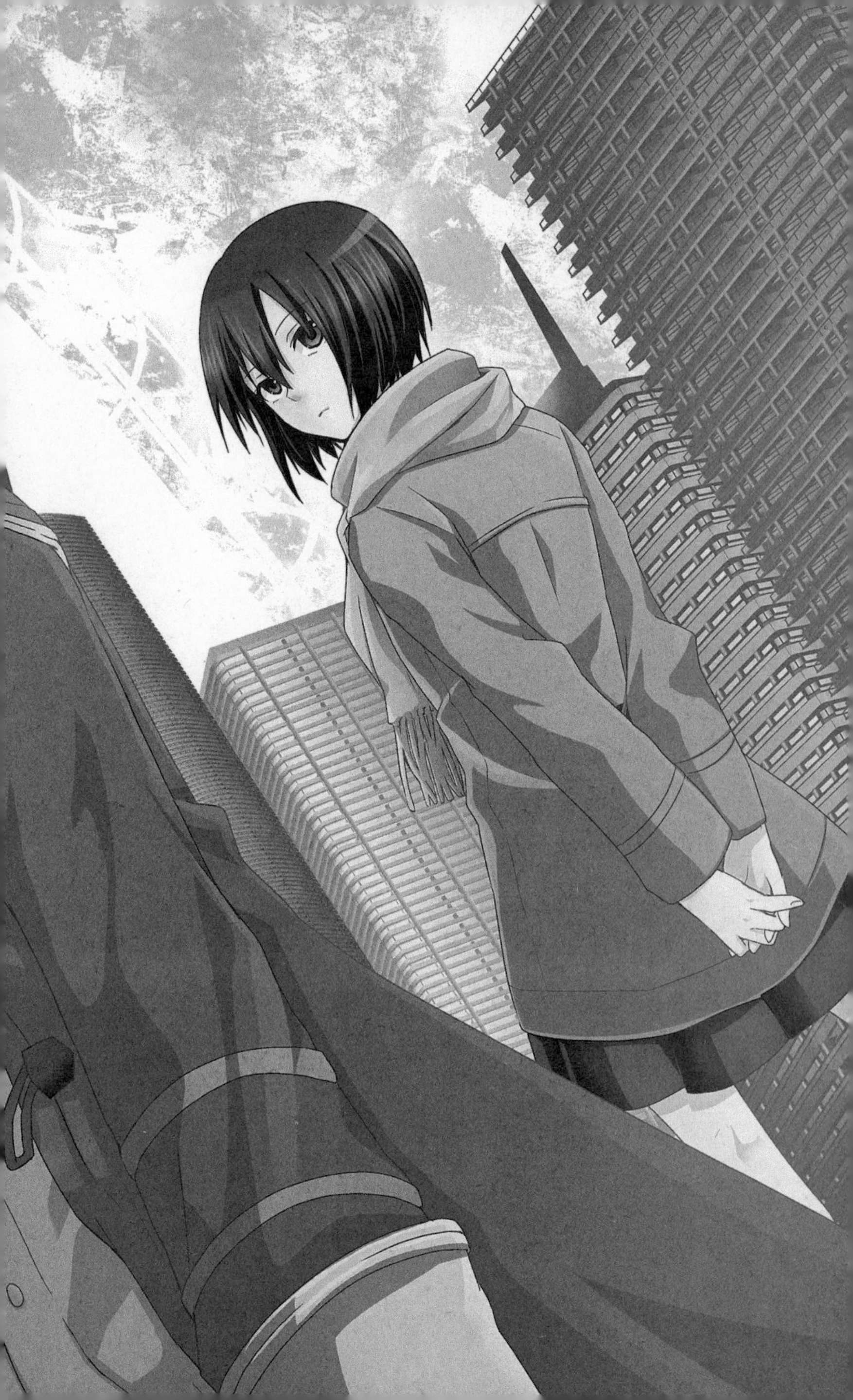

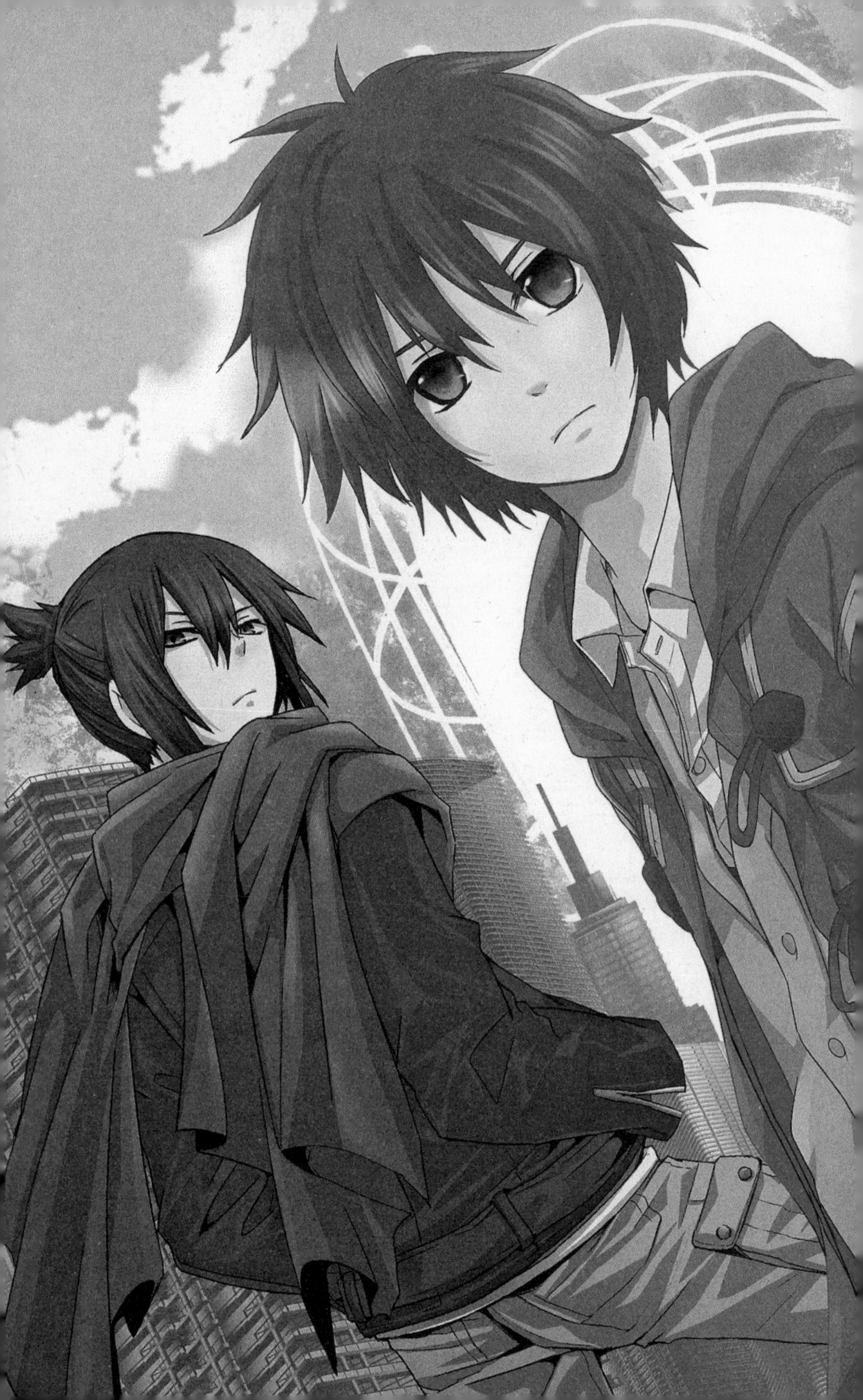

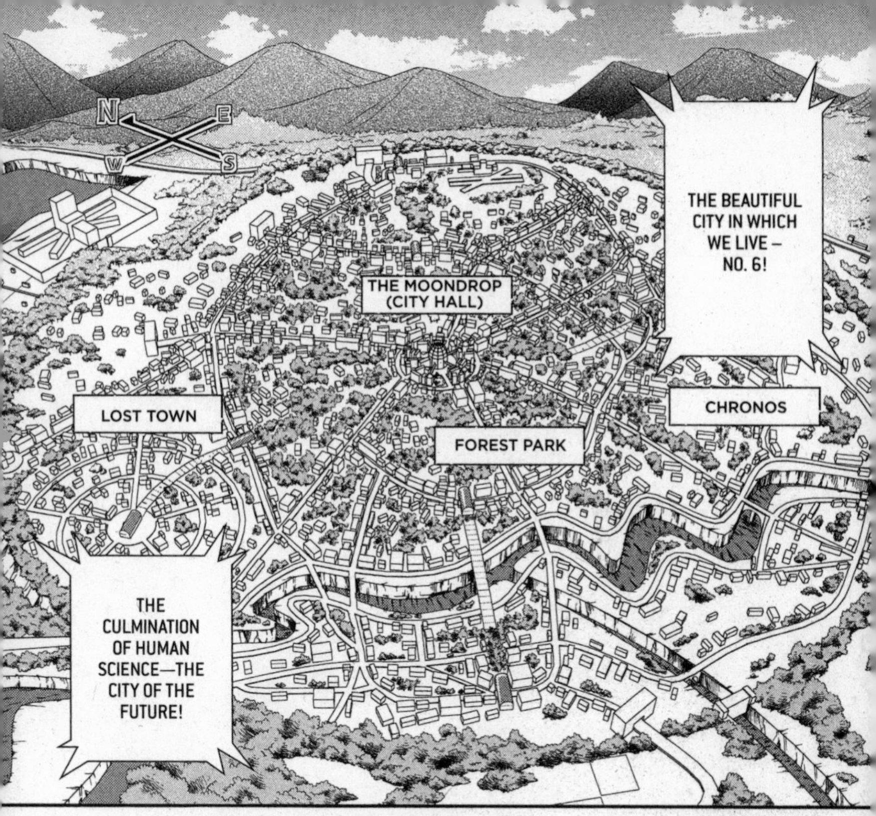
THE BEAUTIFUL CITY IN WHICH WE LIVE — NO. 6!
THE MOONDROP (CITY HALL)
CHRONOS
FOREST PARK
LOST TOWN
THE CULMINATION OF HUMAN SCIENCE—THE CITY OF THE FUTURE!
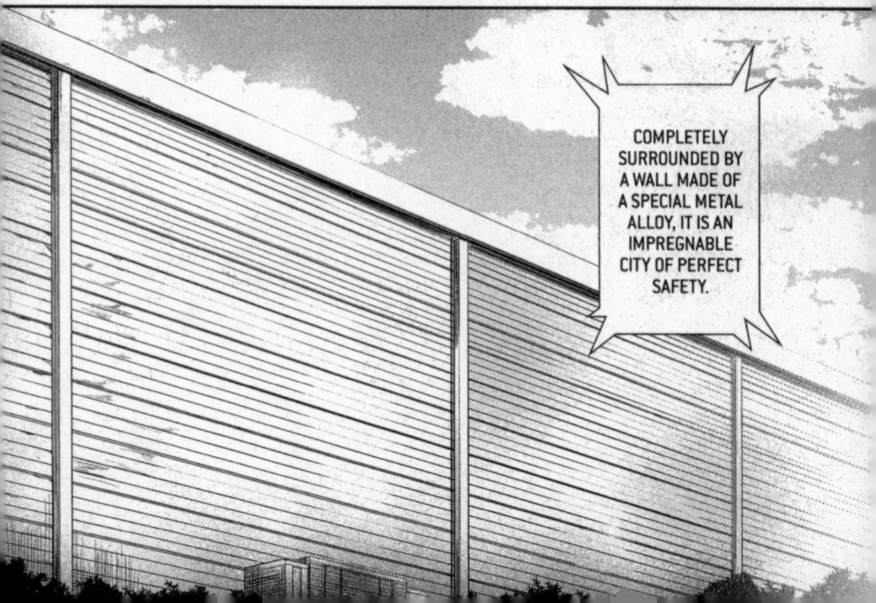
COMPLETELY SURROUNDED BY A WALL MADE OF A SPECIAL METAL ALLOY, IT IS AN IMPREGNABLE CITY OF PERFECT SAFETY.

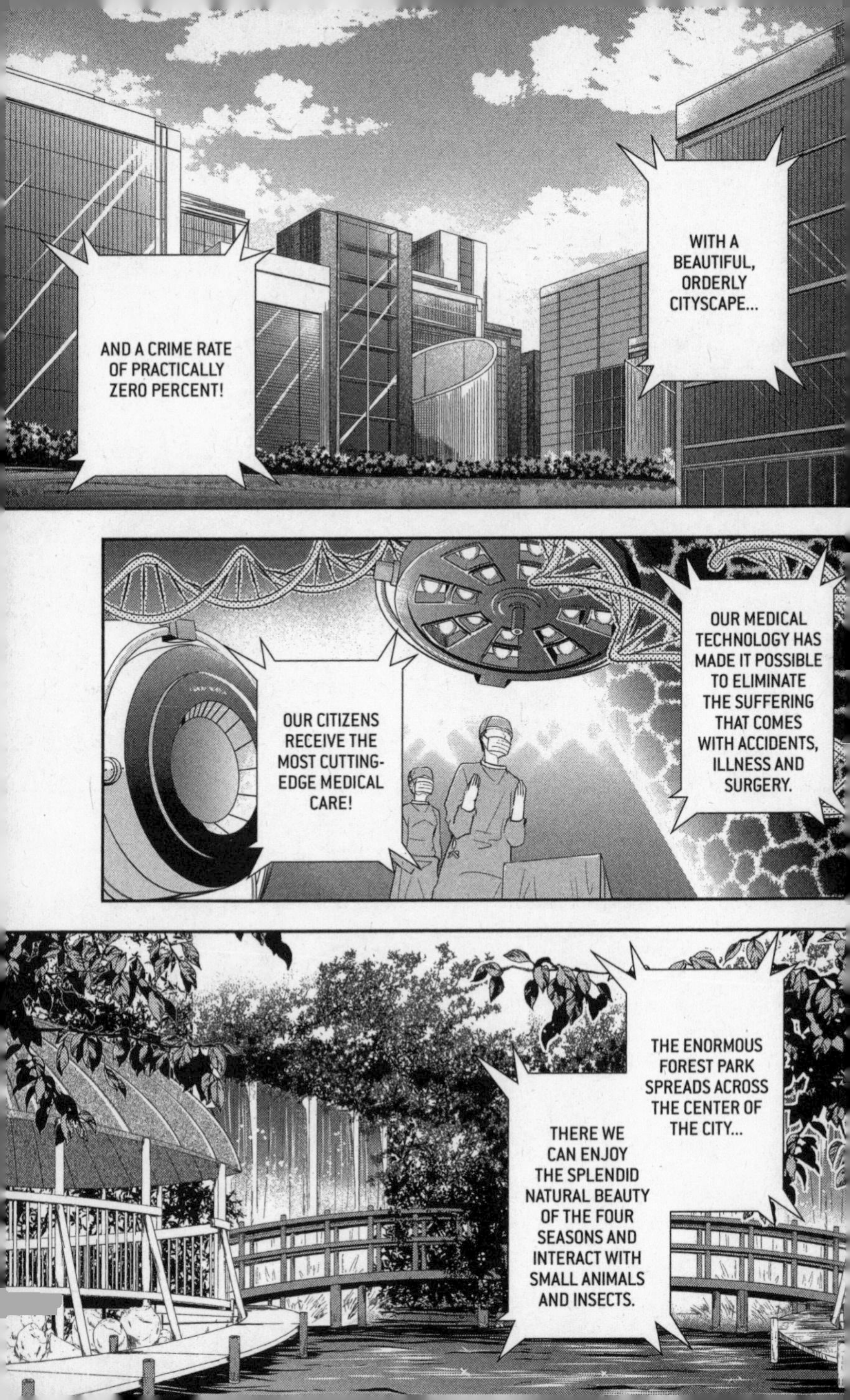
WITH A BEAUTIFUL, ORDERLY CITYSCAPE...
AND A CRIME RATE OF PRACTICALLY ZERO PERCENT!
OUR MEDICAL TECHNOLOGY HAS MADE IT POSSIBLE TO ELIMINATE THE SUFFERING THAT COMES WITH ACCIDENTS, ILLNESS AND SURGERY.
OUR CITIZENS RECEIVE THE MOST CUTTING-EDGE MEDICAL CARE!
THE ENORMOUS FOREST PARK SPREADS ACROSS THE CENTER OF THE CITY...
THERE WE CAN ENJOY THE SPLENDID NATURAL BEAUTY OF THE FOUR SEASONS AND INTERACT WITH SMALL ANIMALS AND INSECTS.

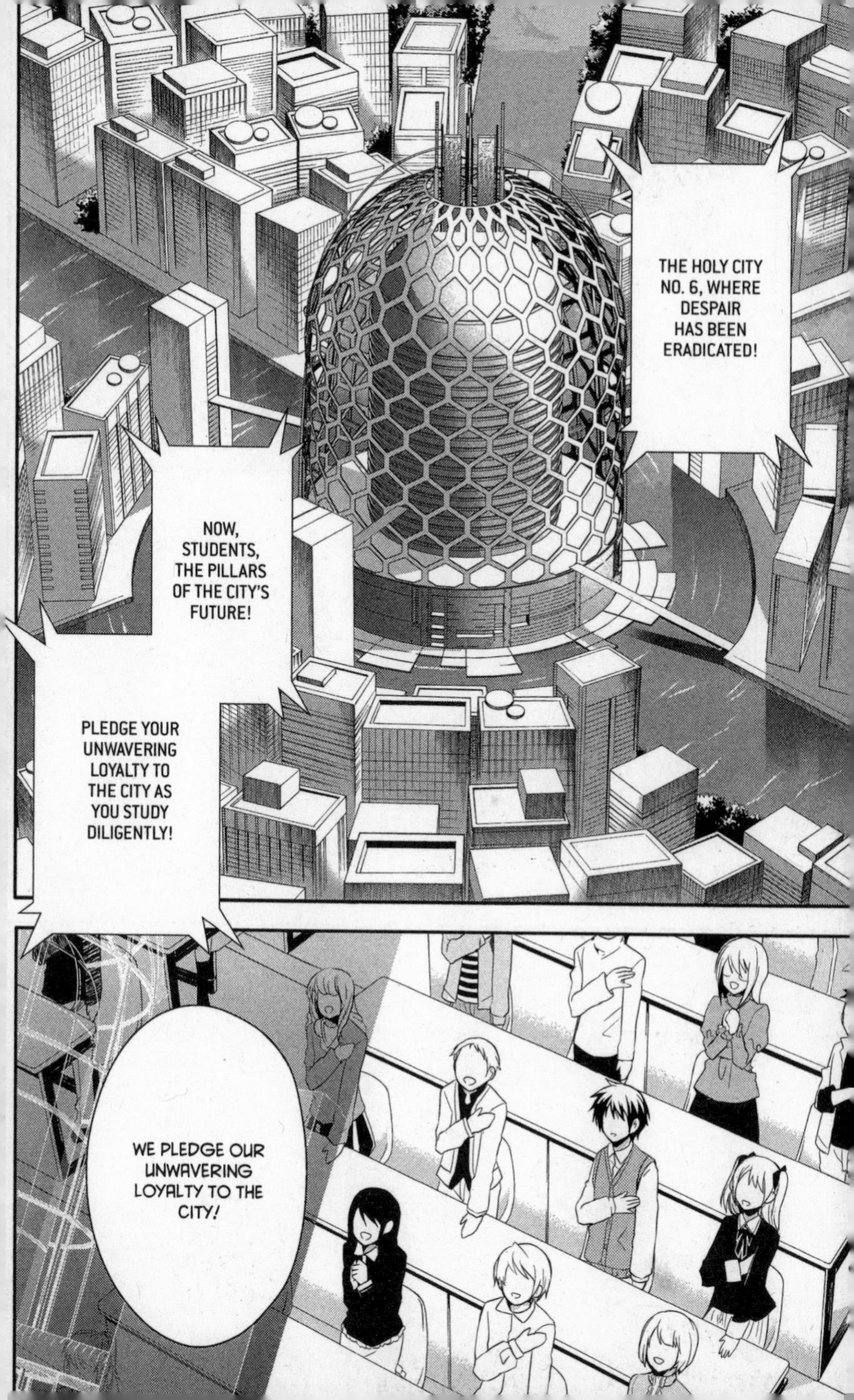
THE HOLY CITY NO. 6, WHERE DESPAIR HAS BEEN ERADICATED!
NOW, STUDENTS, THE PILLARS OF THE CITY'S FUTURE!
PLEDGE YOUR UNWAVERING LOYALTY TO THE CITY AS YOU STUDY DILIGENTLY!
WE PLEDGE OUR UNWAVERING LOYALTY TO THE CITY!

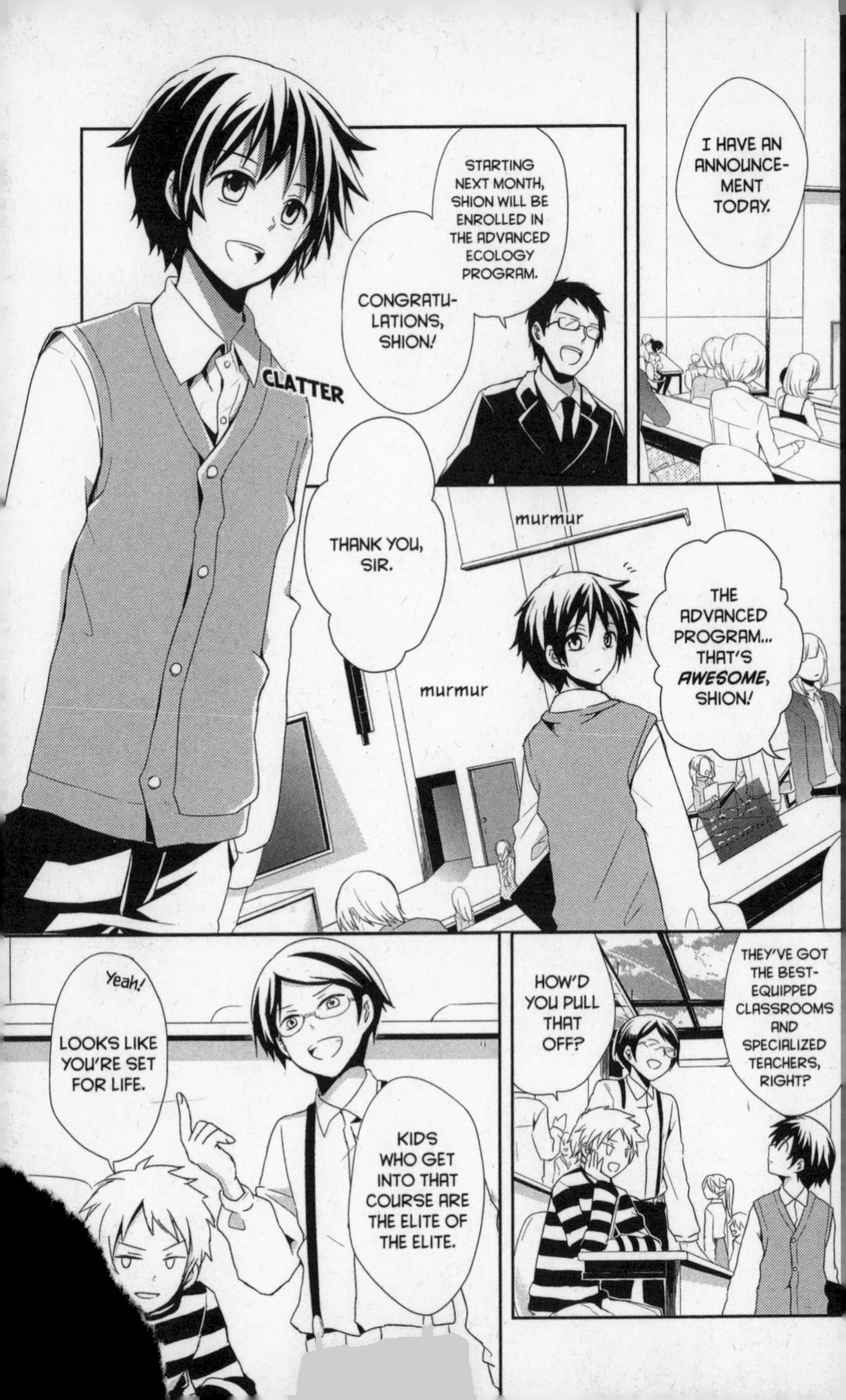
I HAVE AN ANNOUNCEMENT TODAY.
STARTING NEXT MONTH, SHION WILL BE ENROLLED IN THE ADVANCED ECOLOGY PROGRAM.
CONGRATULATIONS, SHION!
THE ADVANCED PROGRAM... THAT'S *AWESOME*, SHION!
murmur
murmur
CLATTER
THANK YOU, SIR.
THEY'VE GOT THE BEST-EQUIPPED CLASSROOMS AND SPECIALIZED TEACHERS, RIGHT?
HOW'D YOU PULL THAT OFF?
KIDS WHO GET INTO THAT COURSE ARE THE ELITE OF THE ELITE.
Yeah!
LOOKS LIKE YOU'RE SET FOR LIFE.

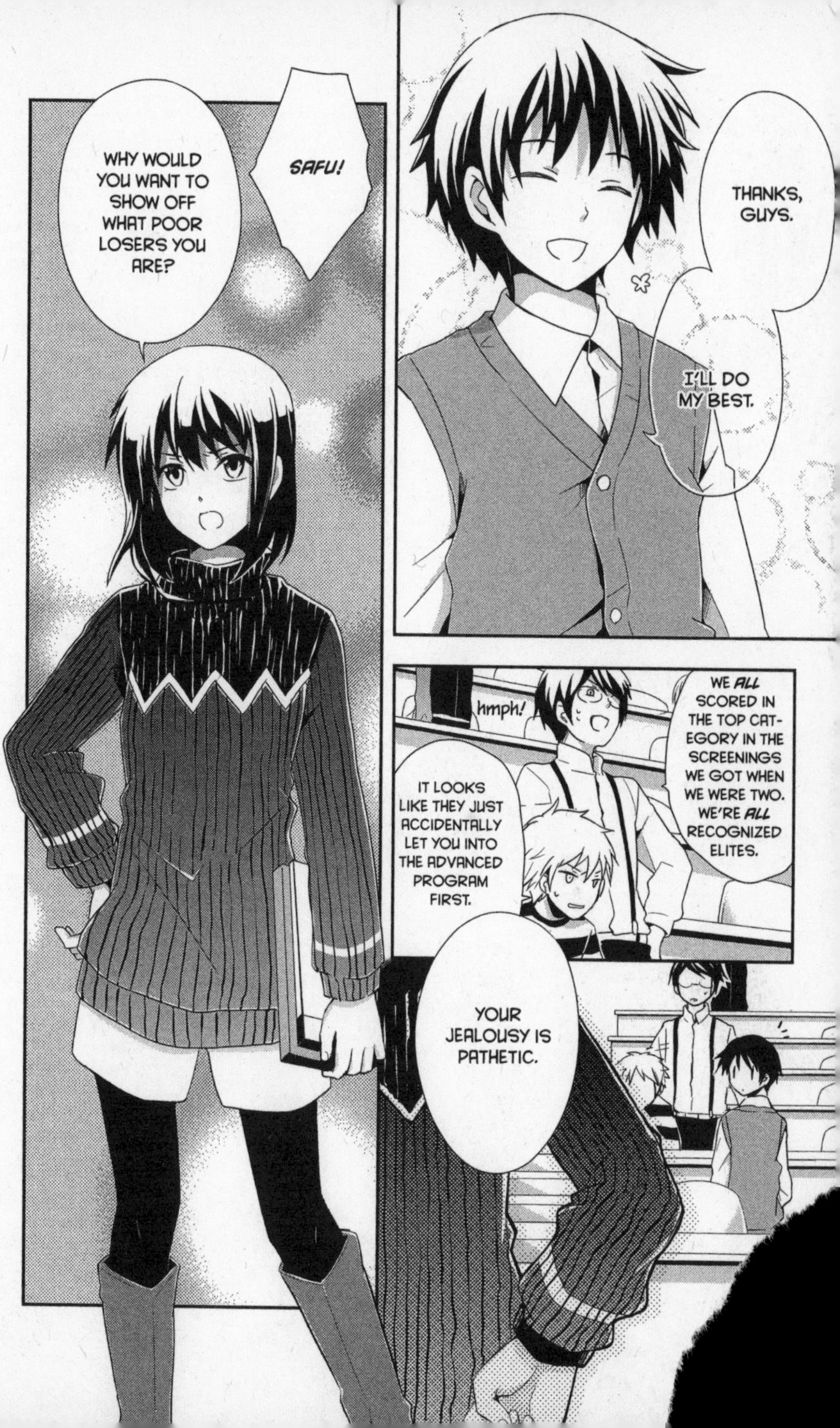
THANKS, GUYS.
I'LL DO MY BEST.
WE ALL SCORED IN THE TOP CATEGORY IN THE SCREENINGS WE GOT WHEN WE WERE TWO. WE'RE ALL RECOGNIZED ELITES.
hmph!
IT LOOKS LIKE THEY JUST ACCIDENTALLY LET YOU INTO THE ADVANCED PROGRAM FIRST.
YOUR JEALOUSY IS PATHETIC.
SAFU!
WHY WOULD YOU WANT TO SHOW OFF WHAT POOR LOSERS YOU ARE?

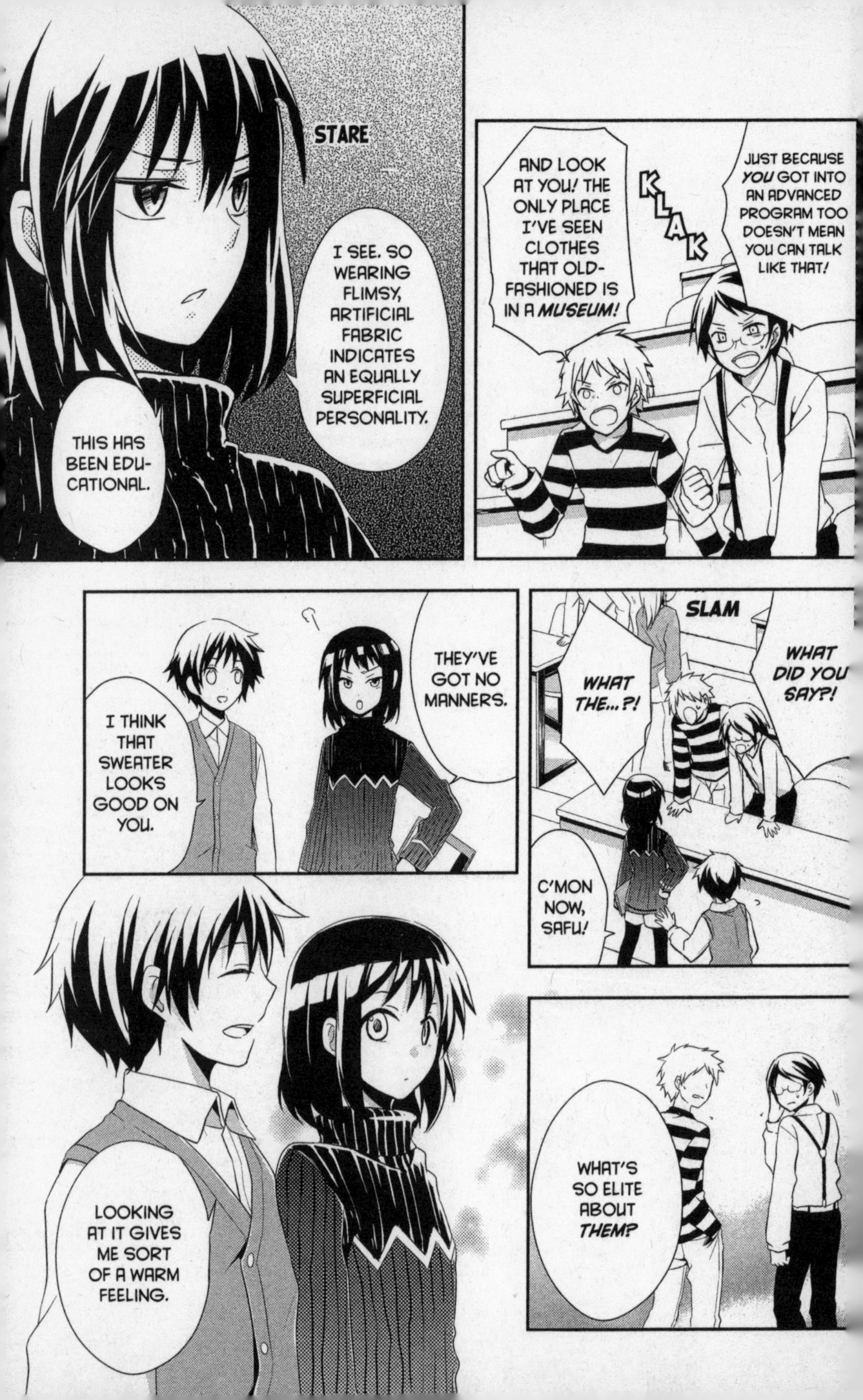
JUST BECAUSE *YOU* GOT INTO AN ADVANCED PROGRAM TOO DOESN'T MEAN YOU CAN TALK LIKE THAT!
KLAK
AND LOOK AT YOU! THE ONLY PLACE I'VE SEEN CLOTHES THAT OLD-FASHIONED IS IN A *MUSEUM!*
STARE
I SEE. SO WEARING FLIMSY, ARTIFICIAL FABRIC INDICATES AN EQUALLY SUPERFICIAL PERSONALITY.
THIS HAS BEEN EDUCATIONAL.
SLAM
WHAT DID YOU SAY?!
WHAT THE...?!
C'MON NOW, SAFU!
THEY'VE GOT NO MANNERS.
I THINK THAT SWEATER LOOKS GOOD ON YOU.
WHAT'S SO ELITE ABOUT *THEM?*
LOOKING AT IT GIVES ME SORT OF A WARM FEELING.

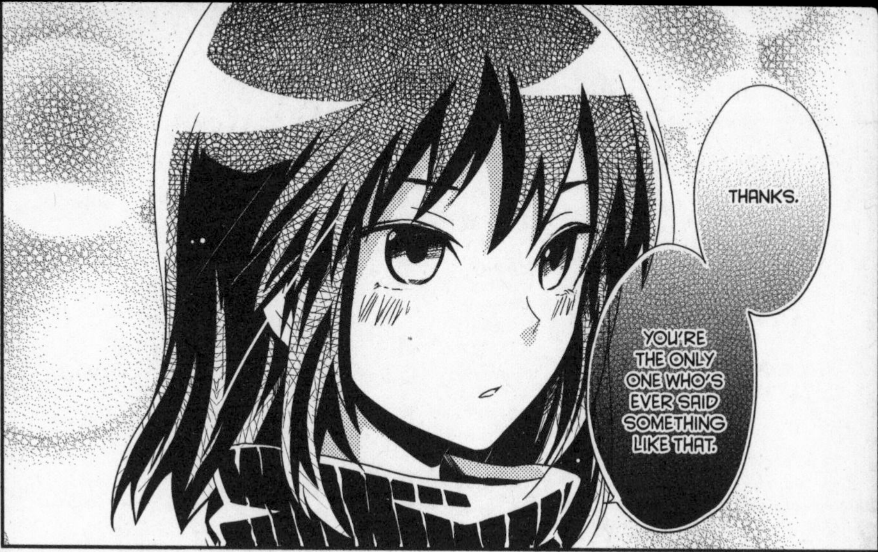
THANKS.
YOU'RE THE ONLY ONE WHO'S EVER SAID SOMETHING LIKE THAT.

SEPT. 7.

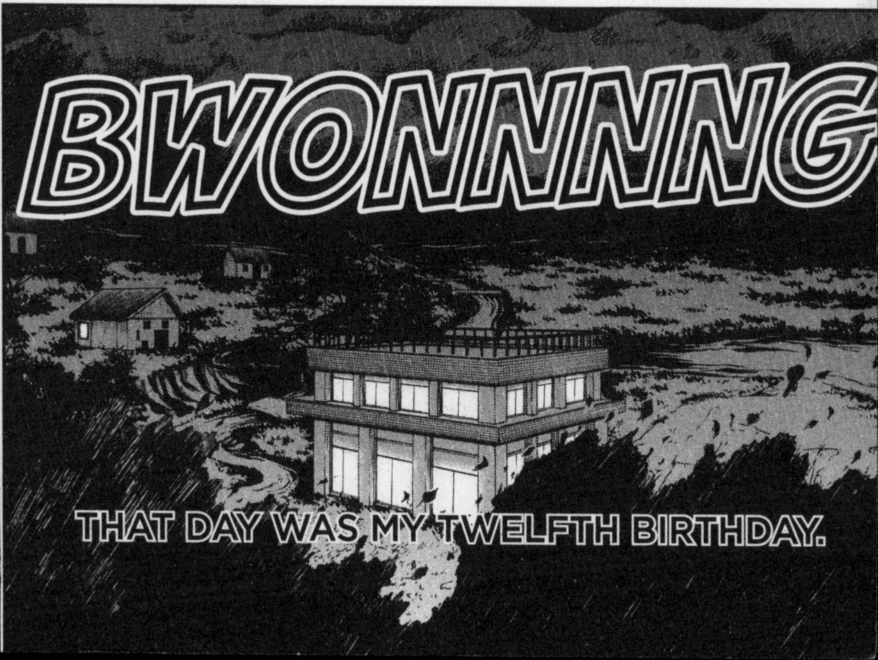
BWONNNNG
THAT DAY WAS MY TWELFTH BIRTHDAY.

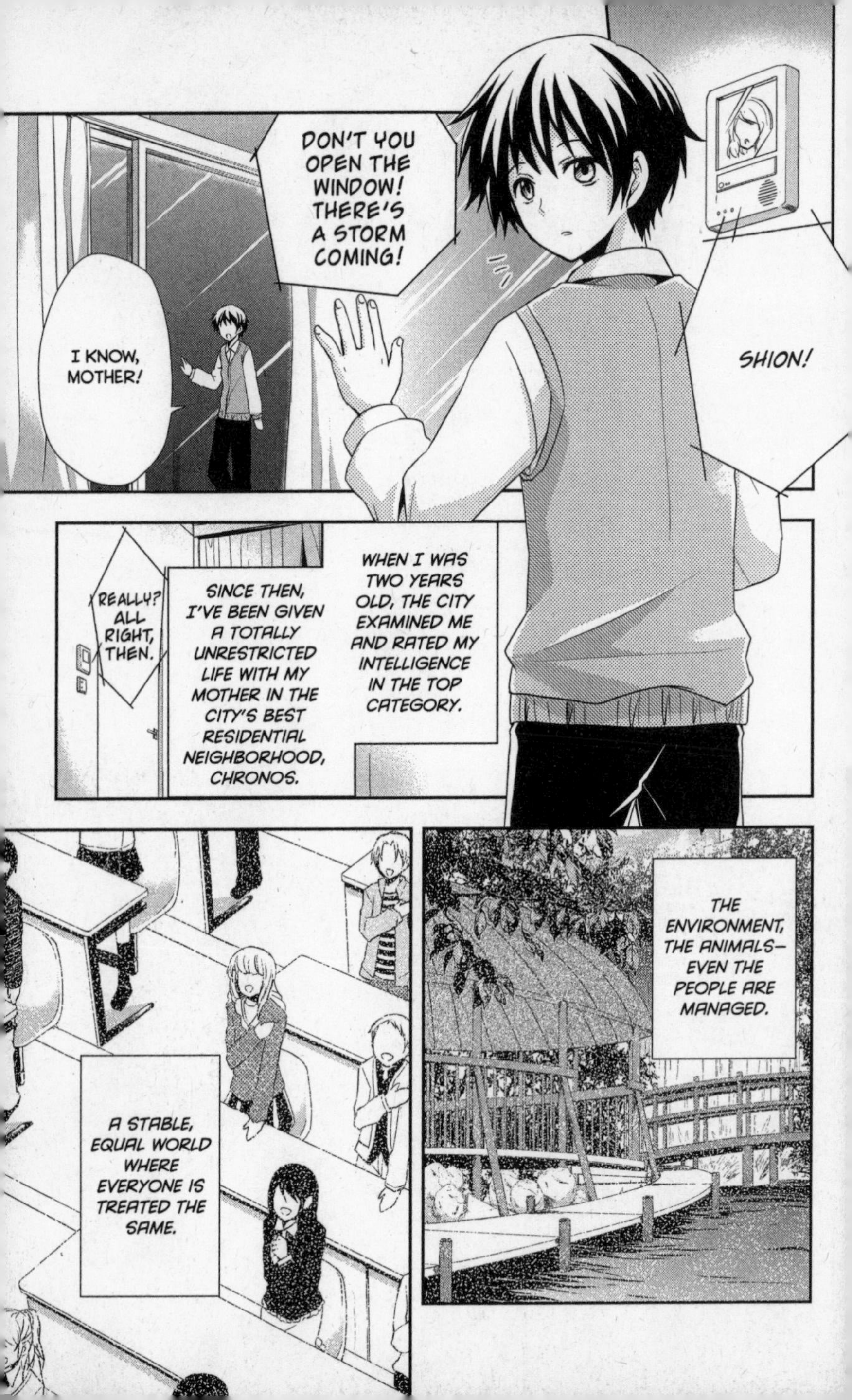
SHION!
DON'T YOU OPEN THE WINDOW! THERE'S A STORM COMING!
I KNOW, MOTHER!
WHEN I WAS TWO YEARS OLD, THE CITY EXAMINED ME AND RATED MY INTELLIGENCE IN THE TOP CATEGORY.
SINCE THEN, I'VE BEEN GIVEN A TOTALLY UNRESTRICTED LIFE WITH MY MOTHER IN THE CITY'S BEST RESIDENTIAL NEIGHBORHOOD, CHRONOS.
REALLY? ALL RIGHT, THEN.
THE ENVIRONMENT, THE ANIMALS— EVEN THE PEOPLE ARE MANAGED.
A STABLE, EQUAL WORLD WHERE EVERYONE IS TREATED THE SAME.

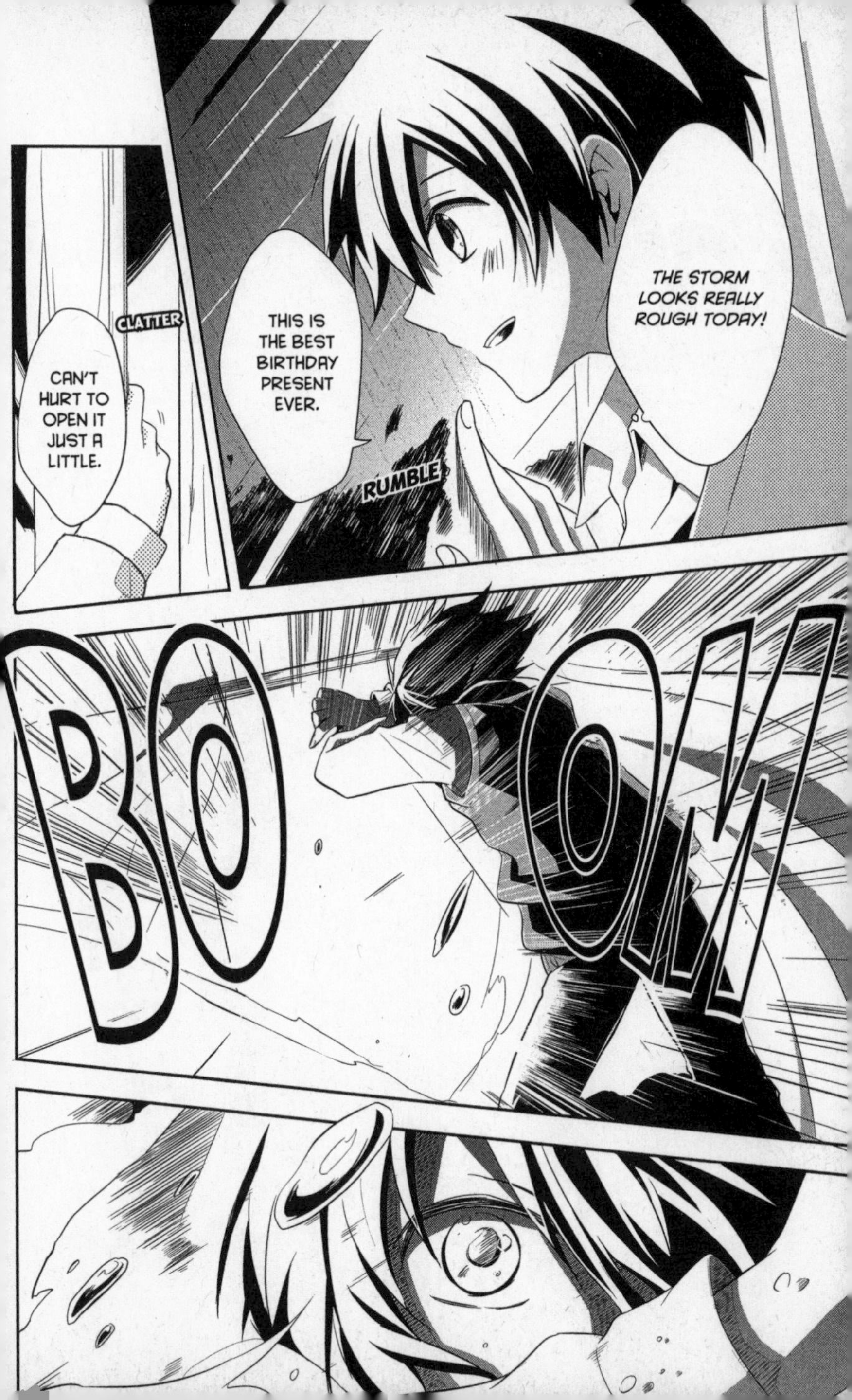
THE STORM LOOKS REALLY ROUGH TODAY!
THIS IS THE BEST BIRTHDAY PRESENT EVER.
RUMBLE
CLATTER
CAN'T HURT TO OPEN IT JUST A LITTLE.
BOOM

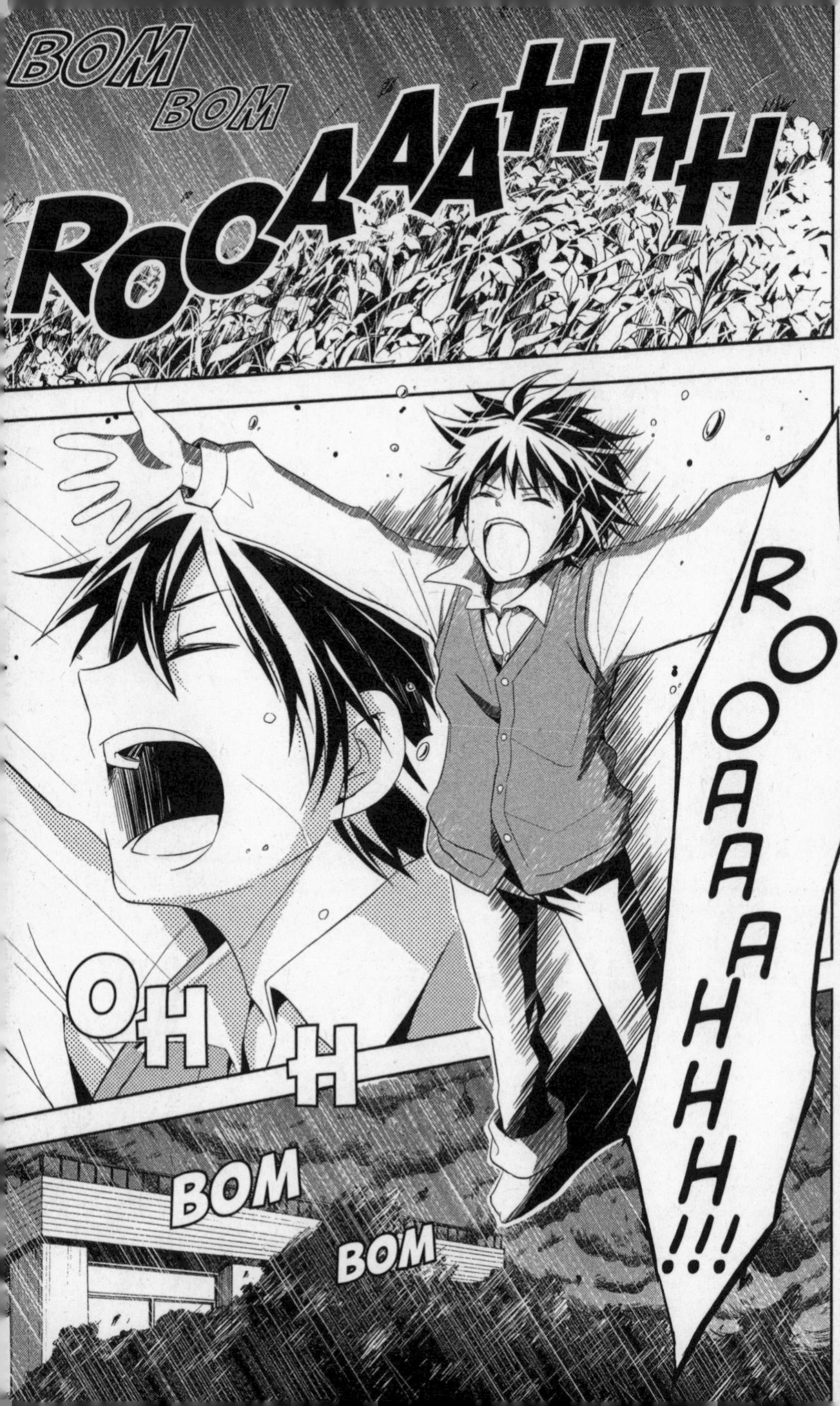
BOM BOM
ROOAAAHHHH
ROOAAAAHHHH!!!
OHH
BOM
BOM

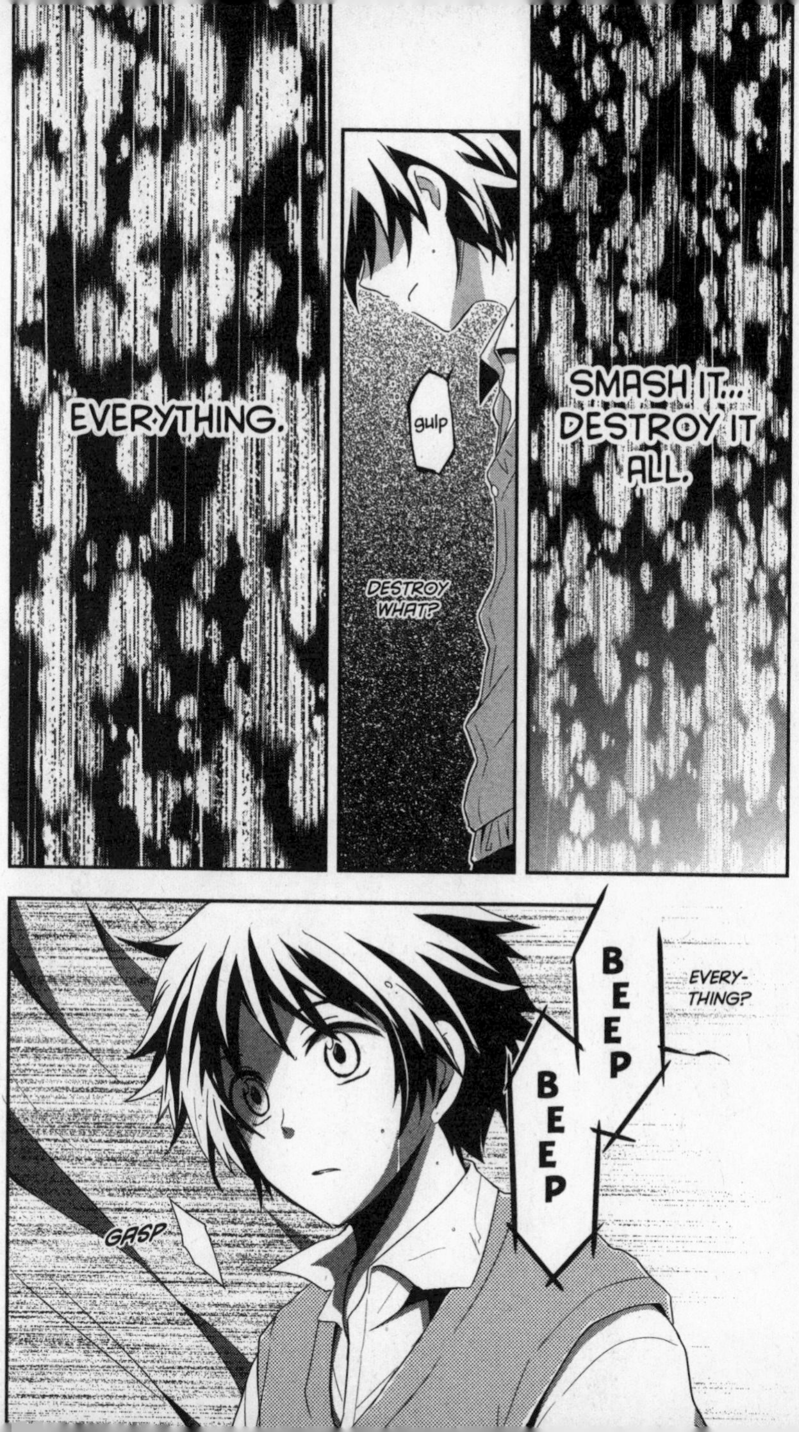
SMASH IT... DESTROY IT ALL.
gulp
DESTROY WHAT?
EVERYTHING.
EVERY-THING?
BEEP
BEEP
GASP

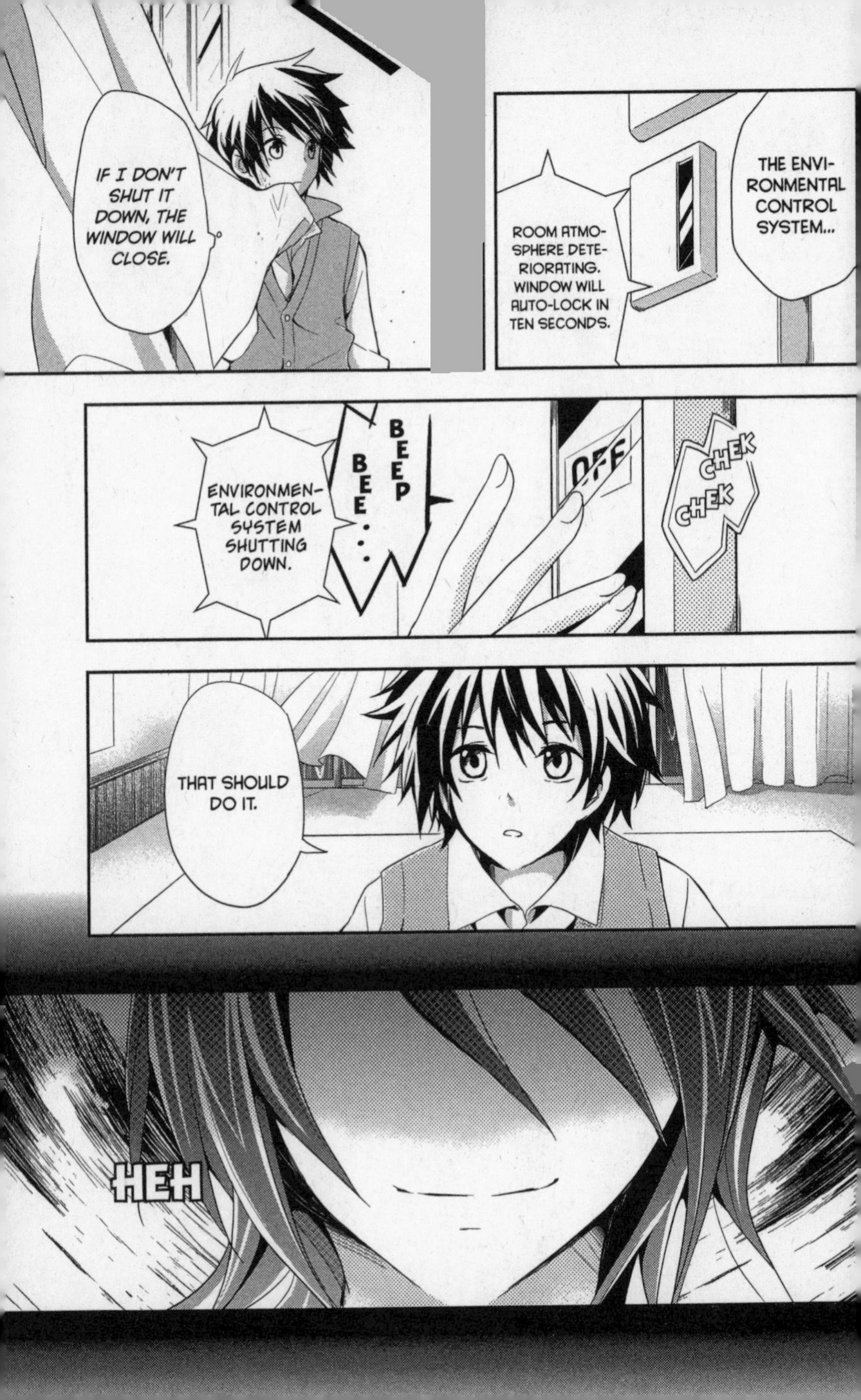
THE ENVI-RONMENTAL CONTROL SYSTEM...
ROOM ATMO-SPHERE DETE-RIORATING. WINDOW WILL AUTO-LOCK IN TEN SECONDS.
IF I DON'T SHUT IT DOWN, THE WINDOW WILL CLOSE.
CHEK CHEK
OFF
BEEP
BEE...
ENVIRONMEN-TAL CONTROL SYSTEM SHUTTING DOWN.
THAT SHOULD DO IT.
HEH

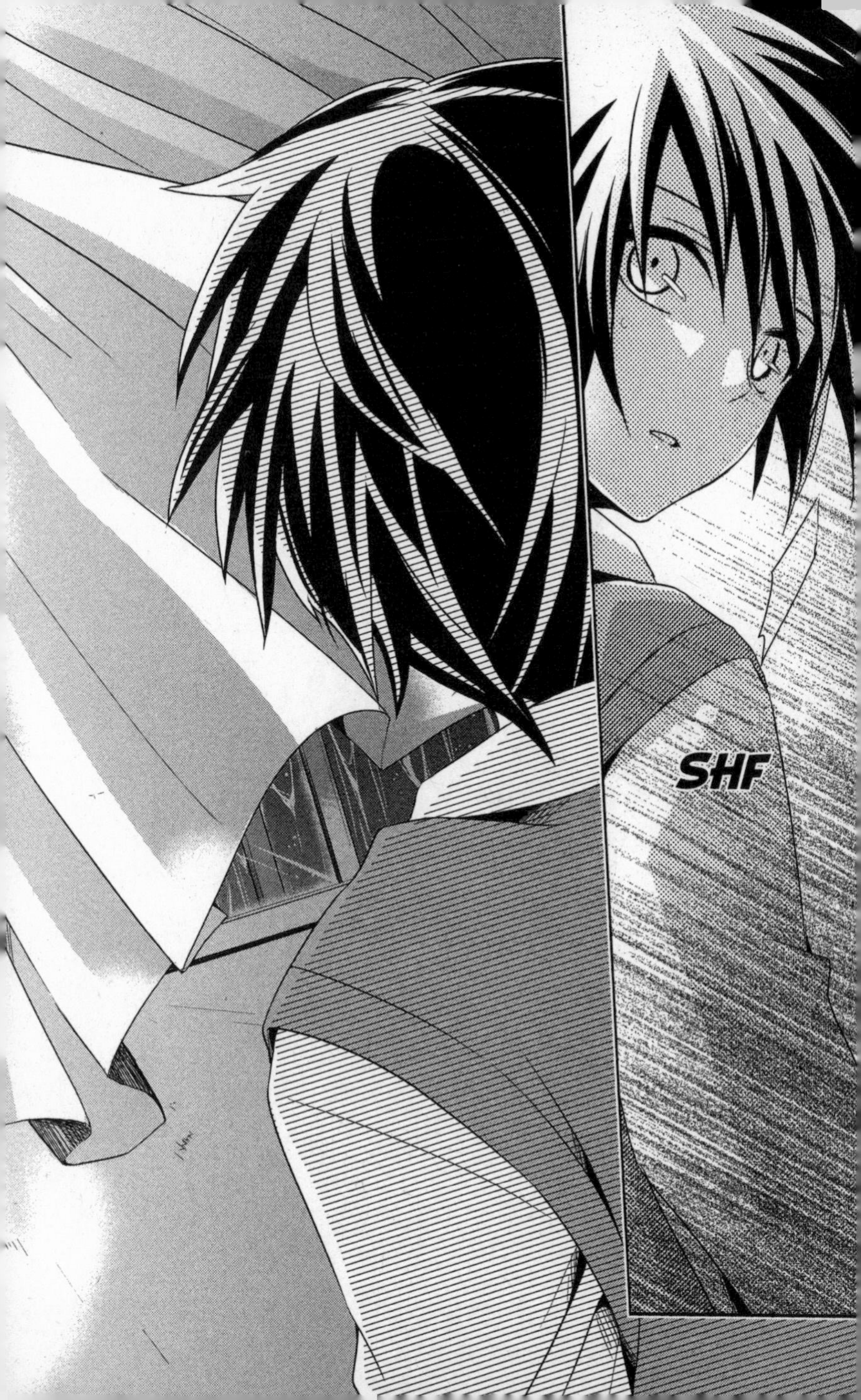
SHF

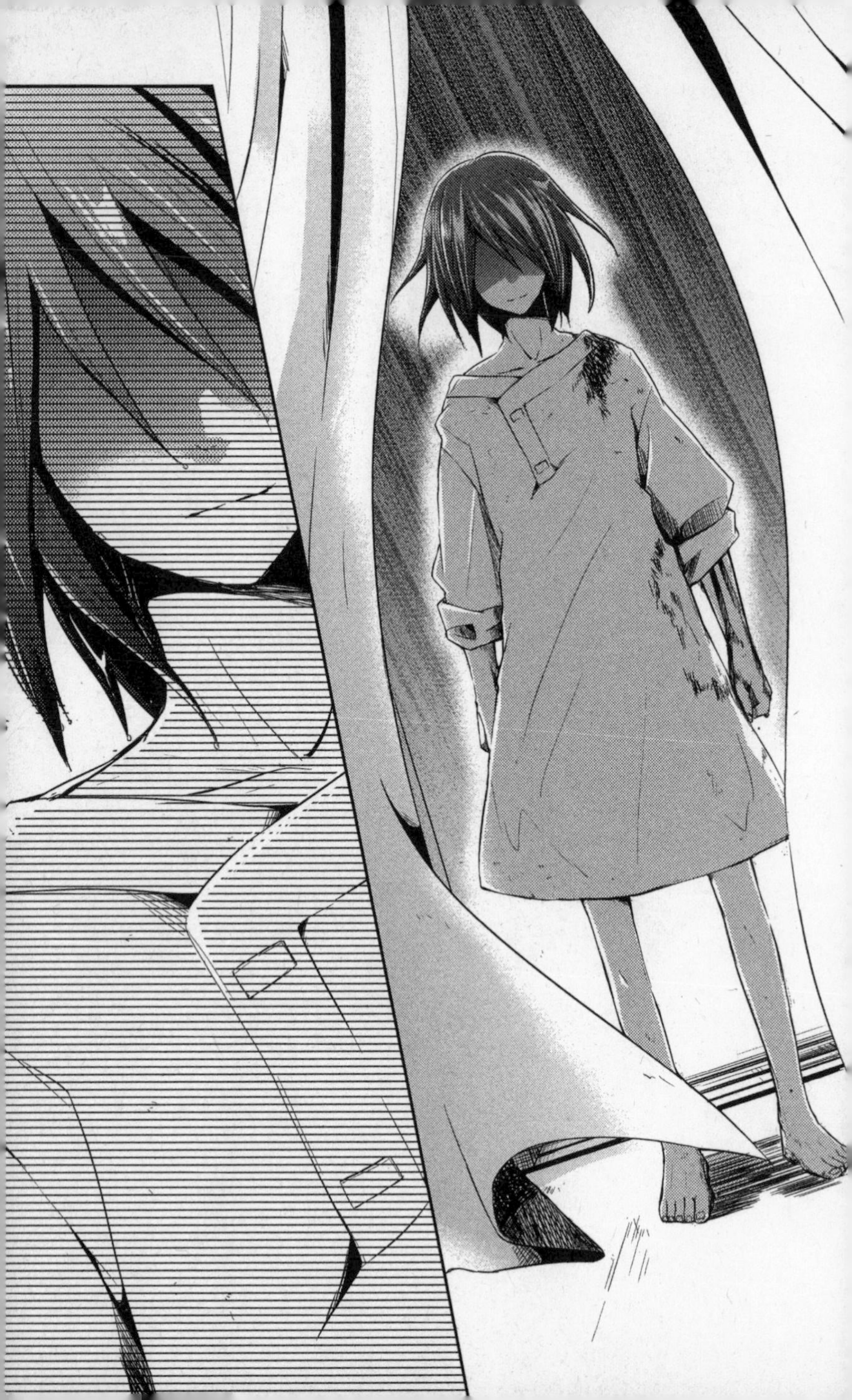

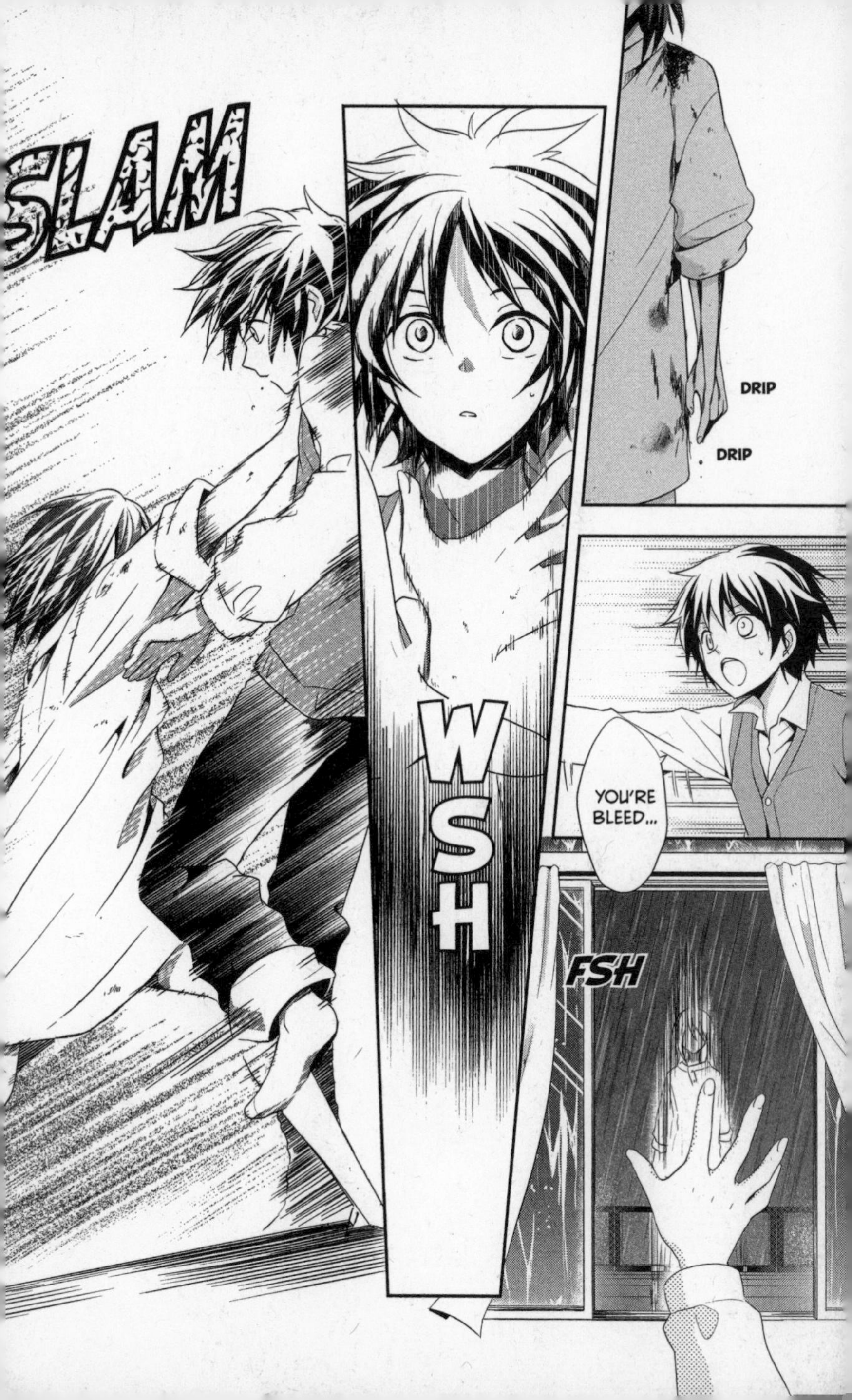
DRIP
DRIP
YOU'RE BLEED...
FSH
WSH
SLAM

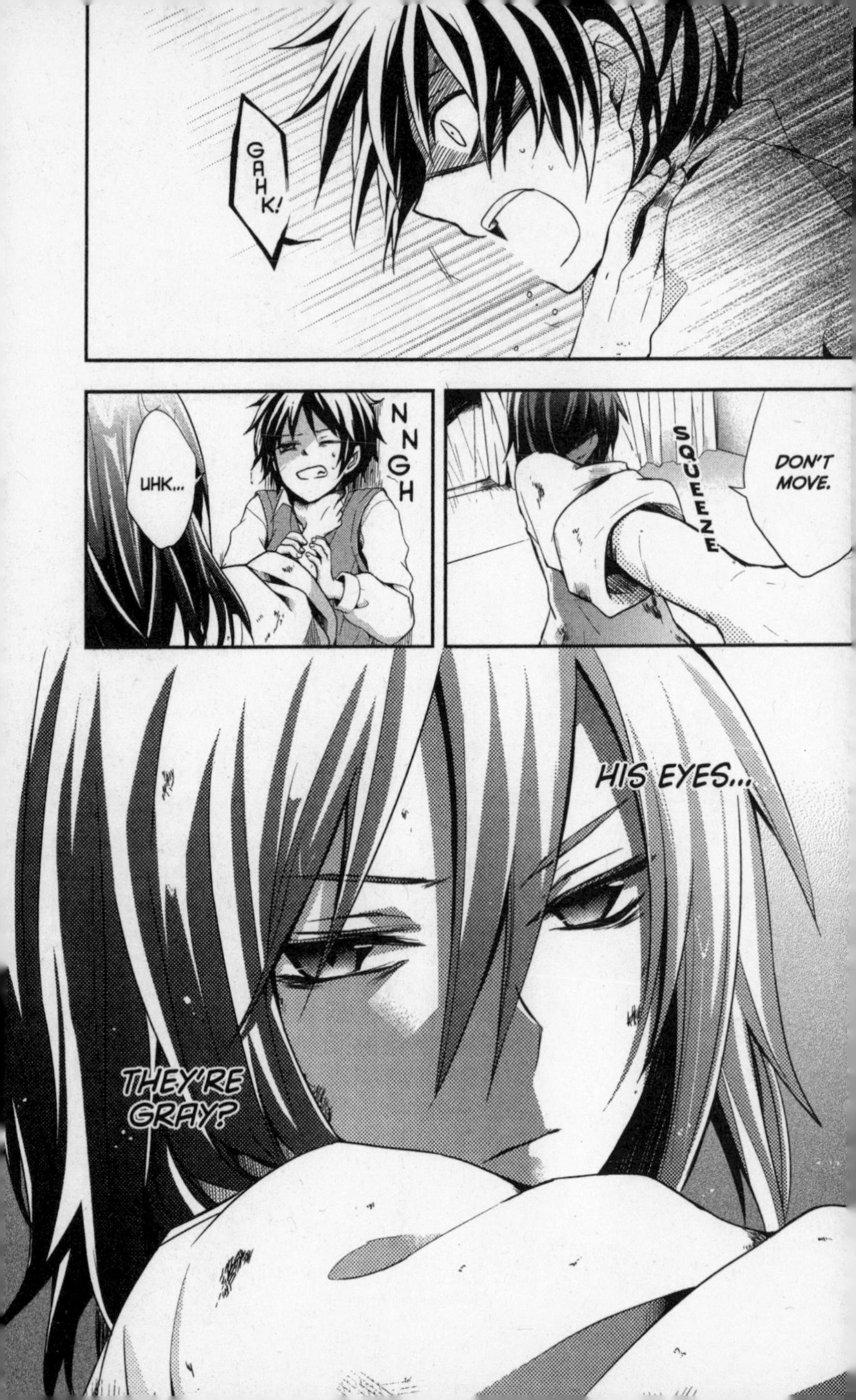
GAHK!
DON'T MOVE.
SQUEEZE
NNGH
UHK...
HIS EYES...
THEY'RE GRAY?

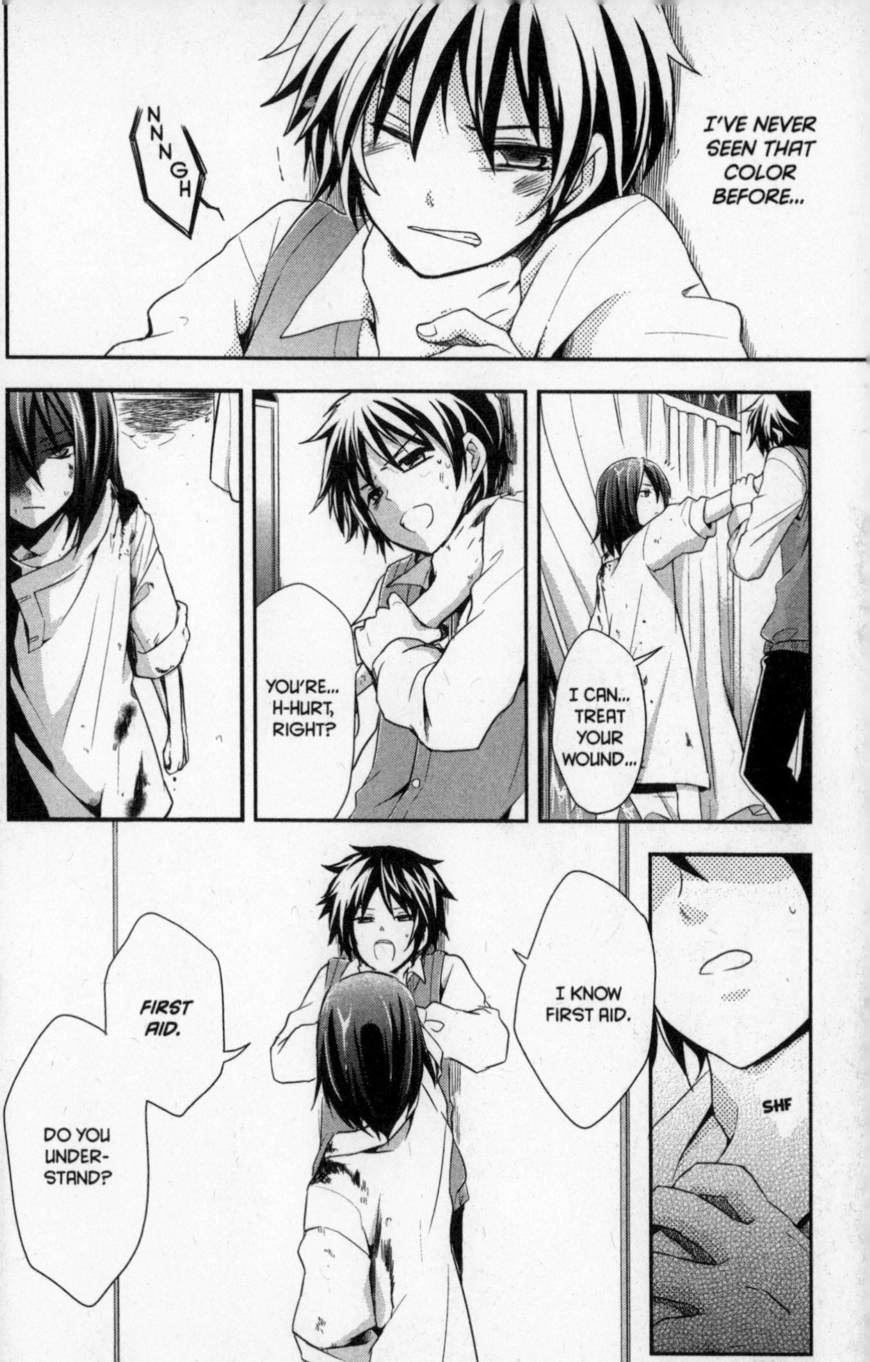
I'VE NEVER SEEN THAT COLOR BEFORE...
NNNGH
I CAN... TREAT YOUR WOUND...
YOU'RE... H-HURT, RIGHT?
SHF
I KNOW FIRST AID.
FIRST AID.
DO YOU UNDER-STAND?

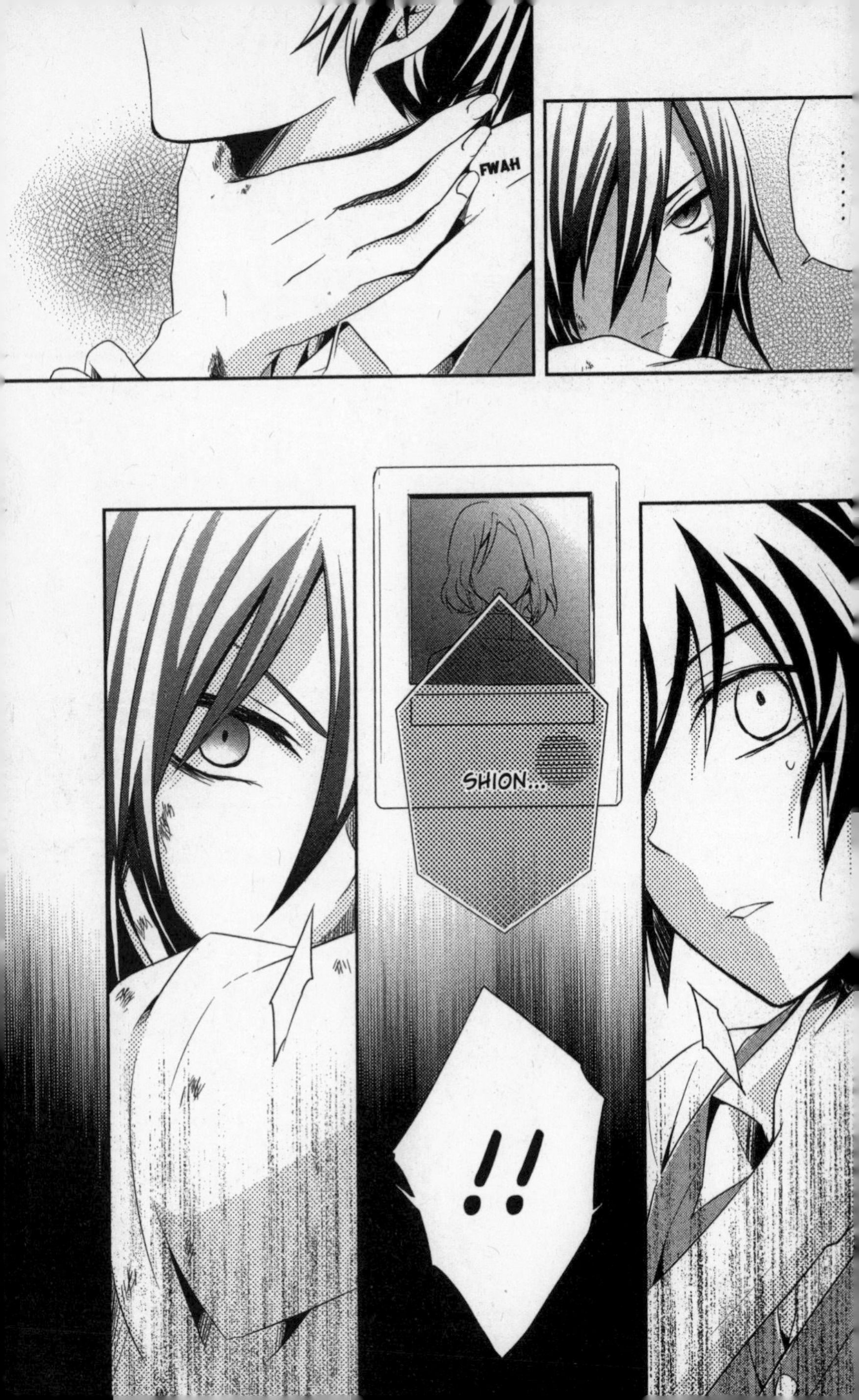
FWAH
SHION...
!!

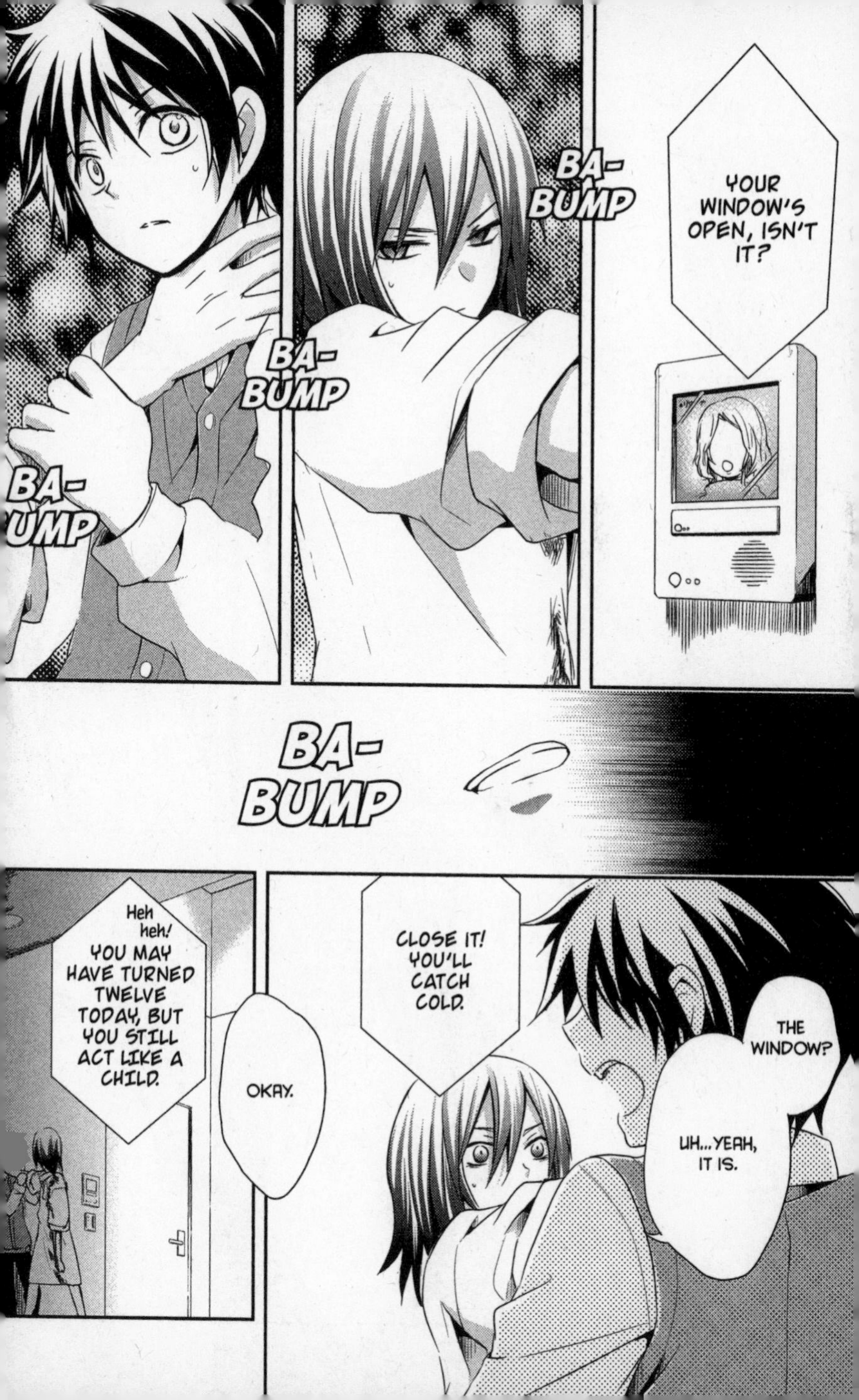
YOUR WINDOW'S OPEN, ISN'T IT?
BA-BUMP
BA-BUMP
BA-UMP
BA-BUMP
THE WINDOW?
UH...YEAH, IT IS.
CLOSE IT! YOU'LL CATCH COLD.
OKAY.
Heh heh!
YOU MAY HAVE TURNED TWELVE TODAY, BUT YOU STILL ACT LIKE A CHILD.

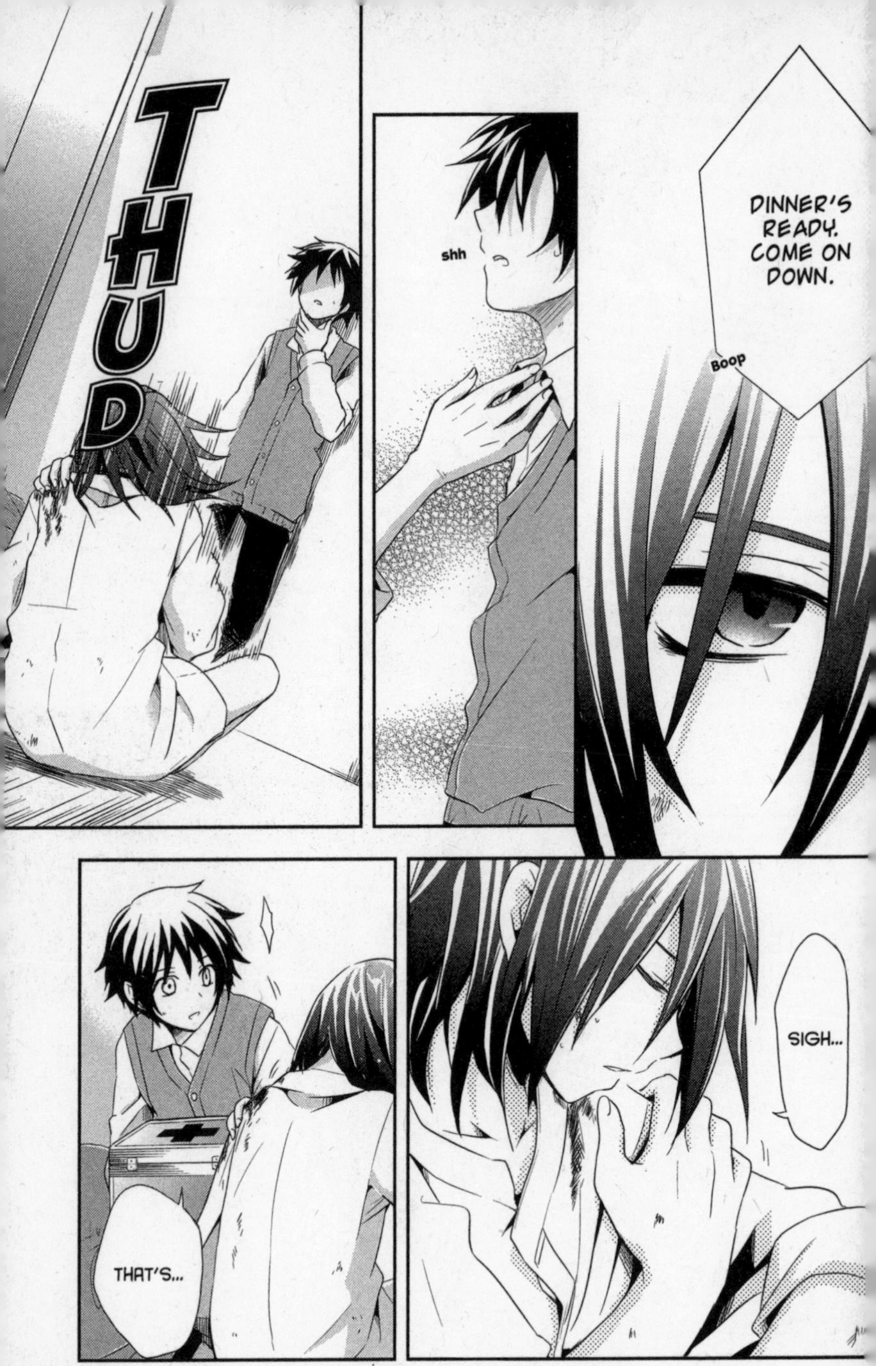
DINNER'S READY. COME ON DOWN.
Boop
shh
THUD
SIGH...
THAT'S...

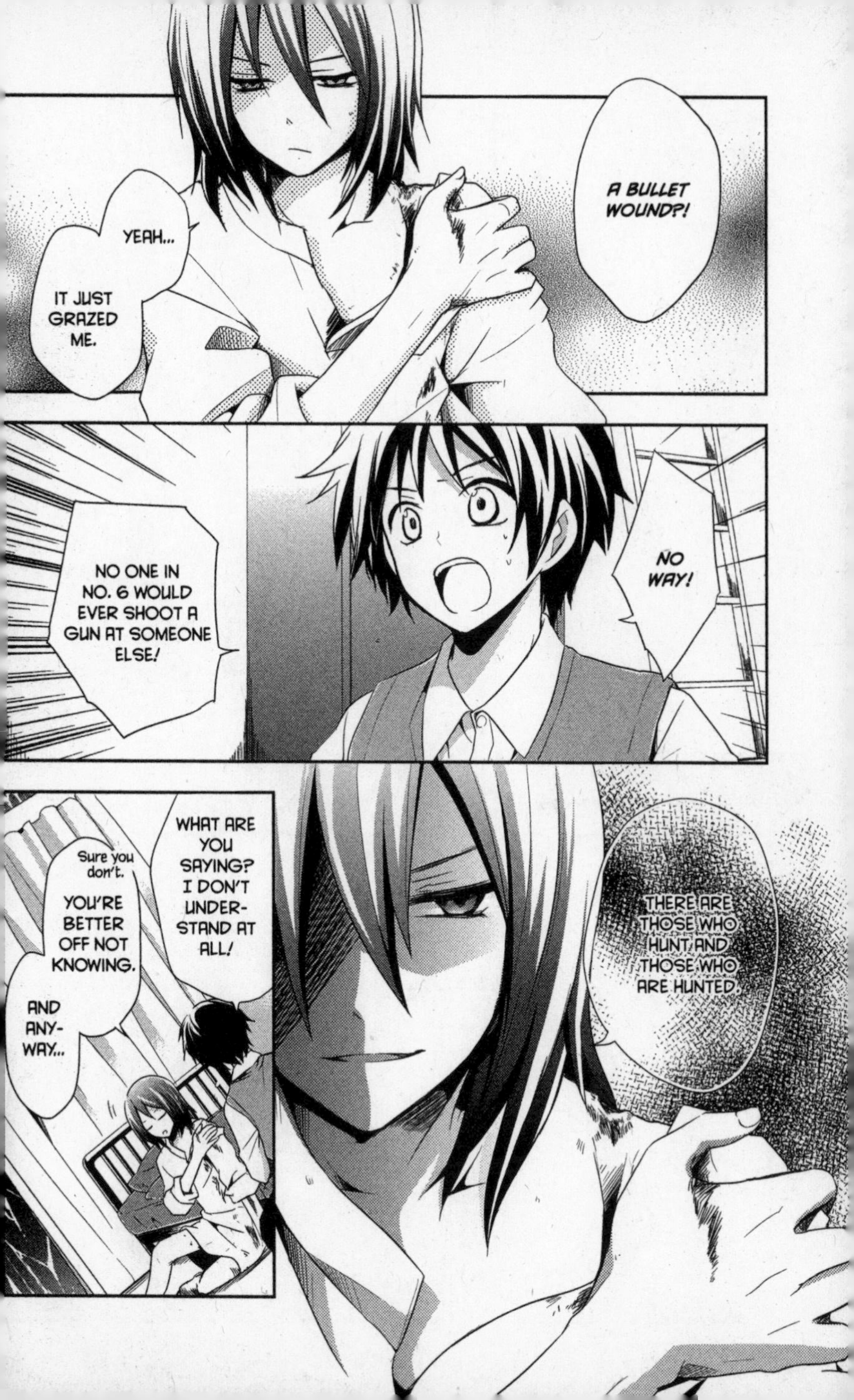
A BULLET WOUND?!
YEAH... IT JUST GRAZED ME.
NO WAY!
NO ONE IN NO. 6 WOULD EVER SHOOT A GUN AT SOMEONE ELSE!
THERE ARE THOSE WHO HUNT AND THOSE WHO ARE HUNTED.
WHAT ARE YOU SAYING? I DON'T UNDER-STAND AT ALL!
Sure you don't.
YOU'RE BETTER OFF NOT KNOWING.
AND ANY-WAY...

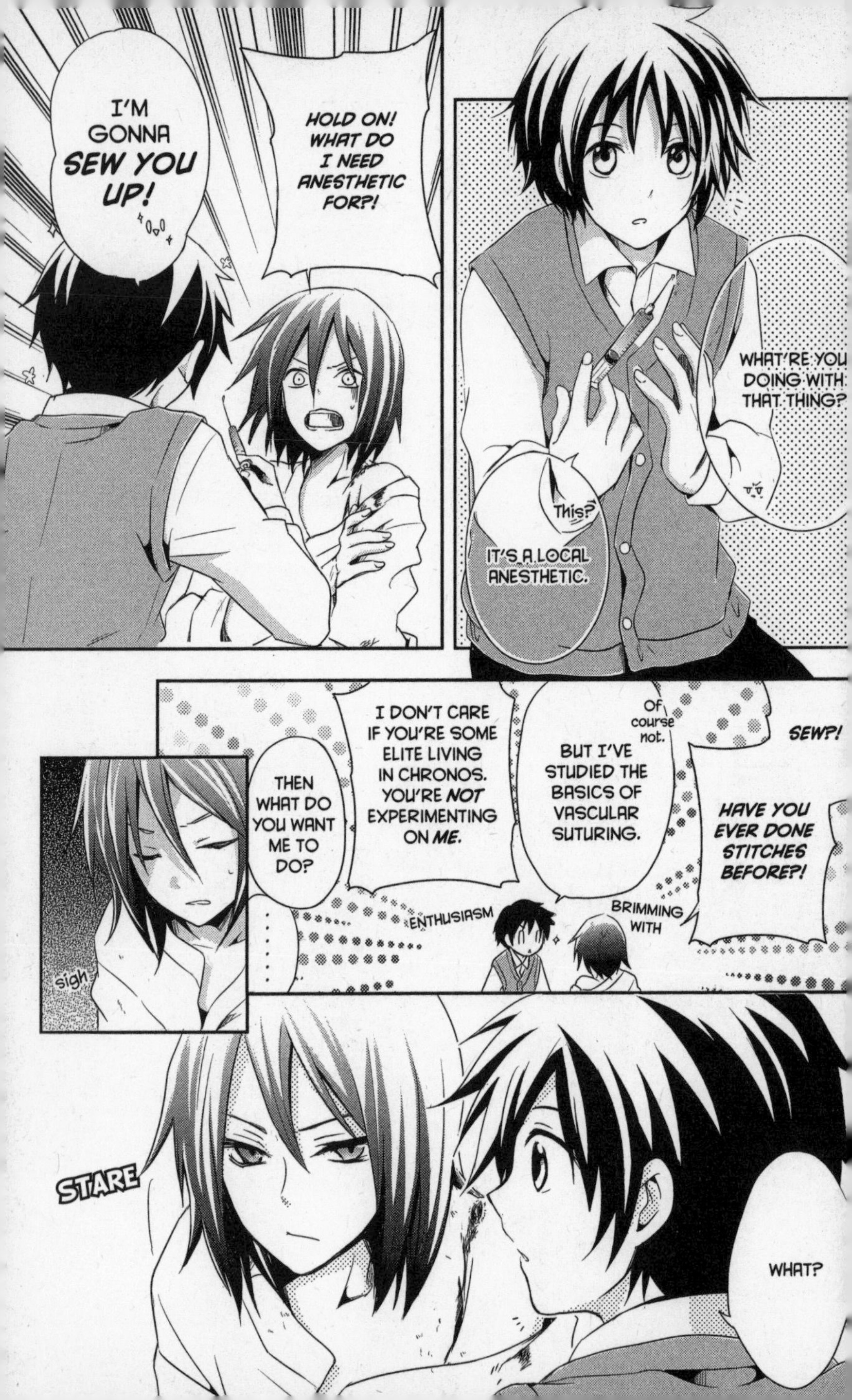
WHAT'RE YOU DOING WITH THAT THING?
This?
IT'S A LOCAL ANESTHETIC.
HOLD ON! WHAT DO I NEED ANESTHETIC FOR?!
I'M GONNA SEW YOU UP!
SEW?!
HAVE YOU EVER DONE STITCHES BEFORE?!
Of course not.
BUT I'VE STUDIED THE BASICS OF VASCULAR SUTURING.
BRIMMING WITH ENTHUSIASM
I DON'T CARE IF YOU'RE SOME ELITE LIVING IN CHRONOS. YOU'RE NOT EXPERIMENTING ON ME.
THEN WHAT DO YOU WANT ME TO DO?
...
sigh
WHAT?
STARE

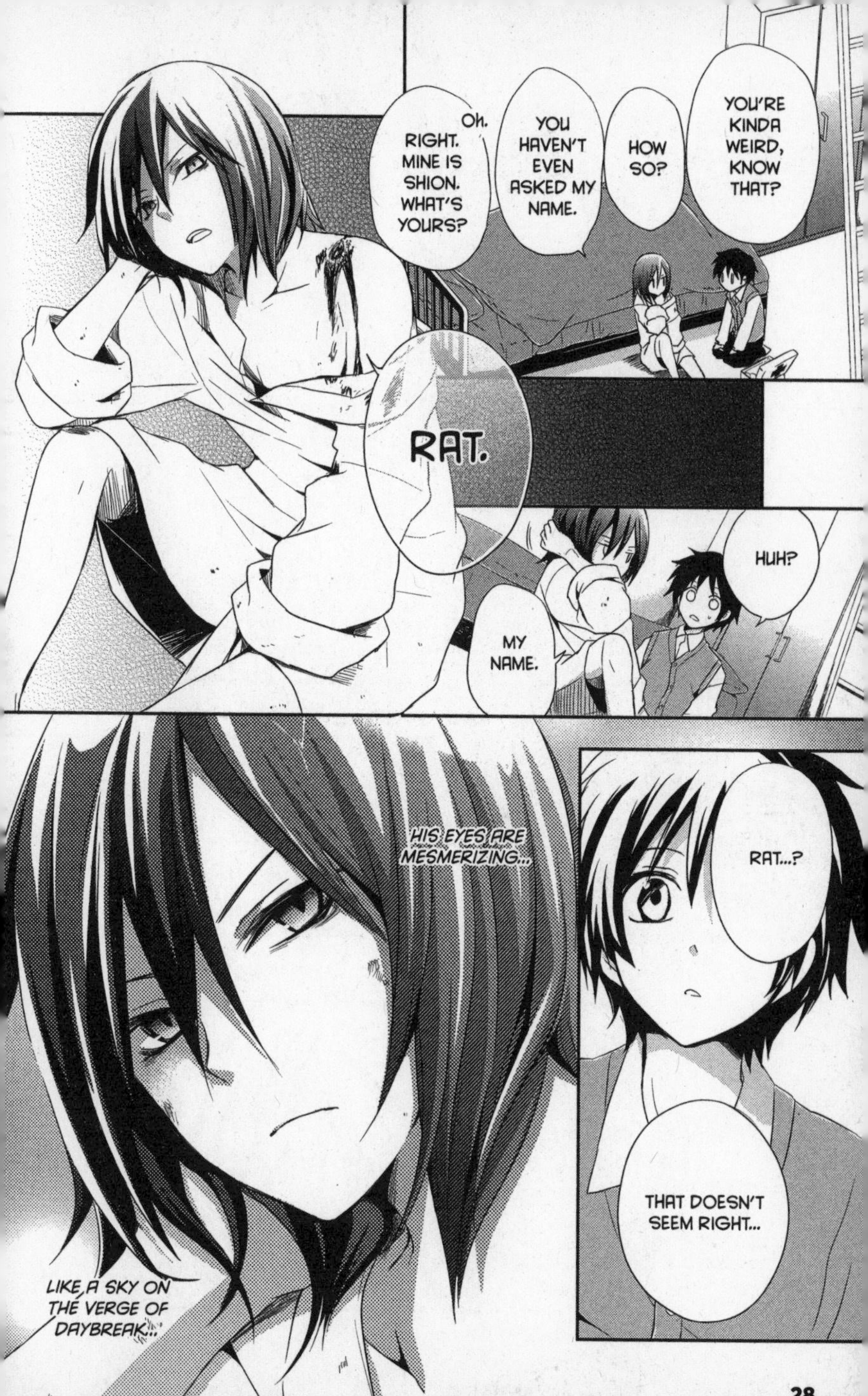
YOU'RE KINDA WEIRD, KNOW THAT?
HOW SO?
YOU HAVEN'T EVEN ASKED MY NAME.
Oh. RIGHT. MINE IS SHION. WHAT'S YOURS?
RAT.
HUH?
MY NAME.
RAT...?
THAT DOESN'T SEEM RIGHT...
HIS EYES ARE MESMERIZING...
LIKE A SKY ON THE VERGE OF DAYBREAK...

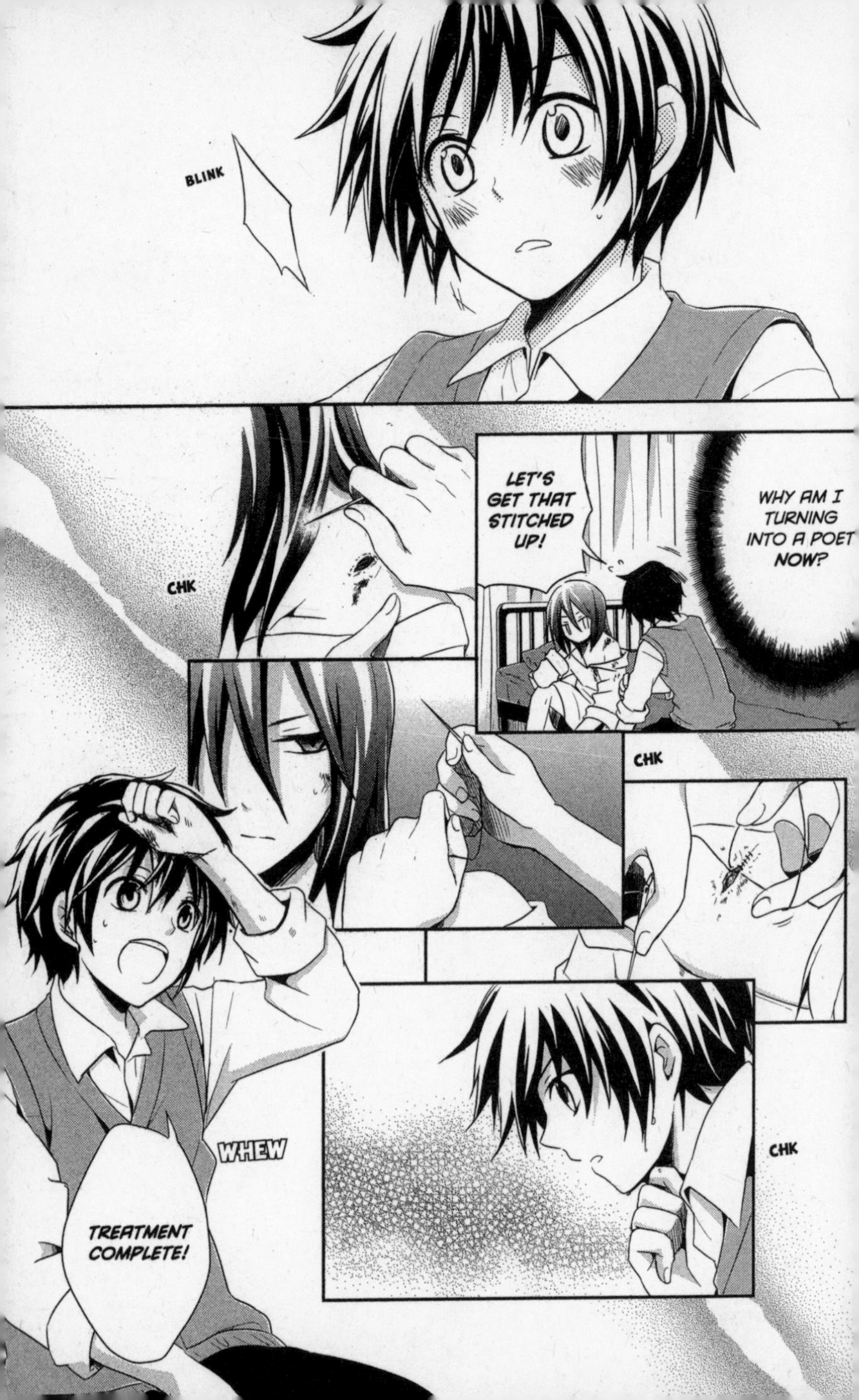
BLINK
WHY AM I TURNING INTO A POET NOW?
LET'S GET THAT STITCHED UP!
CHK
CHK
CHK
WHEW
TREATMENT COMPLETE!

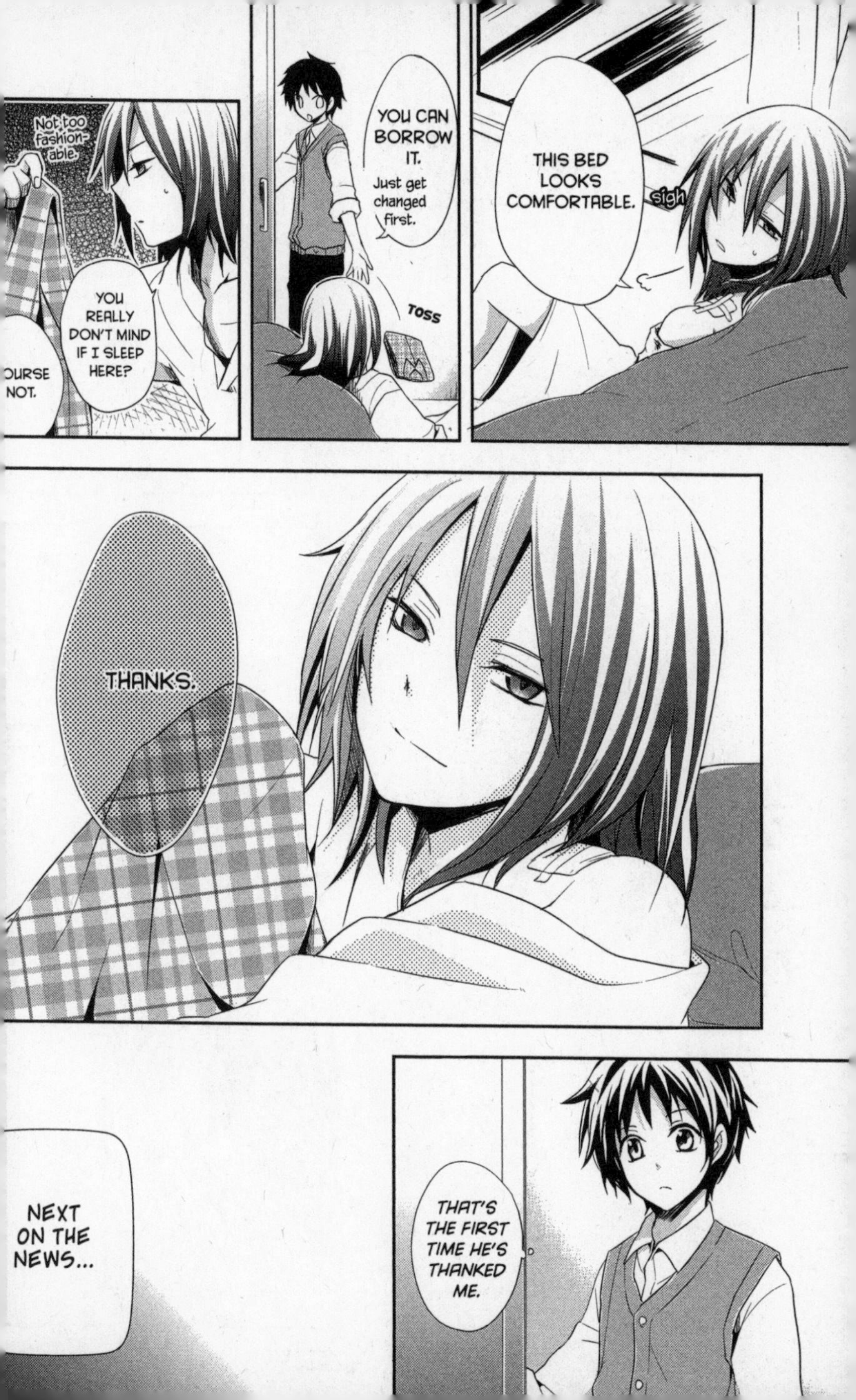
sigh
THIS BED LOOKS COMFORTABLE.
YOU CAN BORROW IT.
Just get changed first.
TOSS
Not too fashion-able.
YOU REALLY DON'T MIND IF I SLEEP HERE?
OURSE NOT.
THANKS.
THAT'S THE FIRST TIME HE'S THANKED ME.
NEXT ON THE NEWS...

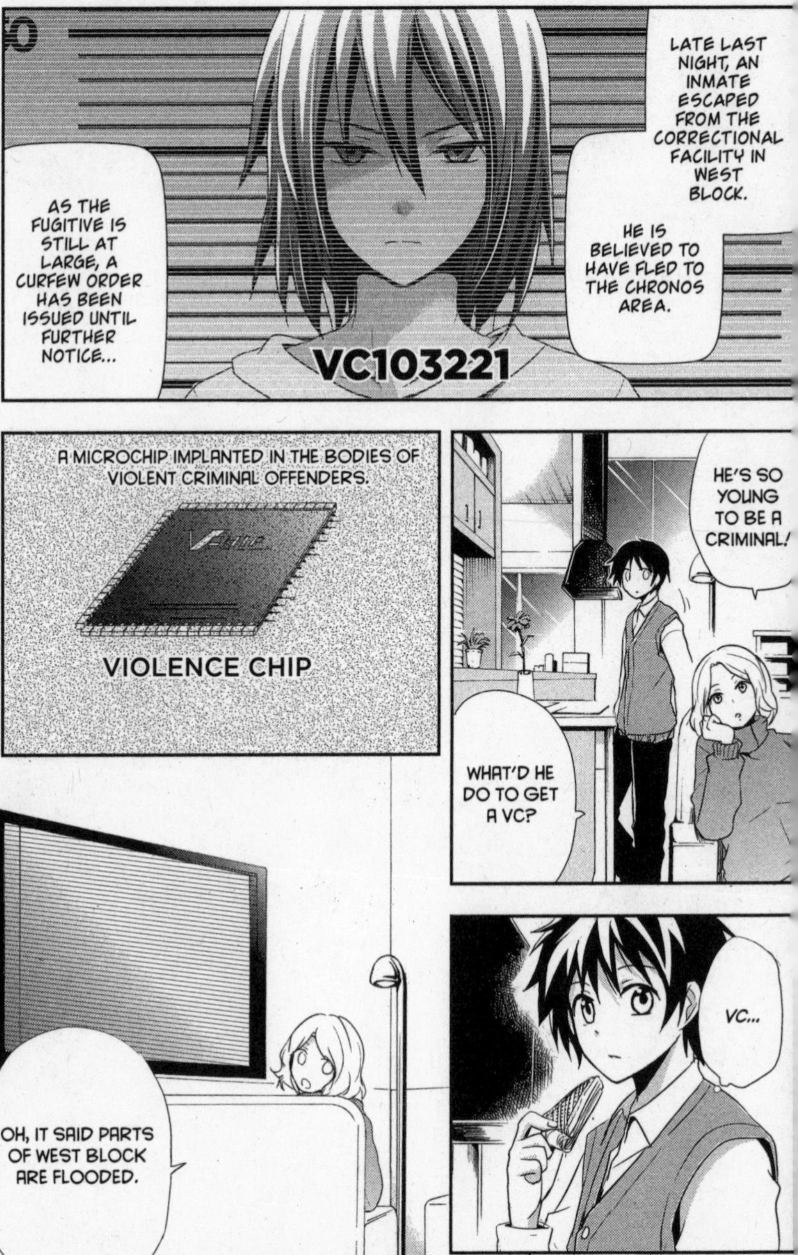
LATE LAST NIGHT, AN INMATE ESCAPED FROM THE CORRECTIONAL FACILITY IN WEST BLOCK.
HE IS BELIEVED TO HAVE FLED TO THE CHRONOS AREA.
VC103221
AS THE FUGITIVE IS STILL AT LARGE, A CURFEW ORDER HAS BEEN ISSUED UNTIL FURTHER NOTICE...
HE'S SO YOUNG TO BE A CRIMINAL!
WHAT'D HE DO TO GET A VC?
A MICROCHIP IMPLANTED IN THE BODIES OF VIOLENT CRIMINAL OFFENDERS.
VIOLENCE CHIP
VC...
OH, IT SAID PARTS OF WEST BLOCK ARE FLOODED.

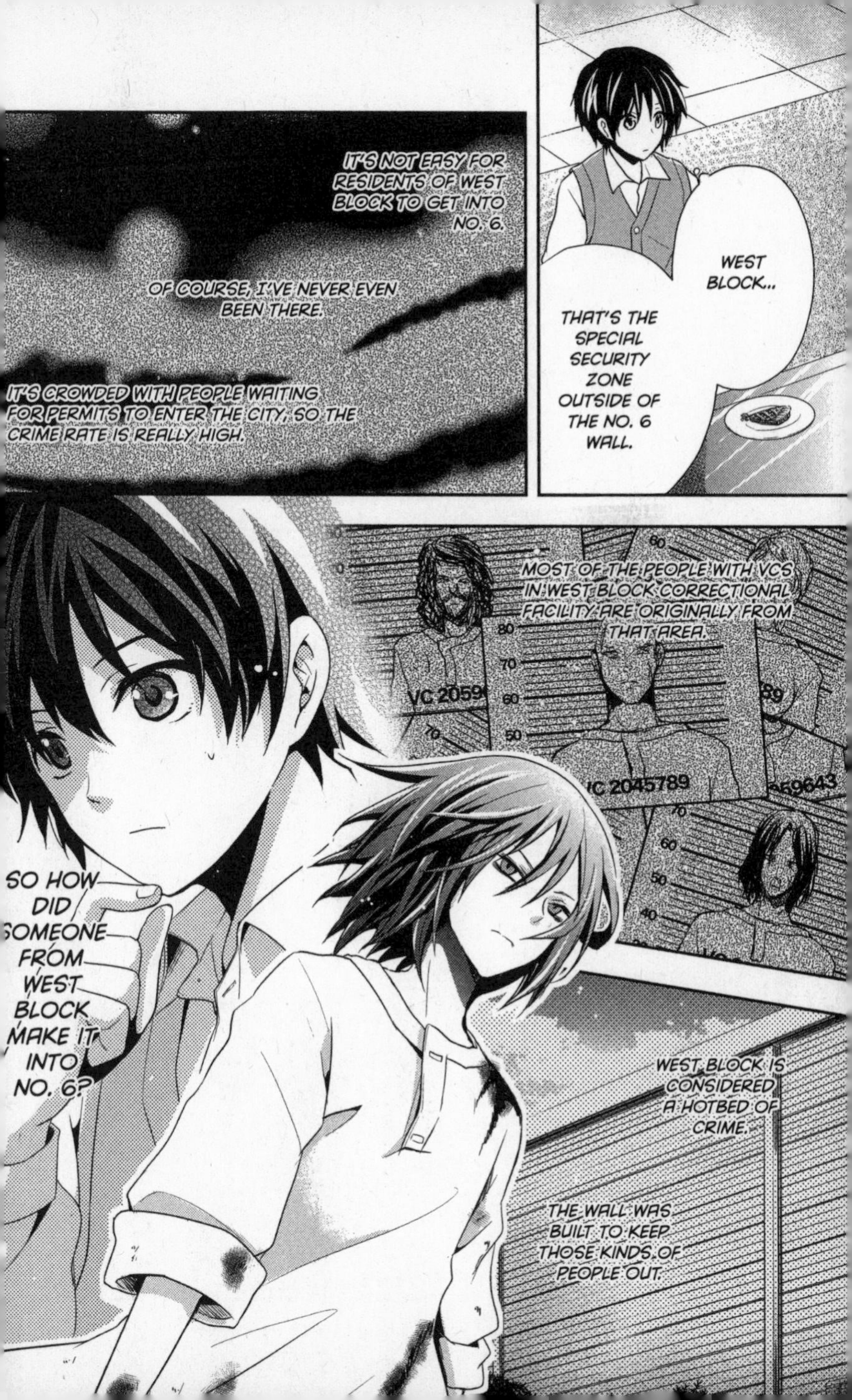
WEST BLOCK...
THAT'S THE SPECIAL SECURITY ZONE OUTSIDE OF THE NO. 6 WALL.
IT'S NOT EASY FOR RESIDENTS OF WEST BLOCK TO GET INTO NO. 6.
OF COURSE, I'VE NEVER EVEN BEEN THERE.
IT'S CROWDED WITH PEOPLE WAITING FOR PERMITS TO ENTER THE CITY, SO THE CRIME RATE IS REALLY HIGH.
MOST OF THE PEOPLE WITH VCS IN WEST BLOCK CORRECTIONAL FACILITY ARE ORIGINALLY FROM THAT AREA.
WEST BLOCK IS CONSIDERED A HOTBED OF CRIME.
THE WALL WAS BUILT TO KEEP THOSE KINDS OF PEOPLE OUT.
SO HOW DID SOMEONE FROM WEST BLOCK MAKE IT INTO NO. 6?

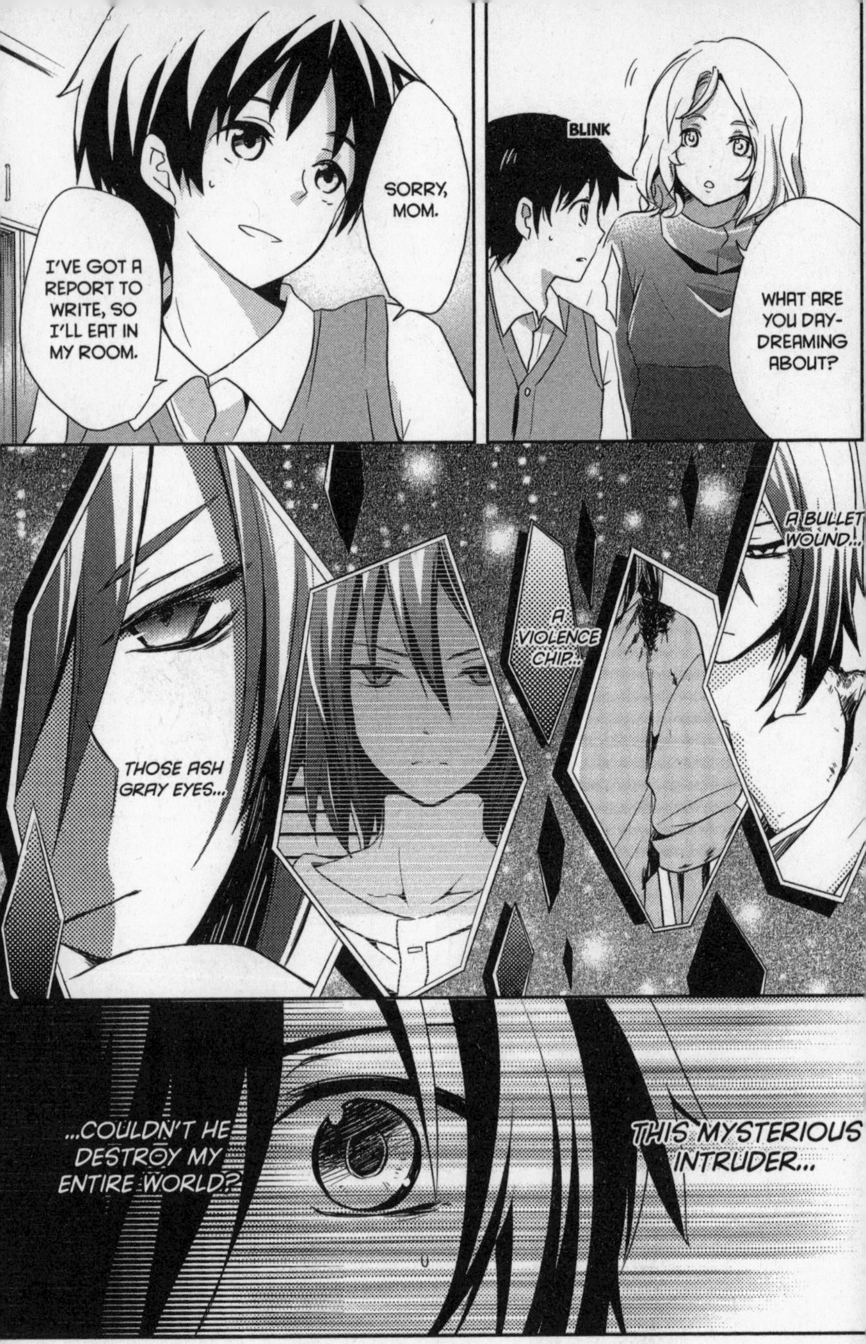
BLINK
WHAT ARE YOU DAY-DREAMING ABOUT?
SORRY, MOM.
I'VE GOT A REPORT TO WRITE, SO I'LL EAT IN MY ROOM.
A BULLET WOUND...
A VIOLENCE CHIP...
THOSE ASH GRAY EYES...
THIS MYSTERIOUS INTRUDER...
...COULDN'T HE DESTROY MY ENTIRE WORLD?

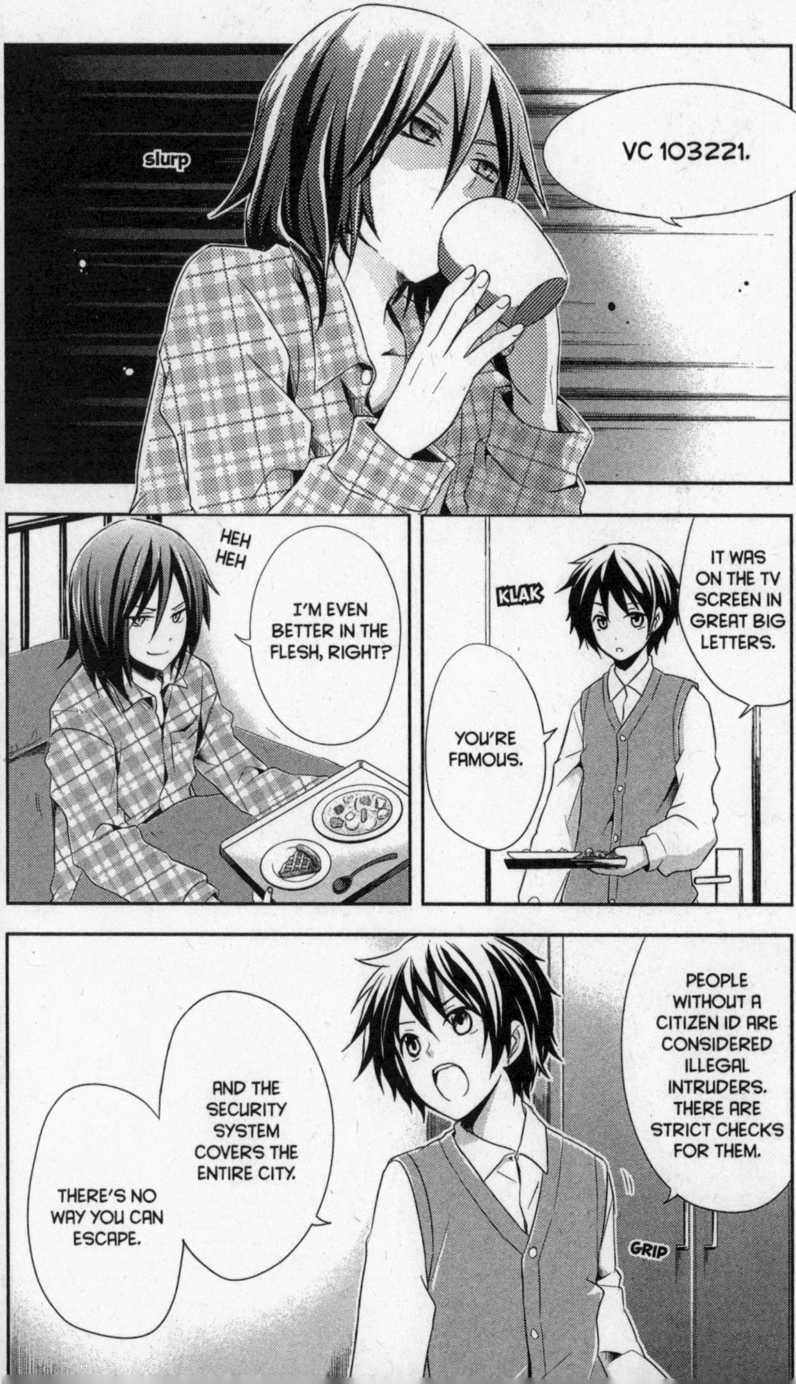
VC 103221.
slurp
IT WAS ON THE TV SCREEN IN GREAT BIG LETTERS.
KLAK
YOU'RE FAMOUS.
HEH HEH
I'M EVEN BETTER IN THE FLESH, RIGHT?
PEOPLE WITHOUT A CITIZEN ID ARE CONSIDERED ILLEGAL INTRUDERS. THERE ARE STRICT CHECKS FOR THEM.
AND THE SECURITY SYSTEM COVERS THE ENTIRE CITY.
THERE'S NO WAY YOU CAN ESCAPE.
GRIP

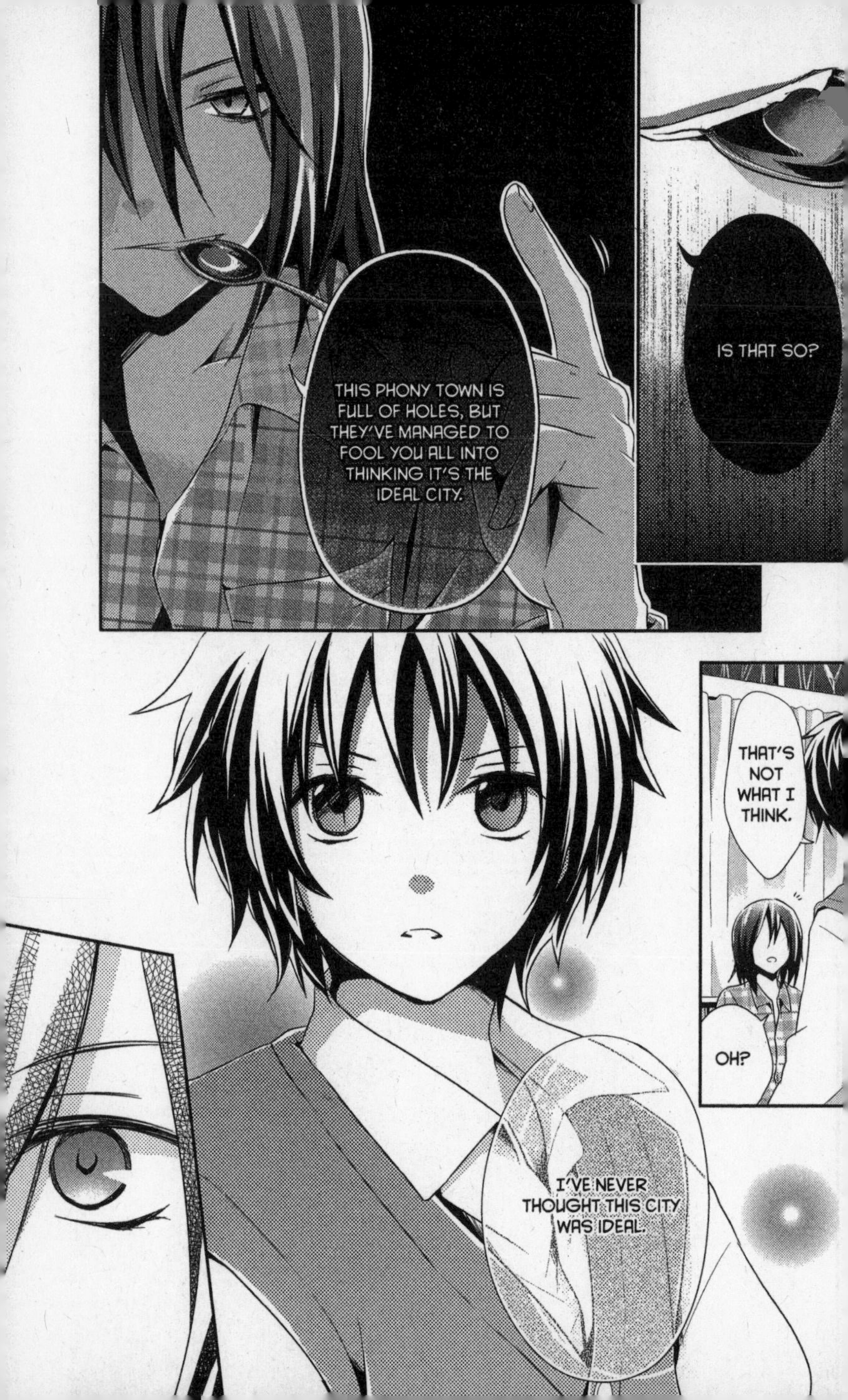
IS THAT SO?
THIS PHONY TOWN IS FULL OF HOLES, BUT THEY'VE MANAGED TO FOOL YOU ALL INTO THINKING IT'S THE IDEAL CITY.
THAT'S NOT WHAT I THINK.
OH?
I'VE NEVER THOUGHT THIS CITY WAS IDEAL.

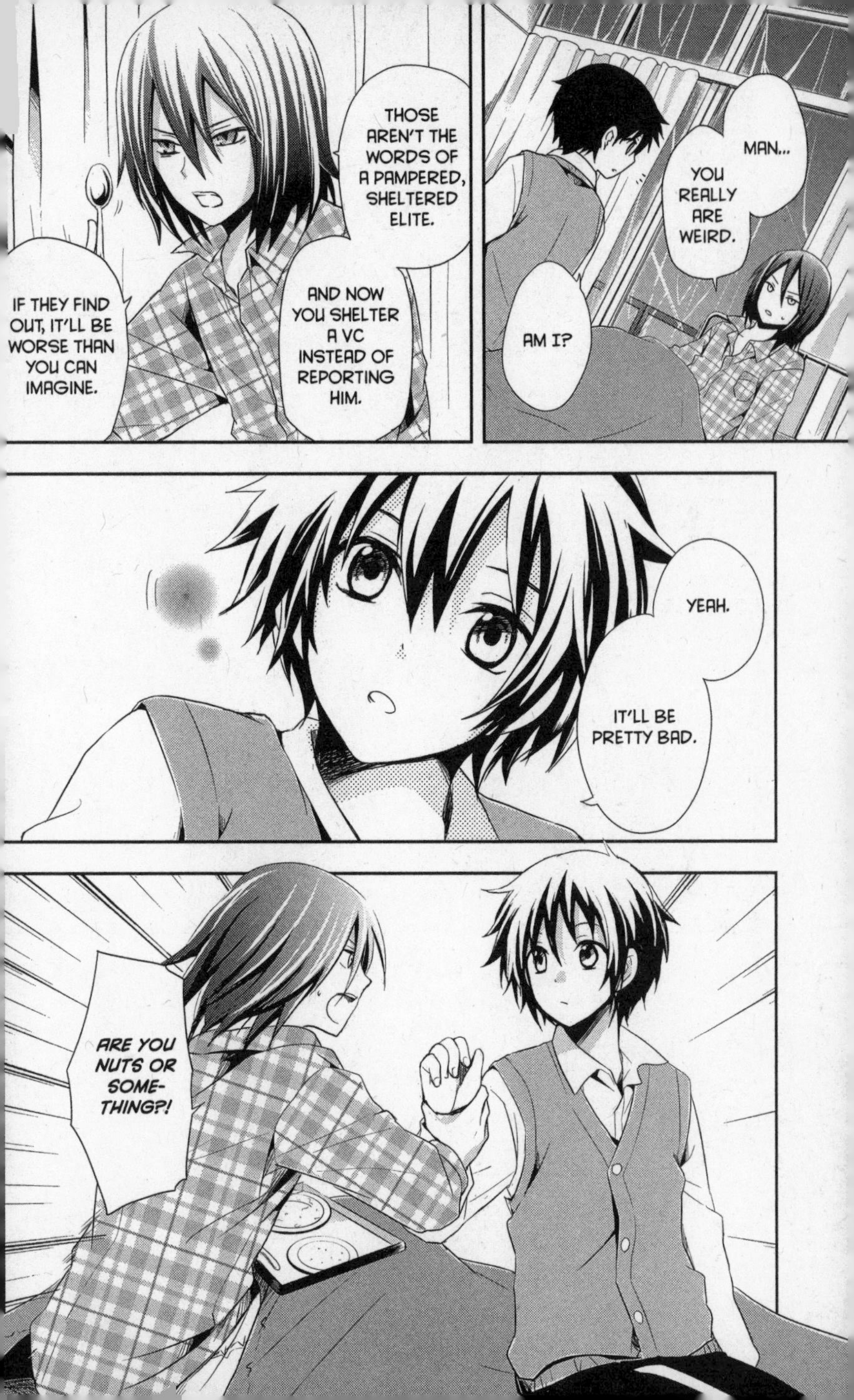
MAN... YOU REALLY ARE WEIRD.
AM I?
THOSE AREN'T THE WORDS OF A PAMPERED, SHELTERED ELITE.
AND NOW YOU SHELTER A VC INSTEAD OF REPORTING HIM.
IF THEY FIND OUT, IT'LL BE WORSE THAN YOU CAN IMAGINE.
YEAH.
IT'LL BE PRETTY BAD.
ARE YOU NUTS OR SOME-THING?!

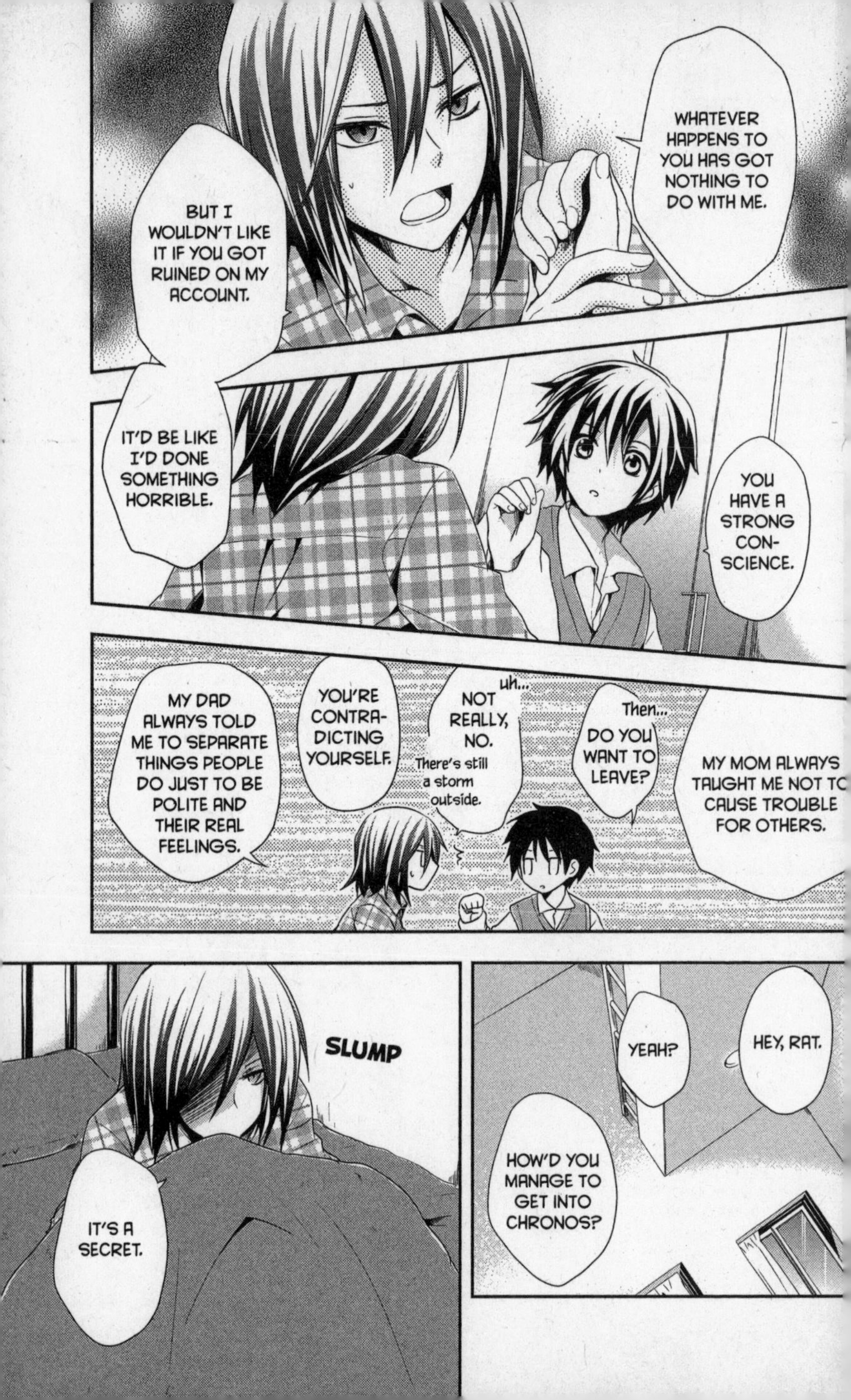
WHATEVER HAPPENS TO YOU HAS GOT NOTHING TO DO WITH ME.
BUT I WOULDN'T LIKE IT IF YOU GOT RUINED ON MY ACCOUNT.
IT'D BE LIKE I'D DONE SOMETHING HORRIBLE.
YOU HAVE A STRONG CON-SCIENCE.
MY MOM ALWAYS TAUGHT ME NOT TO CAUSE TROUBLE FOR OTHERS.
Then...
DO YOU WANT TO LEAVE?
uh...
NOT REALLY, NO.
There's still a storm outside.
YOU'RE CONTRA-DICTING YOURSELF.
MY DAD ALWAYS TOLD ME TO SEPARATE THINGS PEOPLE DO JUST TO BE POLITE AND THEIR REAL FEELINGS.
HEY, RAT.
YEAH?
HOW'D YOU MANAGE TO GET INTO CHRONOS?
SLUMP
IT'S A SECRET.

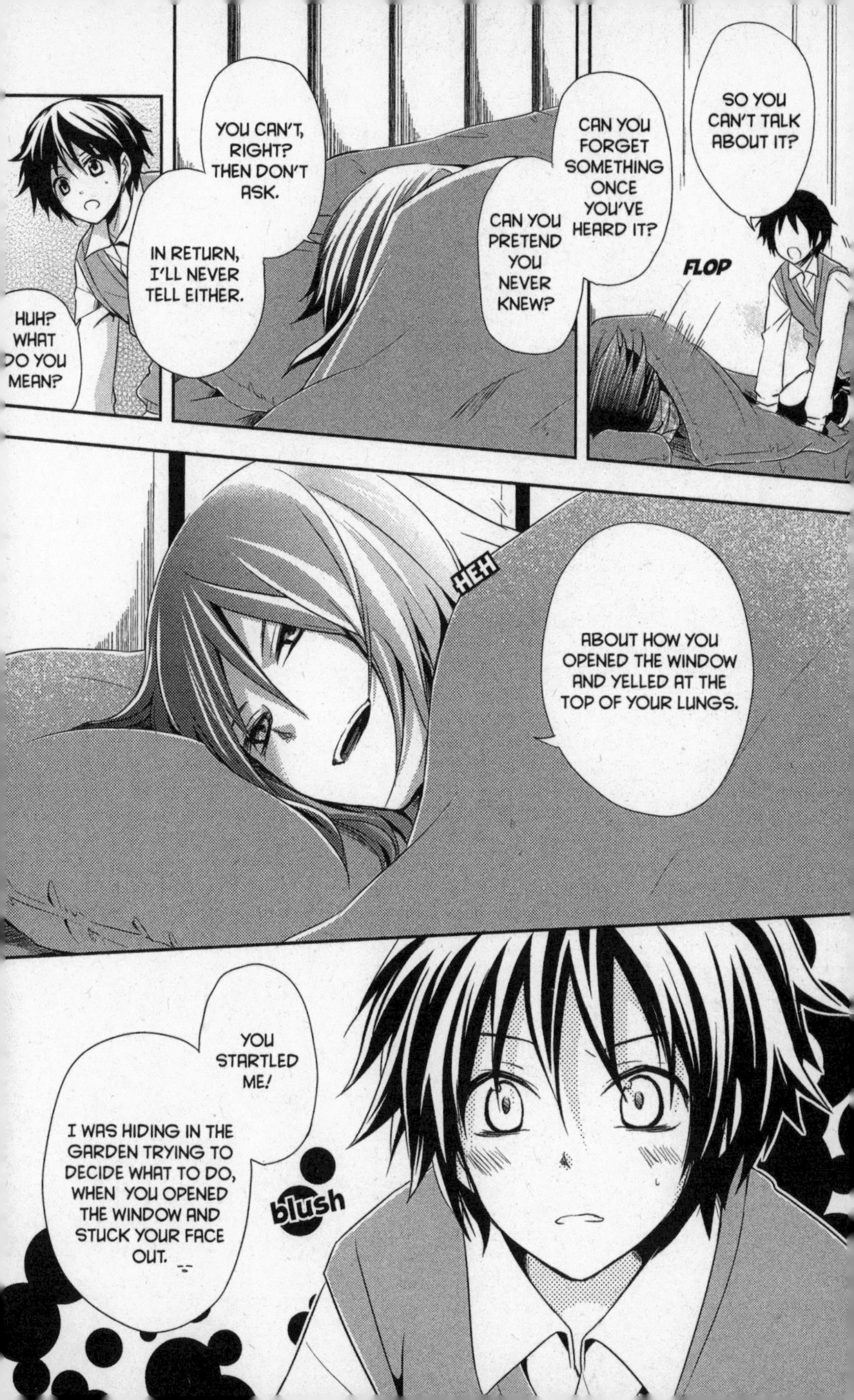
SO YOU CAN'T TALK ABOUT IT?
FLOP
CAN YOU FORGET SOMETHING ONCE YOU'VE HEARD IT?
CAN YOU PRETEND YOU NEVER KNEW?
YOU CAN'T, RIGHT? THEN DON'T ASK.
IN RETURN, I'LL NEVER TELL EITHER.
HUH? WHAT DO YOU MEAN?
HEH
ABOUT HOW YOU OPENED THE WINDOW AND YELLED AT THE TOP OF YOUR LUNGS.
YOU STARTLED ME!
I WAS HIDING IN THE GARDEN TRYING TO DECIDE WHAT TO DO, WHEN YOU OPENED THE WINDOW AND STUCK YOUR FACE OUT.
blush

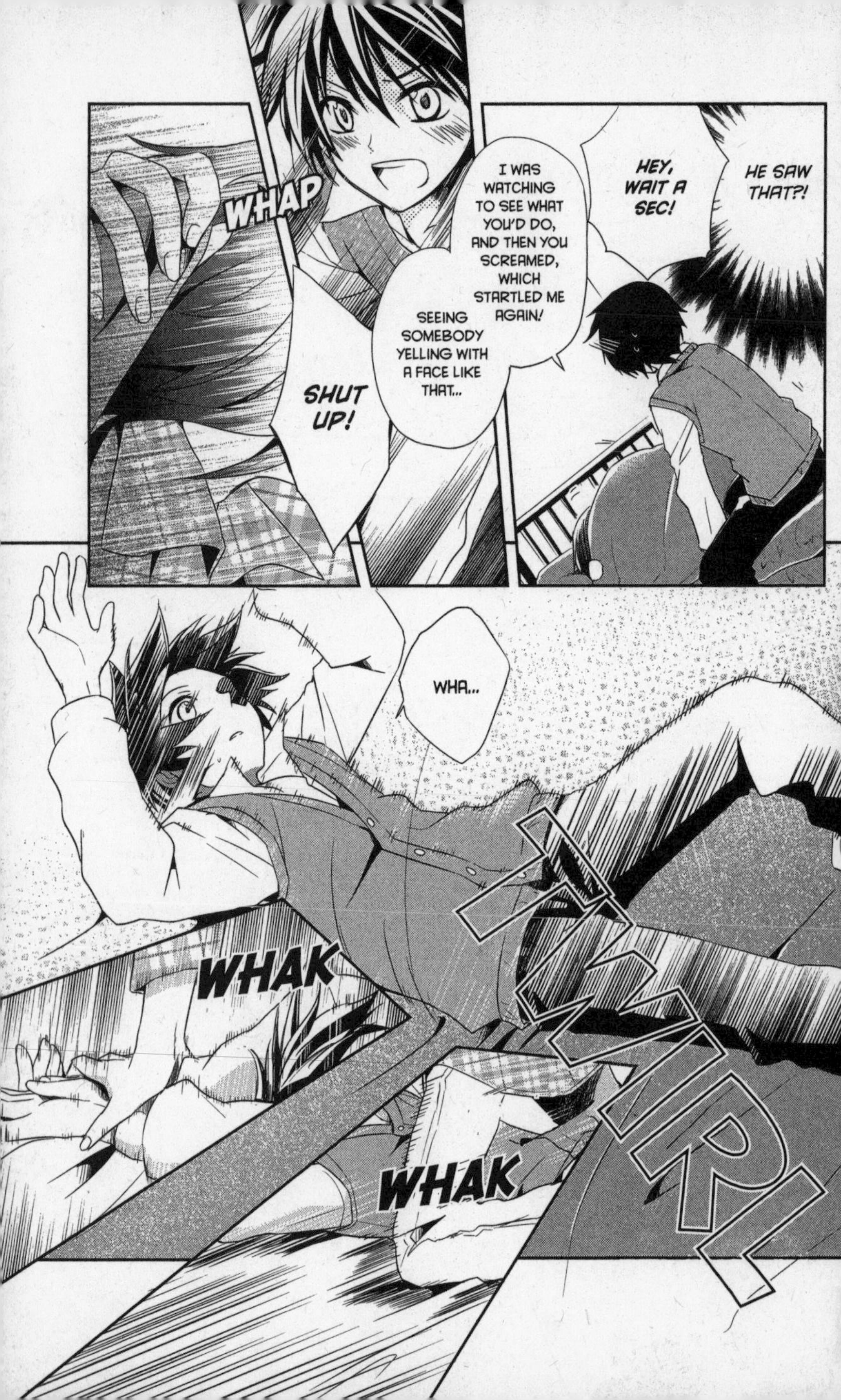
HE SAW THAT?!
HEY, WAIT A SEC!
I WAS WATCHING TO SEE WHAT YOU'D DO, AND THEN YOU SCREAMED, WHICH STARTLED ME AGAIN!
SEEING SOMEBODY YELLING WITH A FACE LIKE THAT...
SHUT UP!
WHAP
WHA...
TWIRL
WHAK
WHAK

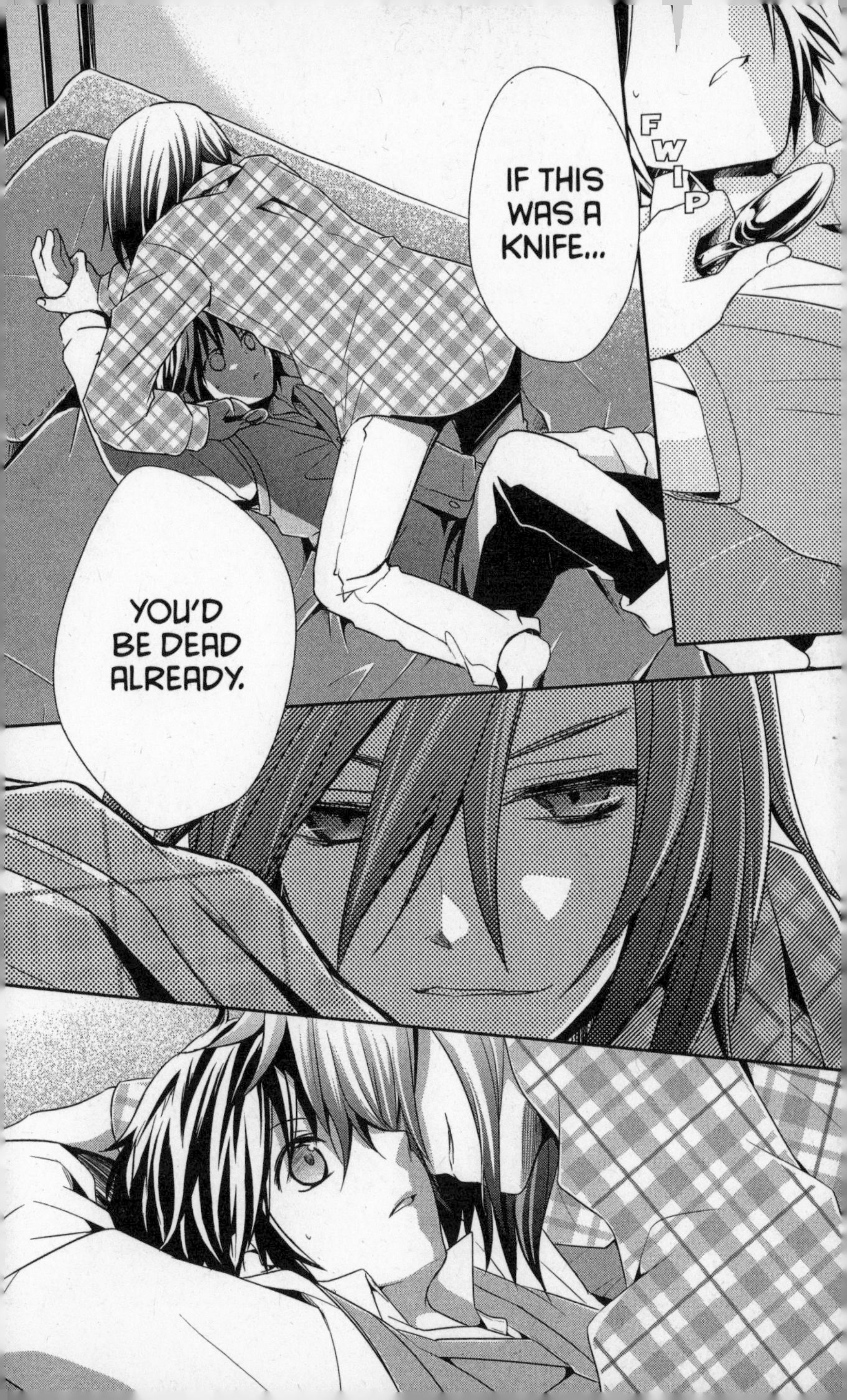
FWIP
IF THIS WAS A KNIFE...
YOU'D BE DEAD ALREADY.

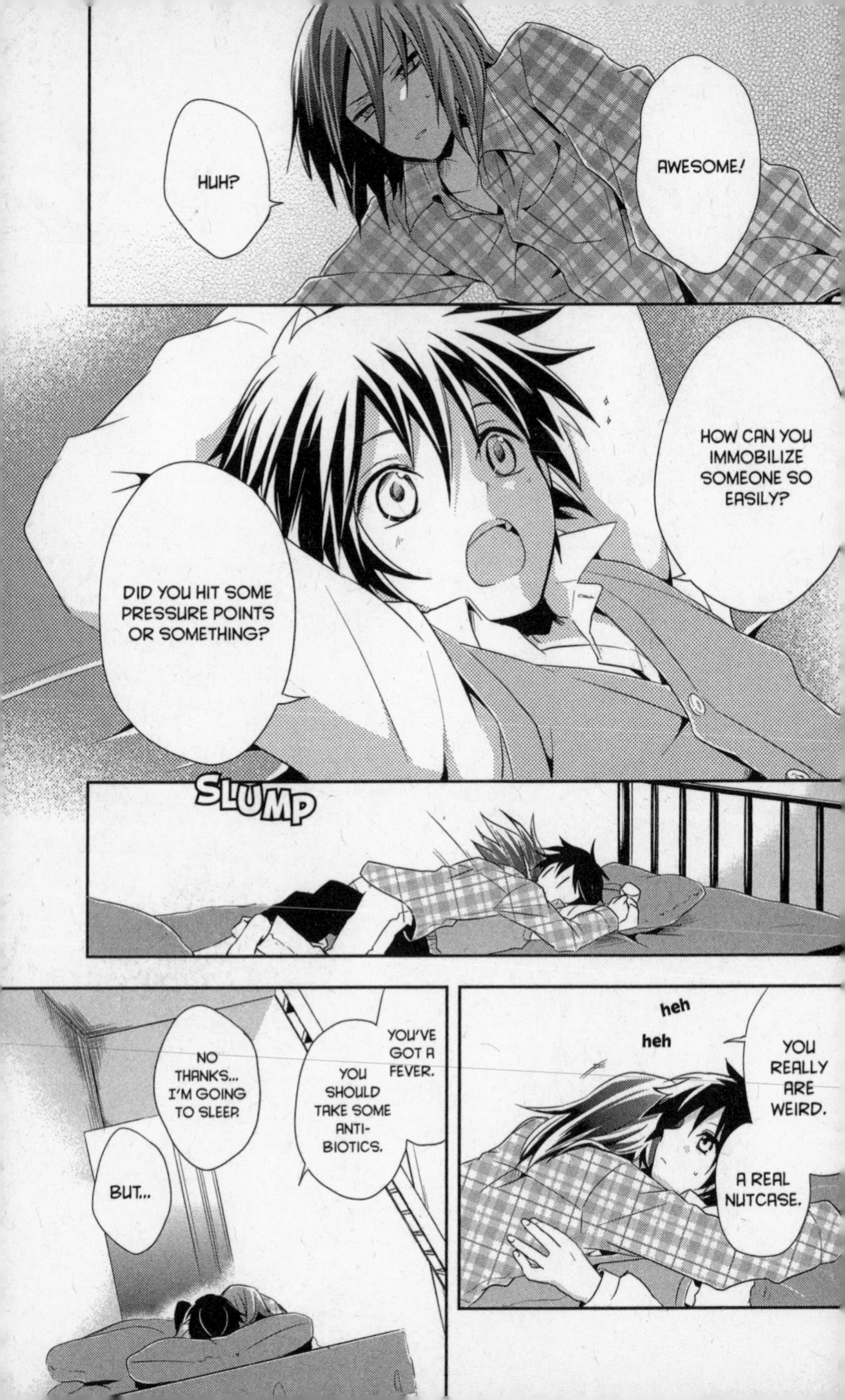
AWESOME!
HUH?
HOW CAN YOU IMMOBILIZE SOMEONE SO EASILY?
DID YOU HIT SOME PRESSURE POINTS OR SOMETHING?
SLUMP
heh
heh
YOU REALLY ARE WEIRD.
A REAL NUTCASE.
YOU'VE GOT A FEVER.
YOU SHOULD TAKE SOME ANTI-BIOTICS.
NO THANKS... I'M GOING TO SLEEP.
BUT...

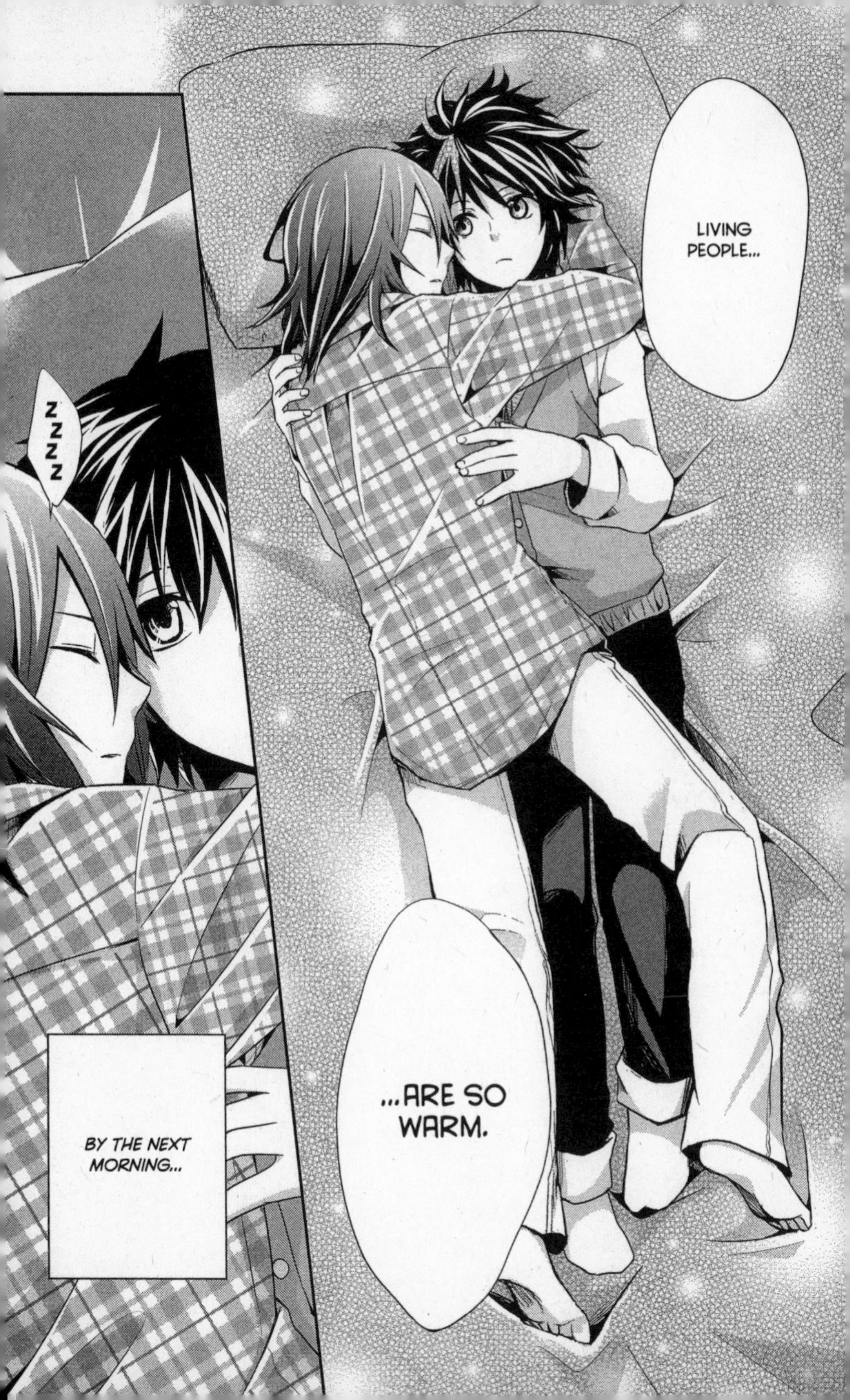
LIVING PEOPLE...
...ARE SO WARM.
ZZZZ
BY THE NEXT MORNING...

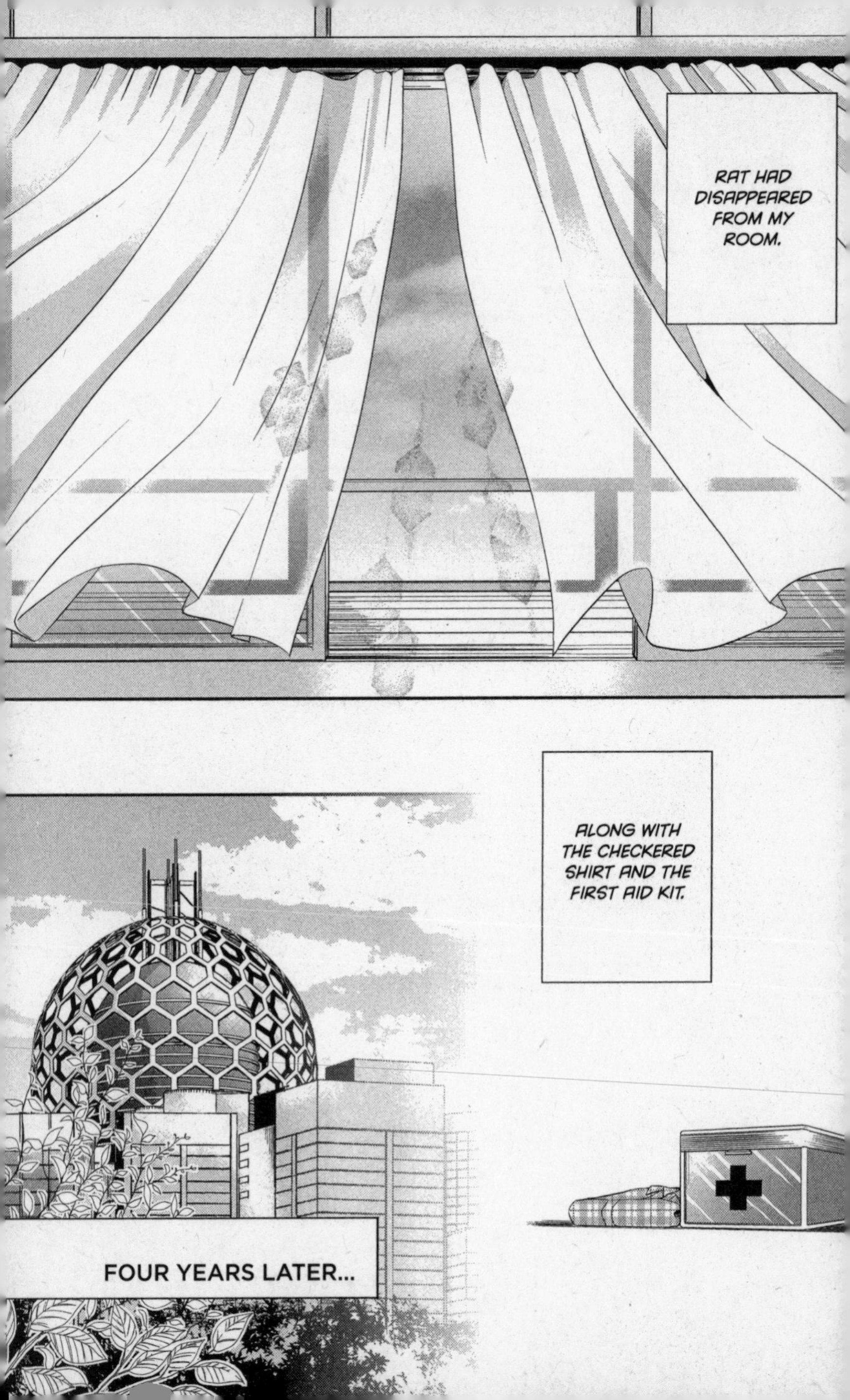
RAT HAD DISAPPEARED FROM MY ROOM.
ALONG WITH THE CHECKERED SHIRT AND THE FIRST AID KIT.
FOUR YEARS LATER...

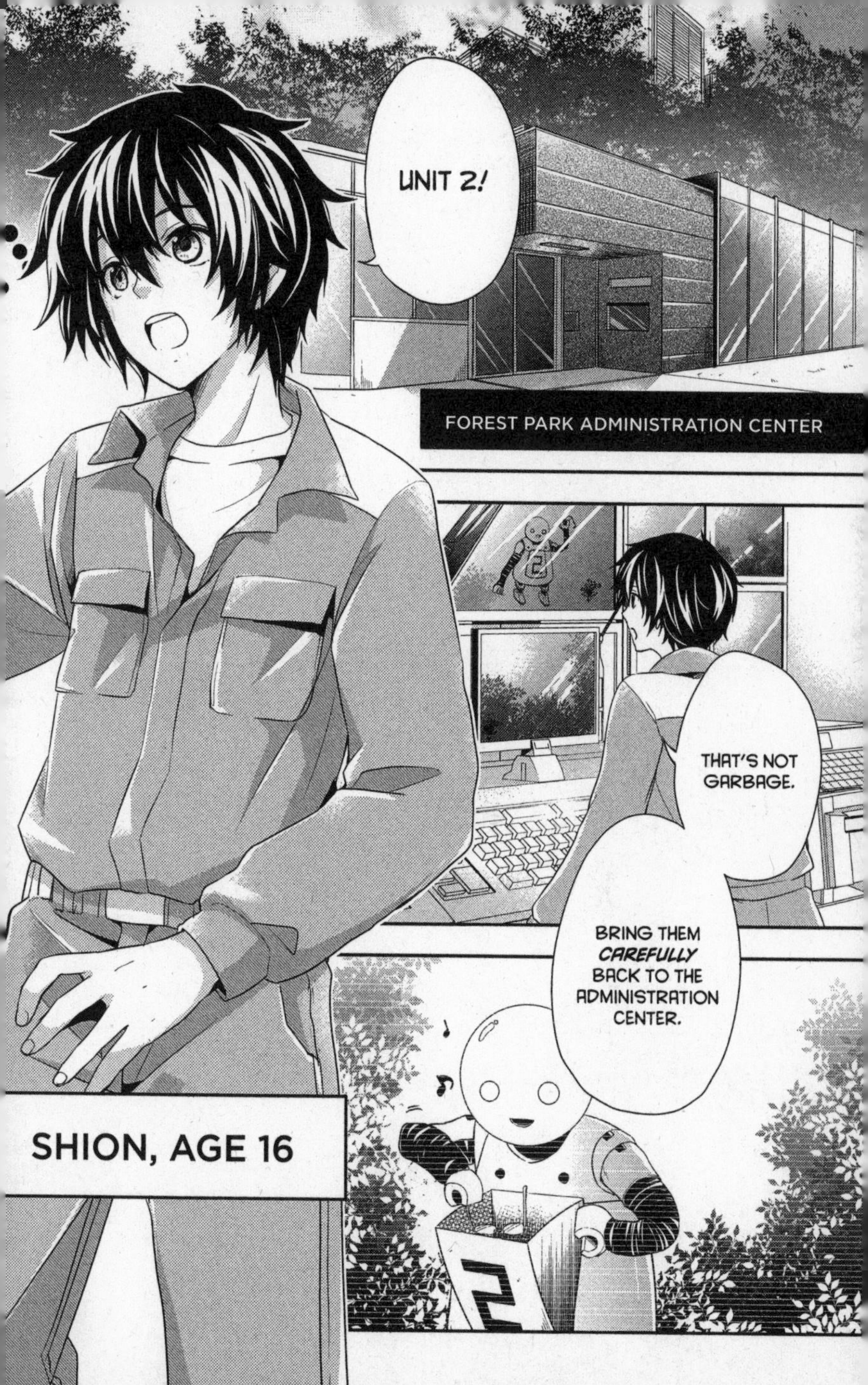
UNIT 2!
FOREST PARK ADMINISTRATION CENTER
THAT'S NOT GARBAGE.
BRING THEM *CAREFULLY* BACK TO THE ADMINISTRATION CENTER.
SHION, AGE 16

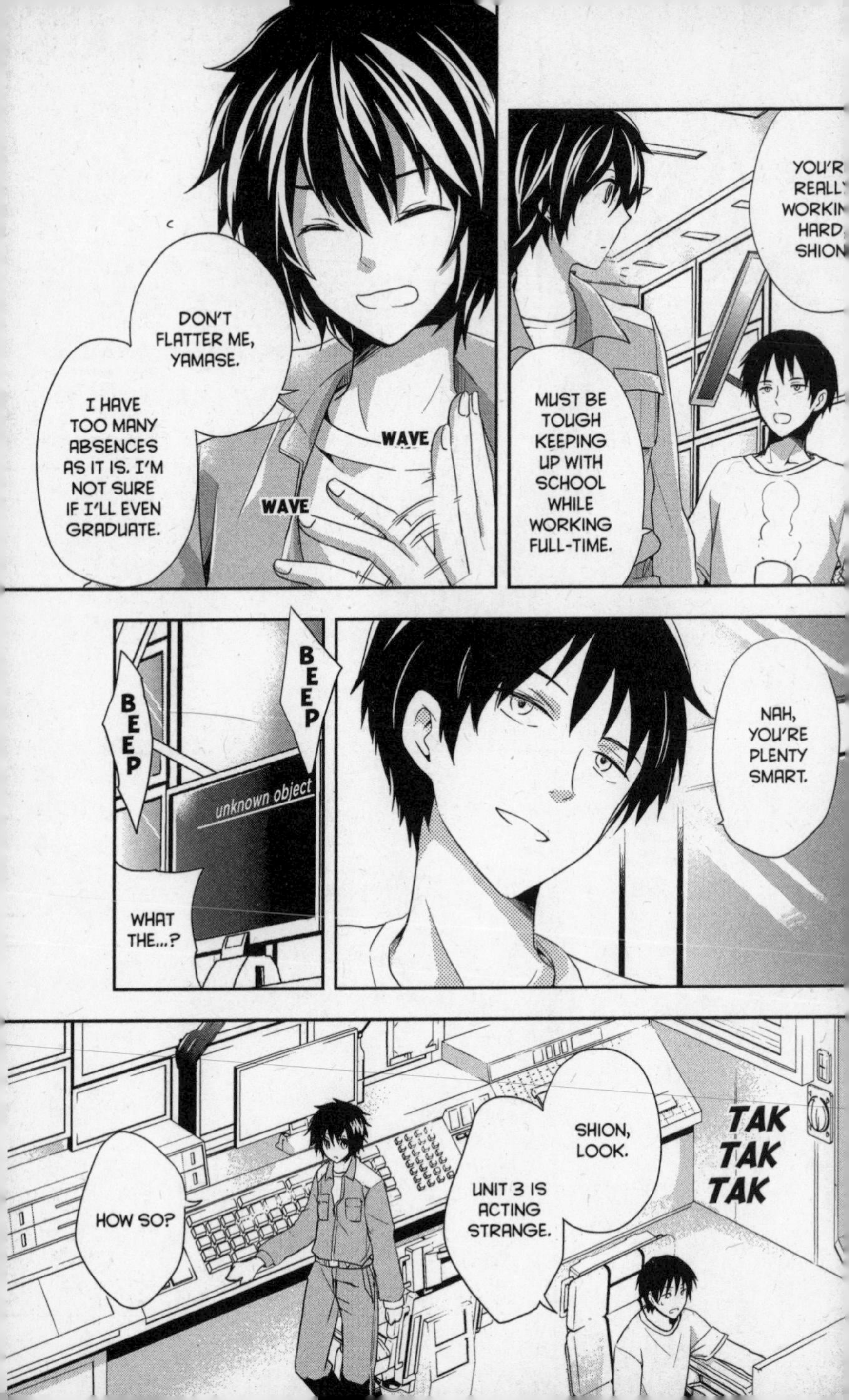

YOU'R REALL WORKIN HARD, SHION
MUST BE TOUGH KEEPING UP WITH SCHOOL WHILE WORKING FULL-TIME.
DON'T FLATTER ME, YAMASE.
I HAVE TOO MANY ABSENCES AS IT IS. I'M NOT SURE IF I'LL EVEN GRADUATE.
WAVE
WAVE
NAH, YOU'RE PLENTY SMART.
BEEP
BEEP
unknown object
WHAT THE...?
TAK TAK TAK
SHION, LOOK.
UNIT 3 IS ACTING STRANGE.
HOW SO?

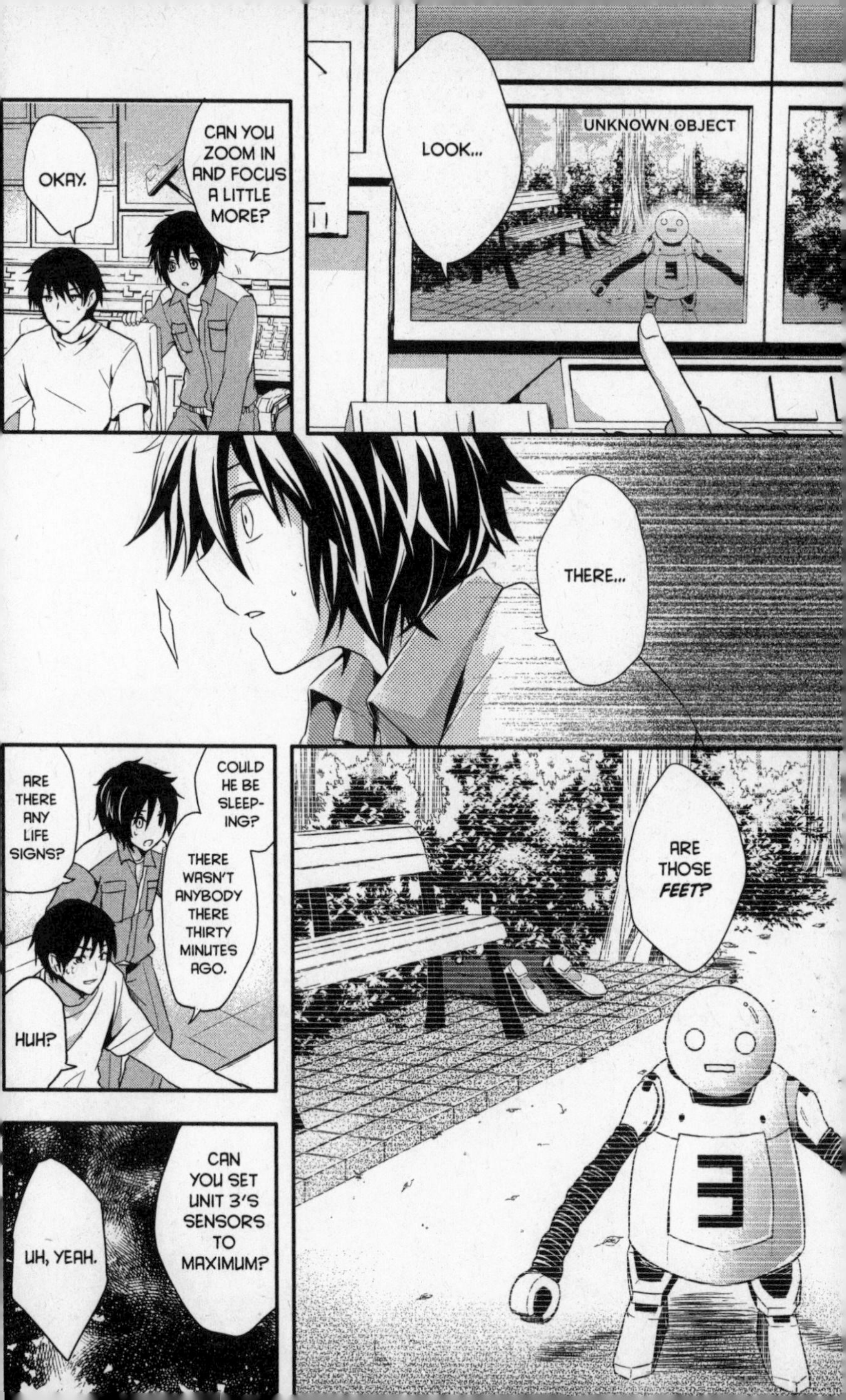
LOOK...
UNKNOWN OBJECT
CAN YOU ZOOM IN AND FOCUS A LITTLE MORE?
OKAY.
THERE...
ARE THOSE *FEET*?
COULD HE BE SLEEP-ING?
THERE WASN'T ANYBODY THERE THIRTY MINUTES AGO.
ARE THERE ANY LIFE SIGNS?
HUH?
CAN YOU SET UNIT 3'S SENSORS TO MAXIMUM?
UH, YEAH.

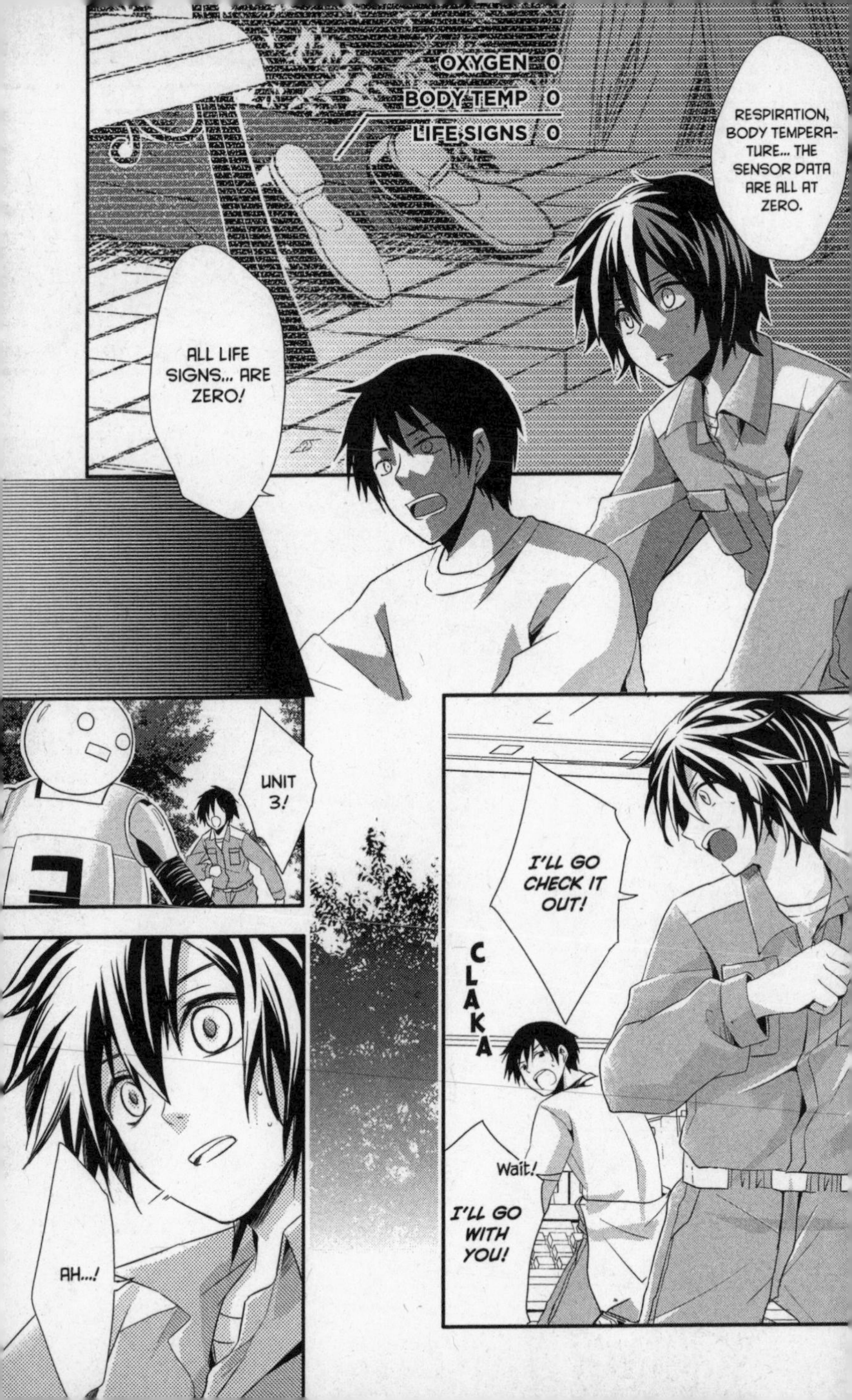
OXYGEN 0
BODY TEMP 0
LIFE SIGNS 0
RESPIRATION, BODY TEMPERATURE... THE SENSOR DATA ARE ALL AT ZERO.
ALL LIFE SIGNS... ARE ZERO!
I'LL GO CHECK IT OUT!
CLAKA
Wait!
I'LL GO WITH YOU!
UNIT 3!
AH...!

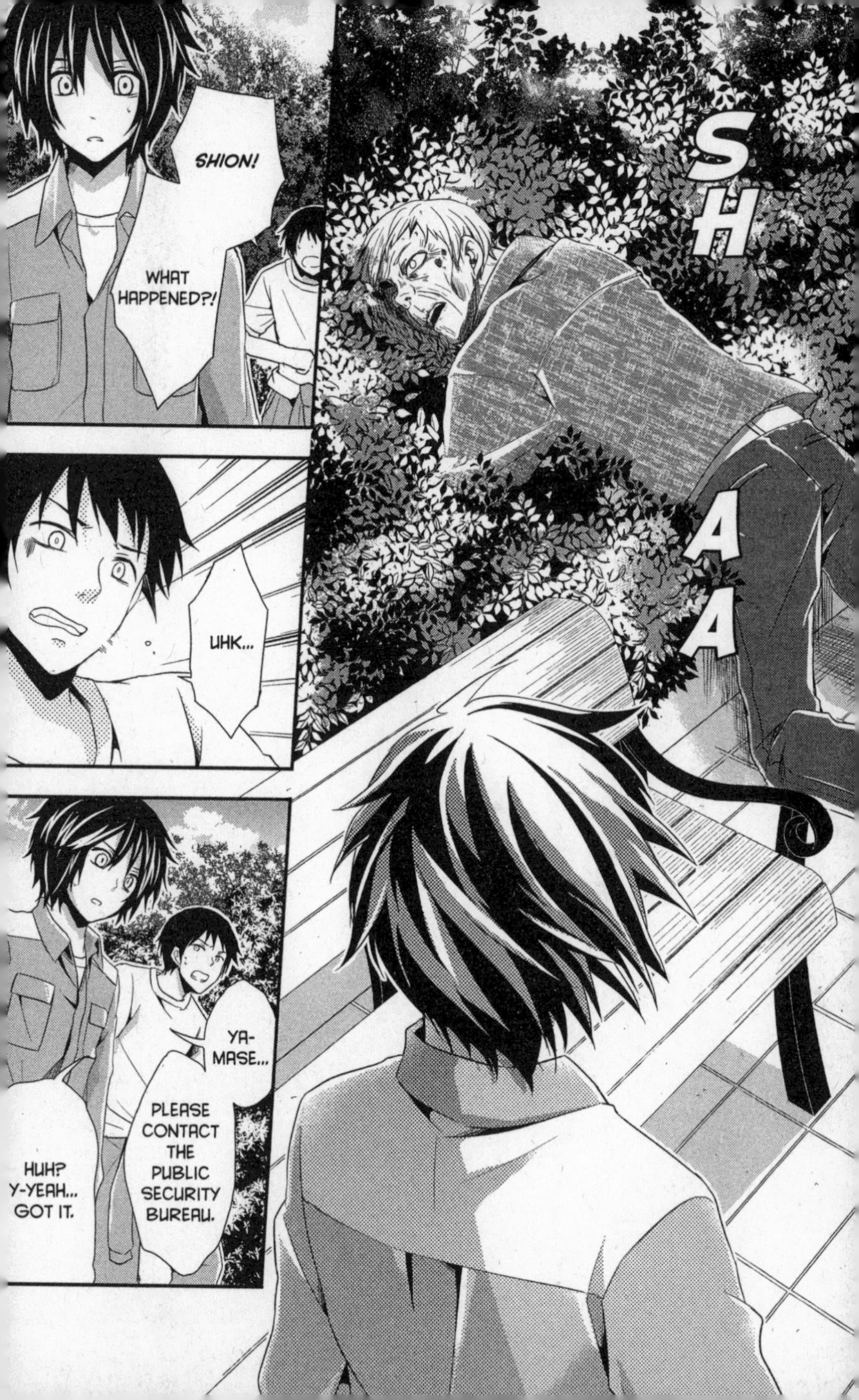
SHAA
SHION!
WHAT HAPPENED?!
UHK...
YA-MASE...
PLEASE CONTACT THE PUBLIC SECURITY BUREAU.
HUH? Y-YEAH... GOT IT.

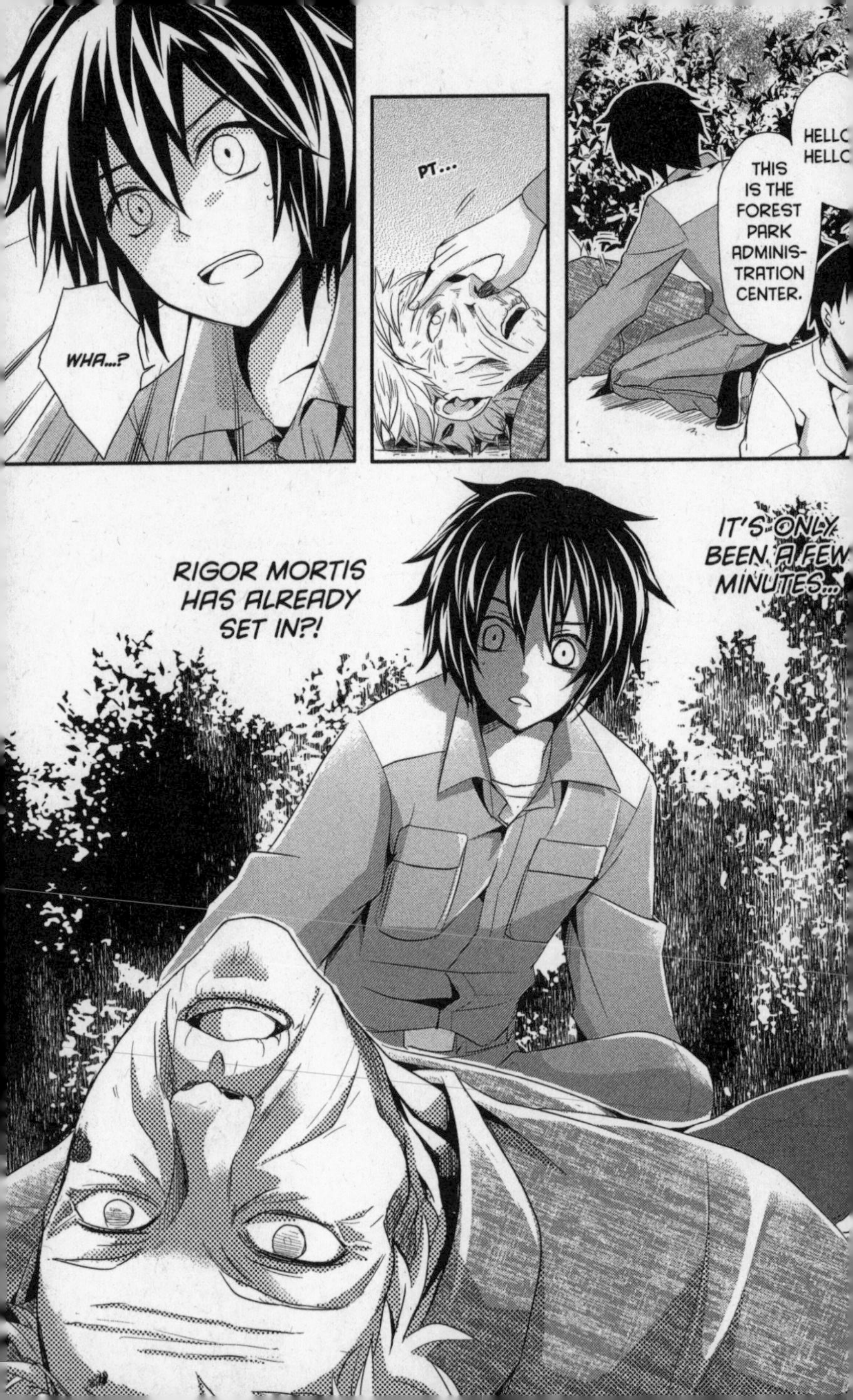
HELLO HELLO
THIS IS THE FOREST PARK ADMINIS-TRATION CENTER.
PT...
WHA...?
IT'S ONLY BEEN A FEW MINUTES...
RIGOR MORTIS HAS ALREADY SET IN?!

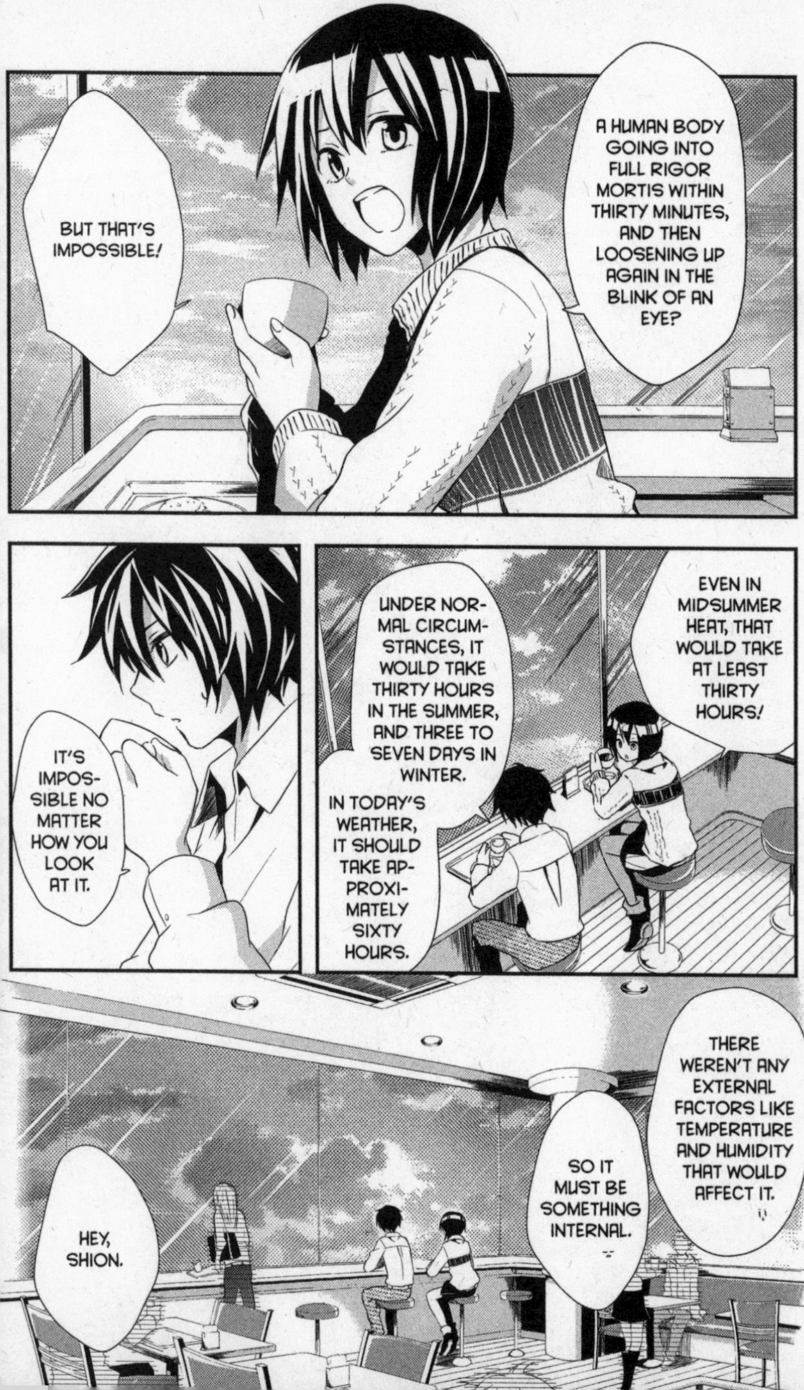
A HUMAN BODY GOING INTO FULL RIGOR MORTIS WITHIN THIRTY MINUTES, AND THEN LOOSENING UP AGAIN IN THE BLINK OF AN EYE?
BUT THAT'S IMPOSSIBLE!
EVEN IN MIDSUMMER HEAT, THAT WOULD TAKE AT LEAST THIRTY HOURS!
UNDER NOR-MAL CIRCUM-STANCES, IT WOULD TAKE THIRTY HOURS IN THE SUMMER, AND THREE TO SEVEN DAYS IN WINTER.
IN TODAY'S WEATHER, IT SHOULD TAKE AP-PROXI-MATELY SIXTY HOURS.
IT'S IMPOS-SIBLE NO MATTER HOW YOU LOOK AT IT.
THERE WEREN'T ANY EXTERNAL FACTORS LIKE TEMPERATURE AND HUMIDITY THAT WOULD AFFECT IT.
SO IT MUST BE SOMETHING INTERNAL.
HEY, SHION.

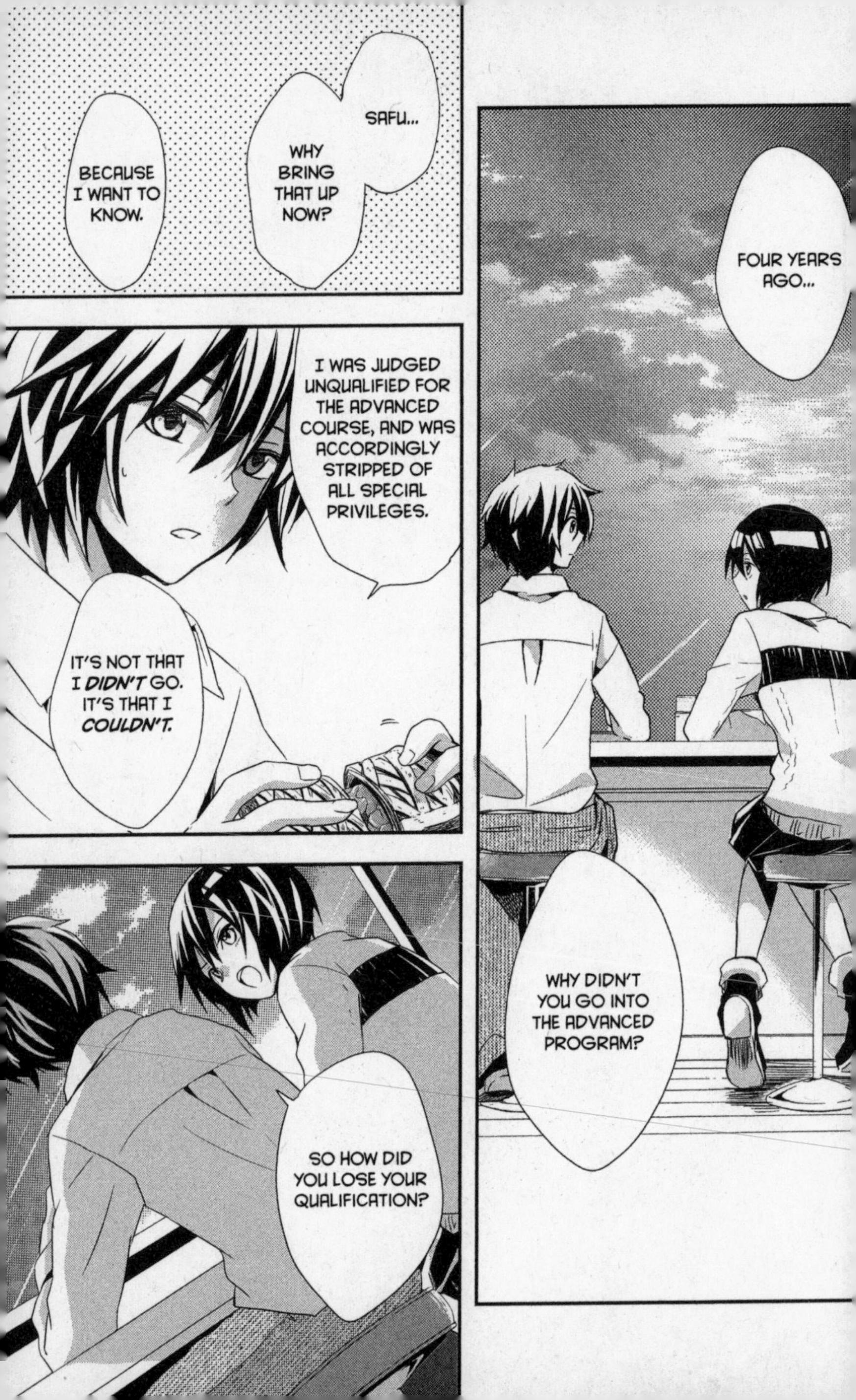
SAFU...
WHY BRING THAT UP NOW?
BECAUSE I WANT TO KNOW.
FOUR YEARS AGO...
WHY DIDN'T YOU GO INTO THE ADVANCED PROGRAM?
I WAS JUDGED UNQUALIFIED FOR THE ADVANCED COURSE, AND WAS ACCORDINGLY STRIPPED OF ALL SPECIAL PRIVILEGES.
IT'S NOT THAT I *DIDN'T* GO. IT'S THAT I *COULDN'T.*
SO HOW DID YOU LOSE YOUR QUALIFICATION?

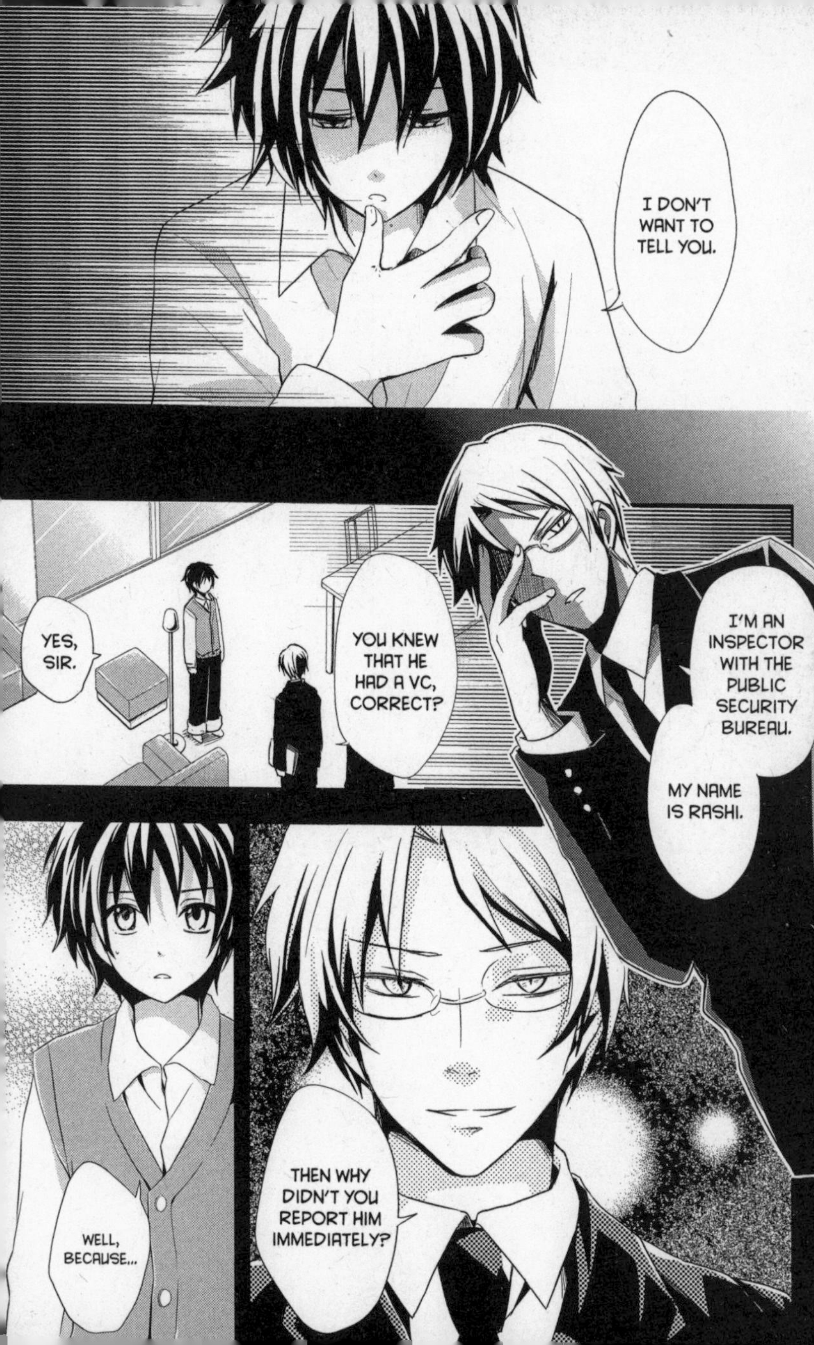
I DON'T WANT TO TELL YOU.
I'M AN INSPECTOR WITH THE PUBLIC SECURITY BUREAU.
MY NAME IS RASHI.
YOU KNEW THAT HE HAD A VC, CORRECT?
YES, SIR.
THEN WHY DIDN'T YOU REPORT HIM IMMEDIATELY?
WELL, BECAUSE...

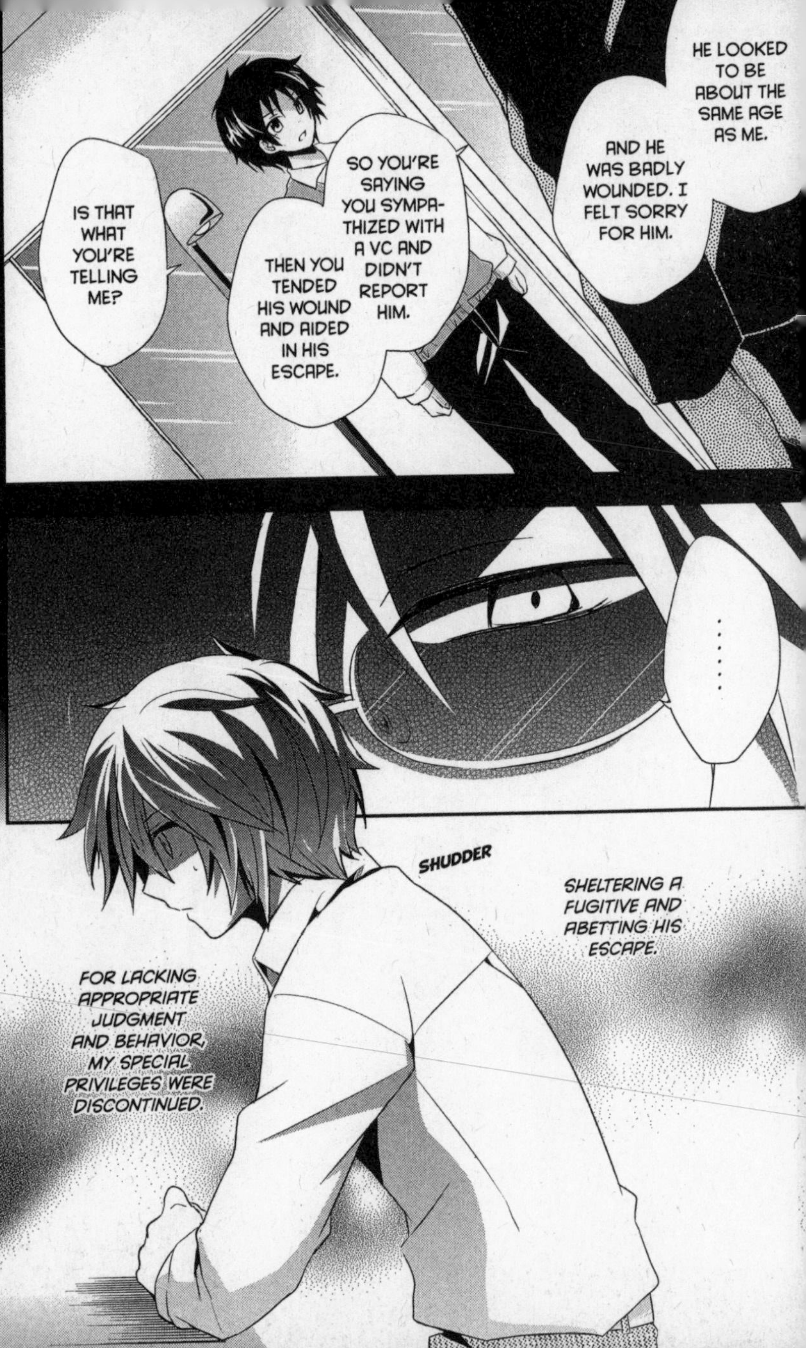
HE LOOKED TO BE ABOUT THE SAME AGE AS ME.
AND HE WAS BADLY WOUNDED. I FELT SORRY FOR HIM.
SO YOU'RE SAYING YOU SYMPATHIZED WITH A VC AND DIDN'T REPORT HIM.
THEN YOU TENDED HIS WOUND AND AIDED IN HIS ESCAPE.
IS THAT WHAT YOU'RE TELLING ME?
......
SHUDDER
SHELTERING A FUGITIVE AND ABETTING HIS ESCAPE.
FOR LACKING APPROPRIATE JUDGMENT AND BEHAVIOR, MY SPECIAL PRIVILEGES WERE DISCONTINUED.

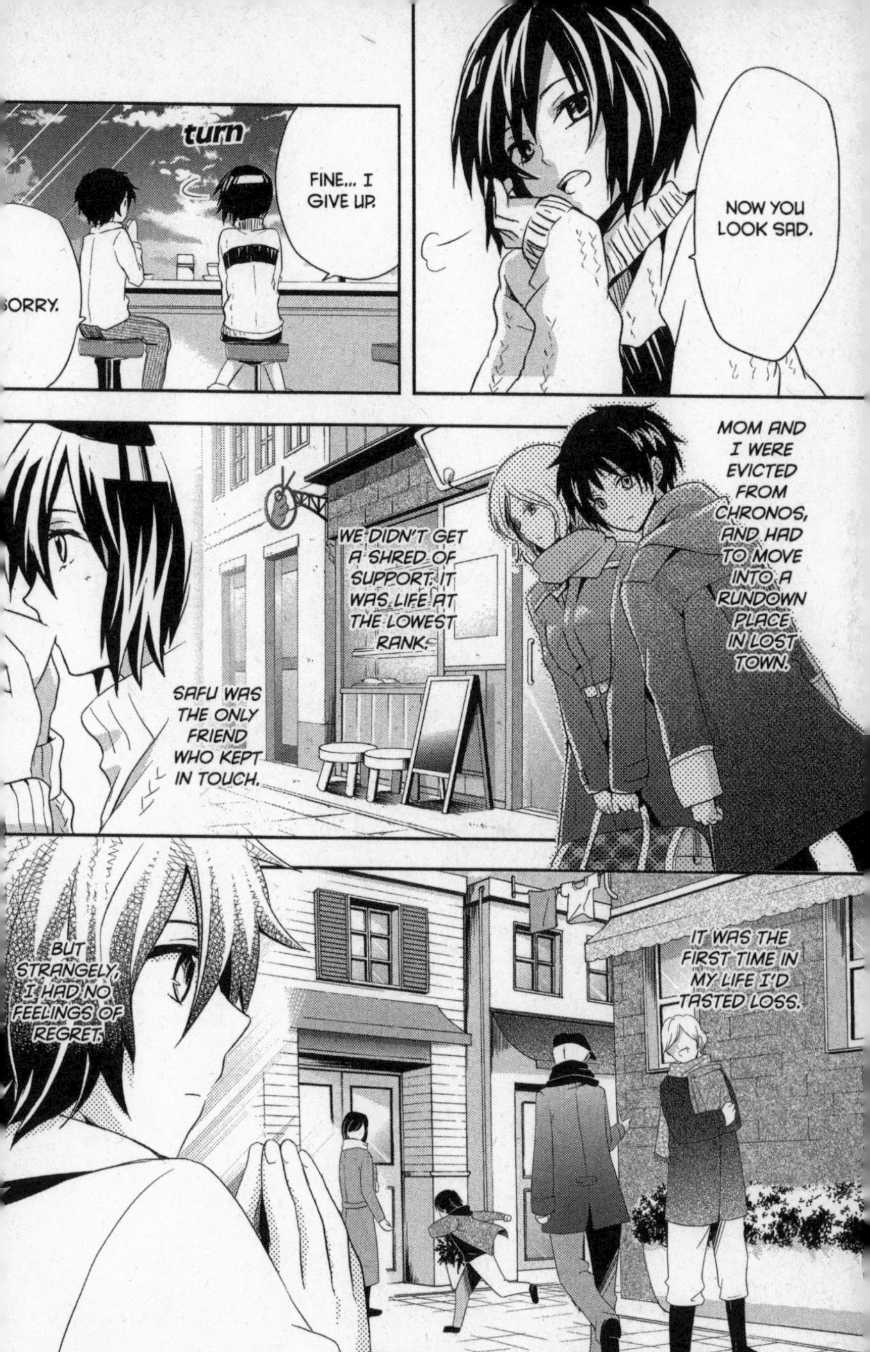
NOW YOU LOOK SAD.
FINE... I GIVE UP.
turn
SORRY.
MOM AND I WERE EVICTED FROM CHRONOS, AND HAD TO MOVE INTO A RUNDOWN PLACE IN LOST TOWN.
WE DIDN'T GET A SHRED OF SUPPORT. IT WAS LIFE AT THE LOWEST RANK.
SAFU WAS THE ONLY FRIEND WHO KEPT IN TOUCH.
IT WAS THE FIRST TIME IN MY LIFE I'D TASTED LOSS.
BUT STRANGELY, I HAD NO FEELINGS OF REGRET.

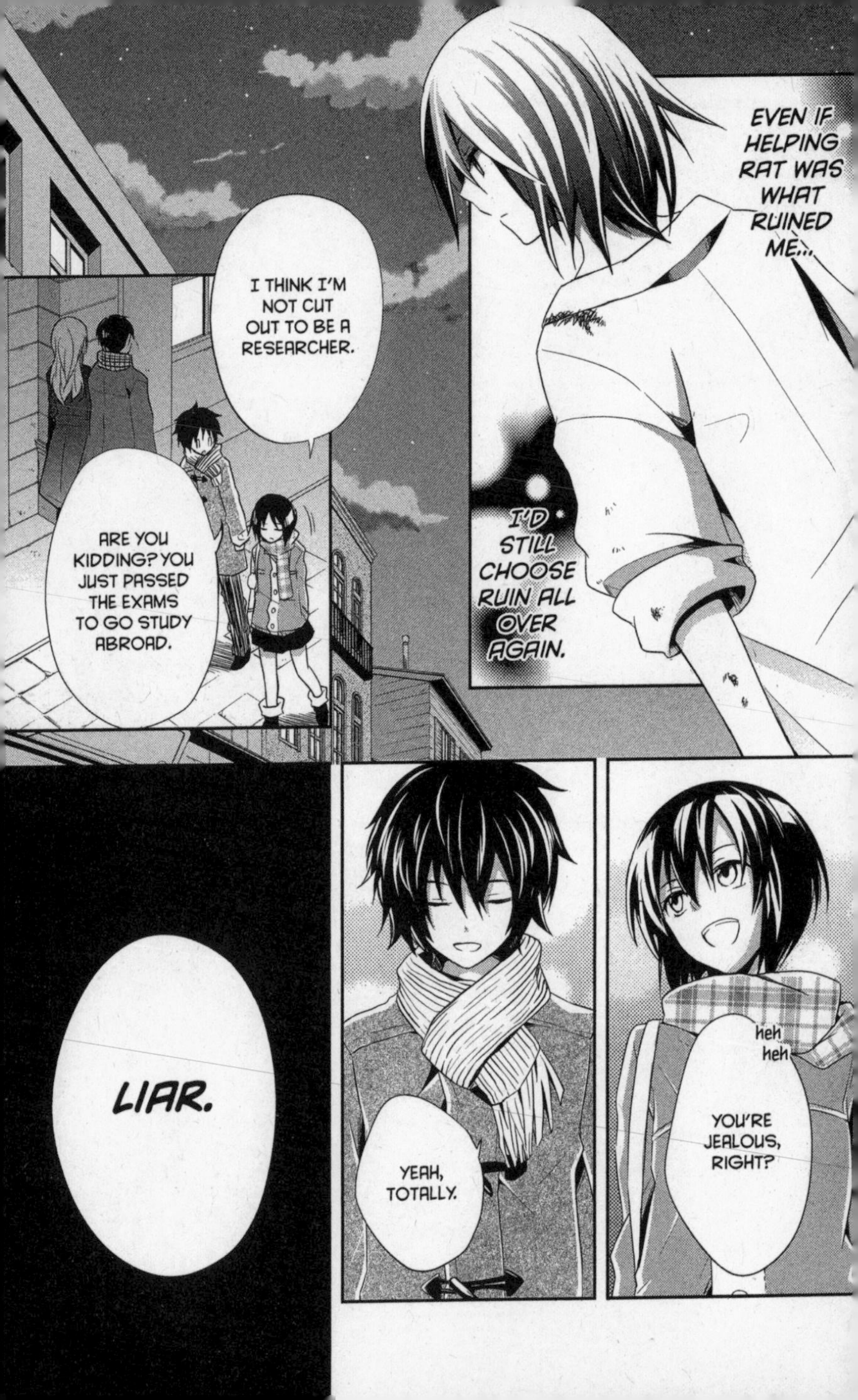
EVEN IF HELPING RAT WAS WHAT RUINED ME...
I'D STILL CHOOSE RUIN ALL OVER AGAIN.
I THINK I'M NOT CUT OUT TO BE A RESEARCHER.
ARE YOU KIDDING? YOU JUST PASSED THE EXAMS TO GO STUDY ABROAD.
heh heh
YOU'RE JEALOUS, RIGHT?
YEAH, TOTALLY.
LIAR.

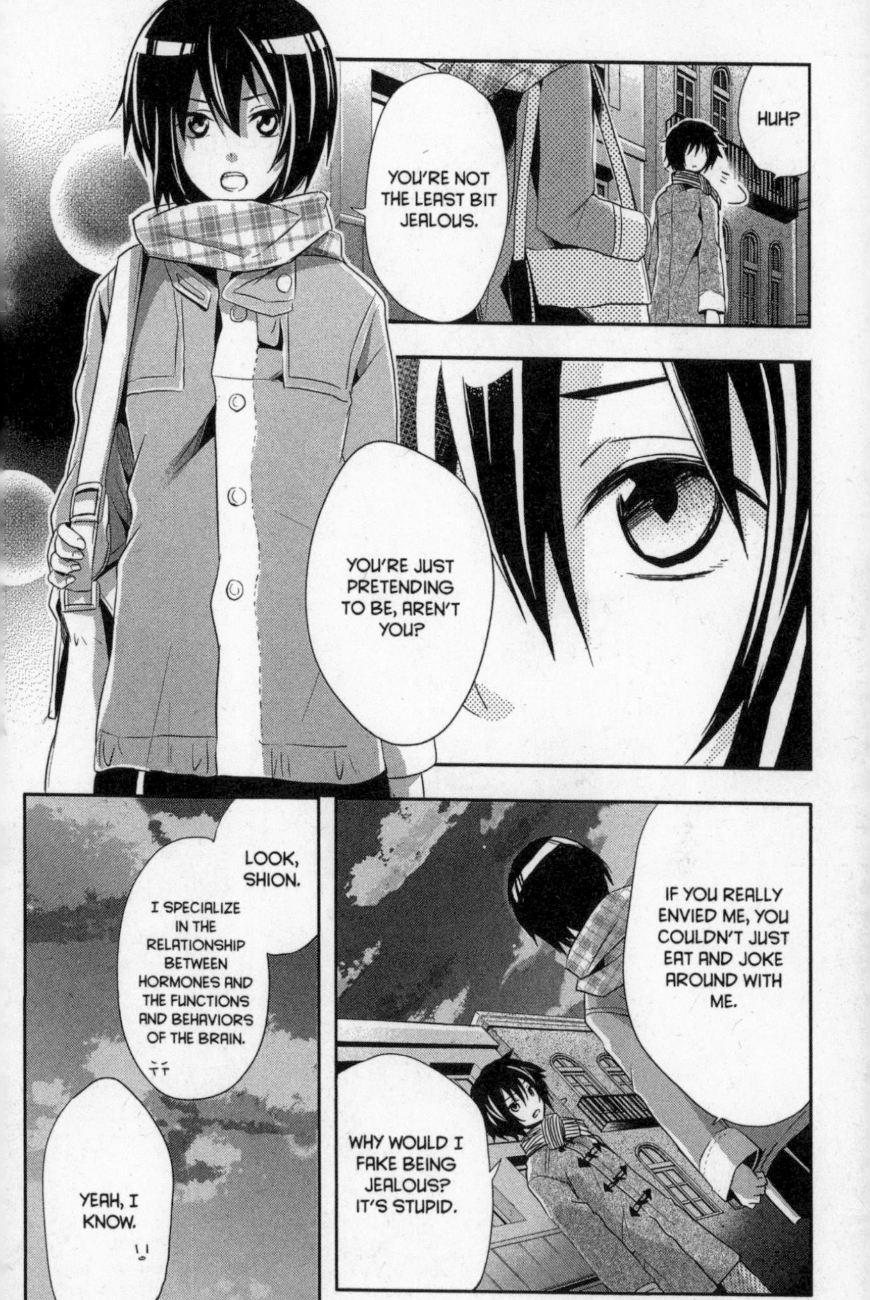

HUH?
YOU'RE NOT THE LEAST BIT JEALOUS.
YOU'RE JUST PRETENDING TO BE, AREN'T YOU?
IF YOU REALLY ENVIED ME, YOU COULDN'T JUST EAT AND JOKE AROUND WITH ME.
WHY WOULD I FAKE BEING JEALOUS? IT'S STUPID.
LOOK, SHION.
I SPECIALIZE IN THE RELATIONSHIP BETWEEN HORMONES AND THE FUNCTIONS AND BEHAVIORS OF THE BRAIN.
YEAH, I KNOW.

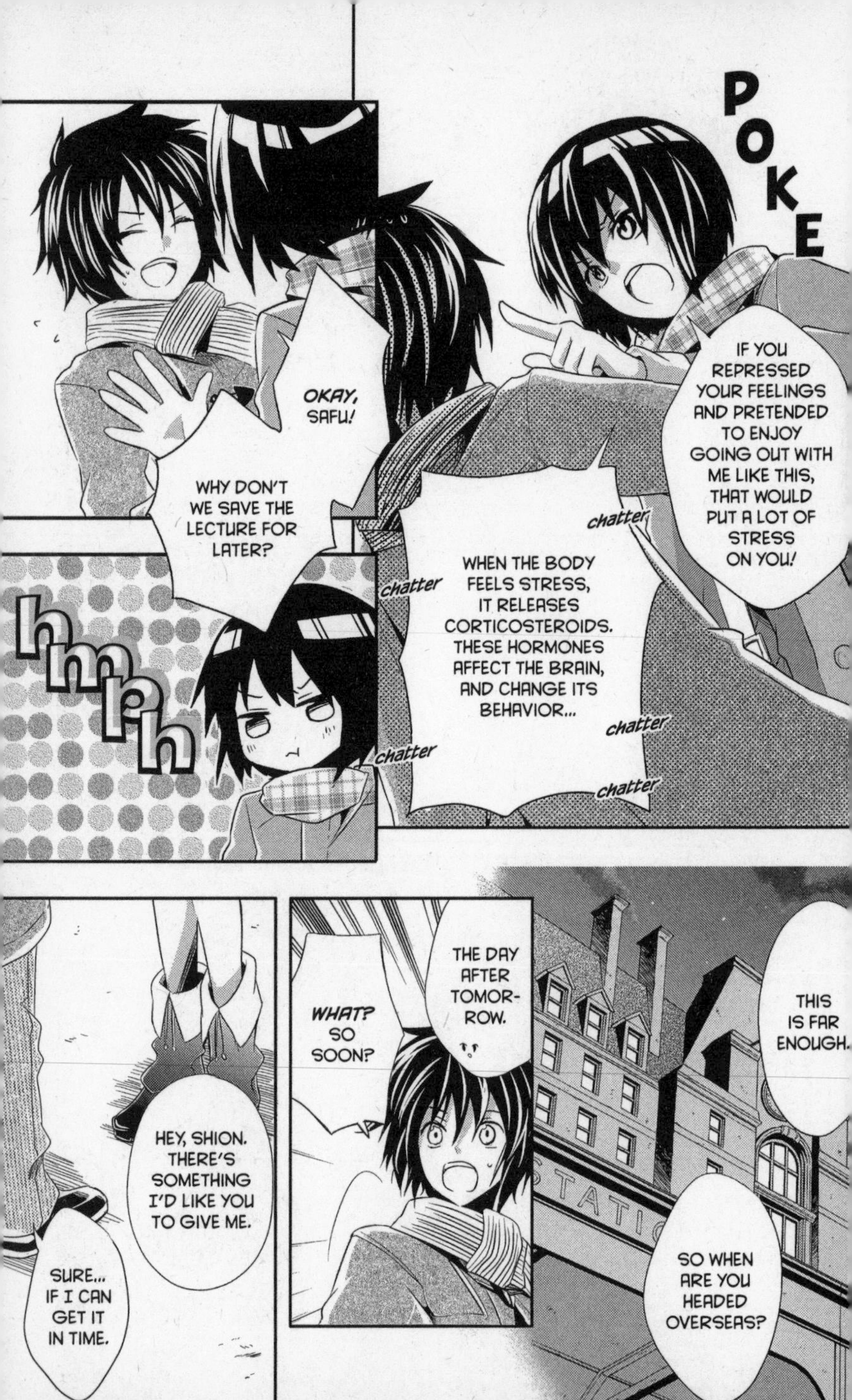
POKE
IF YOU REPRESSED YOUR FEELINGS AND PRETENDED TO ENJOY GOING OUT WITH ME LIKE THIS, THAT WOULD PUT A LOT OF STRESS ON YOU!
WHEN THE BODY FEELS STRESS, IT RELEASES CORTICOSTEROIDS. THESE HORMONES AFFECT THE BRAIN, AND CHANGE ITS BEHAVIOR...
chatter
chatter
chatter
chatter
chatter
OKAY, SAFU!
WHY DON'T WE SAVE THE LECTURE FOR LATER?
hmph
THIS IS FAR ENOUGH.
SO WHEN ARE YOU HEADED OVERSEAS?
THE DAY AFTER TOMOR-ROW.
WHAT? SO SOON?
HEY, SHION. THERE'S SOMETHING I'D LIKE YOU TO GIVE ME.
SURE... IF I CAN GET IT IN TIME.

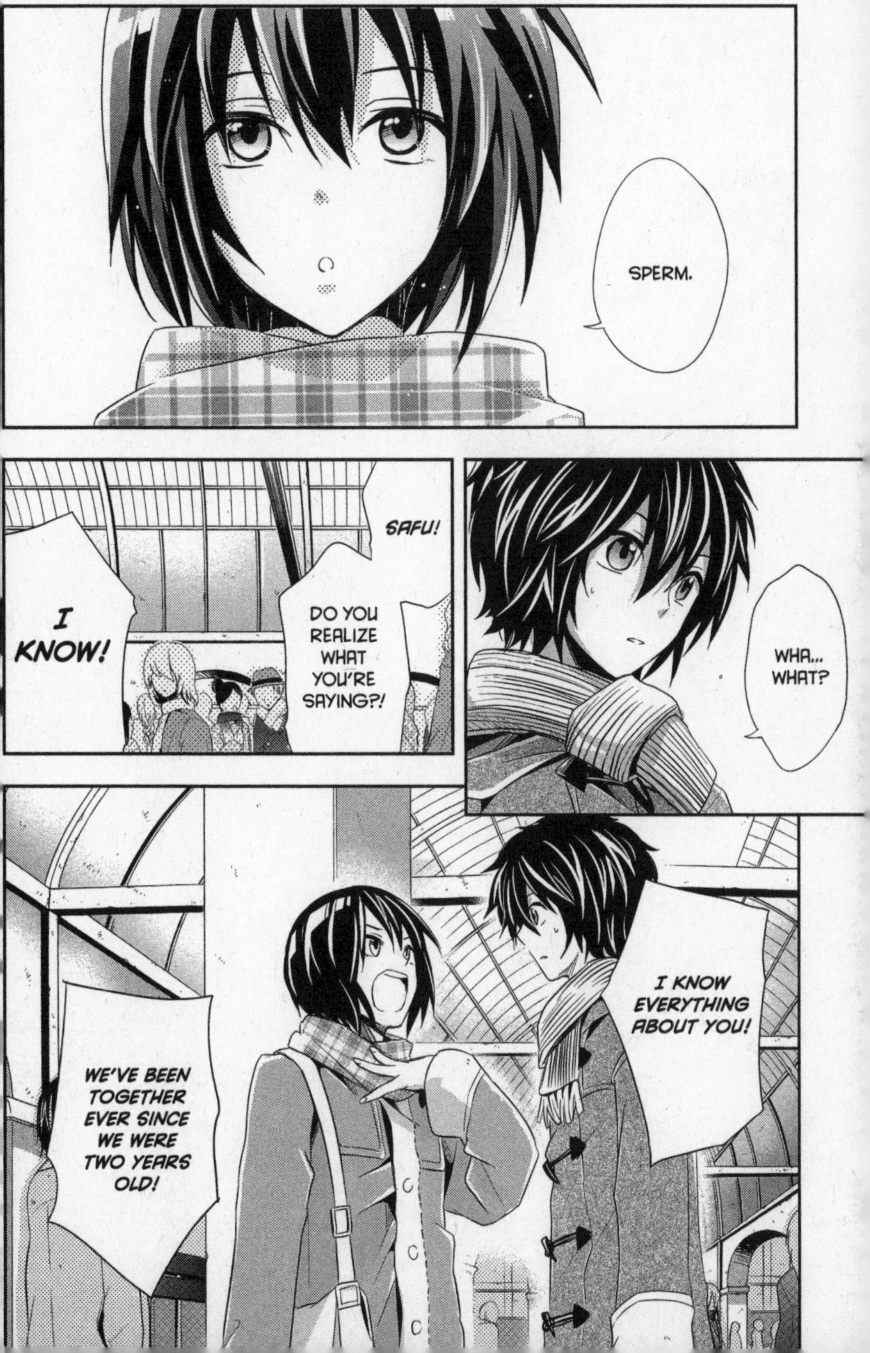
SPERM.
WHA... WHAT?
SAFU!
DO YOU REALIZE WHAT YOU'RE SAYING?!
I KNOW!
I KNOW EVERYTHING ABOUT YOU!
WE'VE BEEN TOGETHER EVER SINCE WE WERE TWO YEARS OLD!

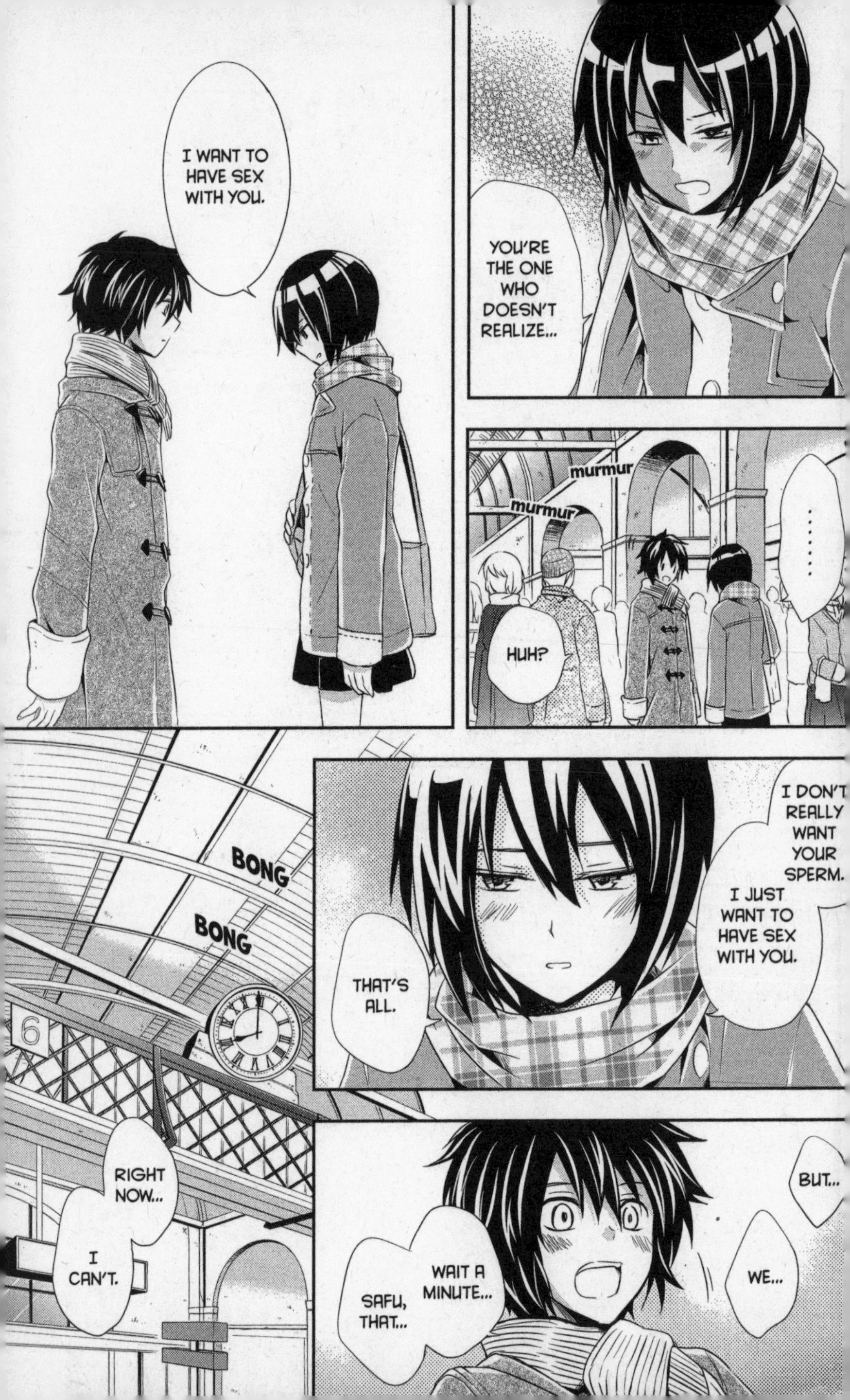

YOU'RE THE ONE WHO DOESN'T REALIZE...
......
murmur
murmur
HUH?
I WANT TO HAVE SEX WITH YOU.
I DON'T REALLY WANT YOUR SPERM.
I JUST WANT TO HAVE SEX WITH YOU.
THAT'S ALL.
BUT...
WE...
WAIT A MINUTE...
SAFU, THAT...
BONG
BONG
RIGHT NOW...
I CAN'T.

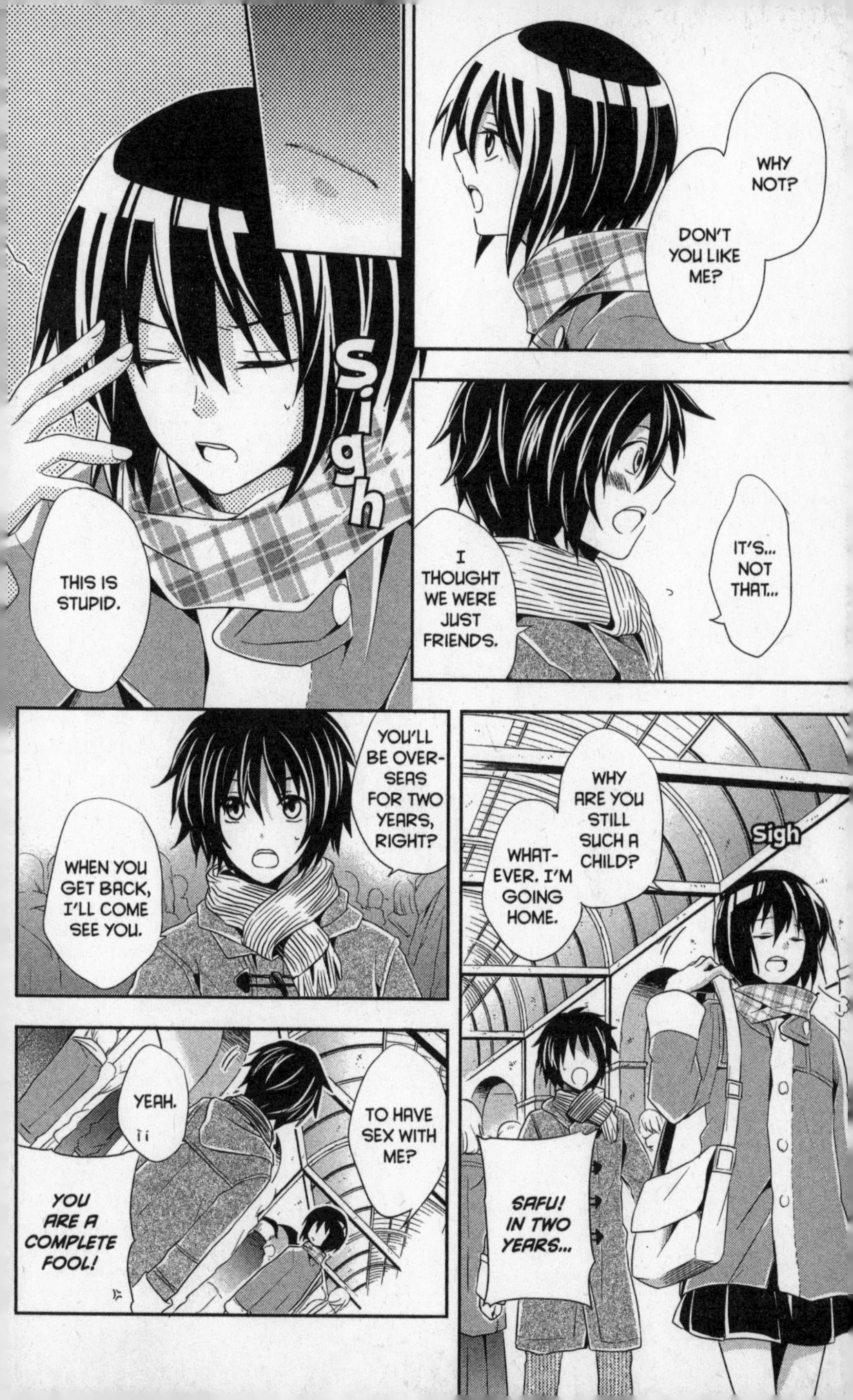
WHY NOT?
DON'T YOU LIKE ME?
IT'S... NOT THAT...
I THOUGHT WE WERE JUST FRIENDS.
Sigh
THIS IS STUPID.
WHY ARE YOU STILL SUCH A CHILD?
Sigh
WHAT-EVER. I'M GOING HOME.
SAFU! IN TWO YEARS...
YOU'LL BE OVER-SEAS FOR TWO YEARS, RIGHT?
WHEN YOU GET BACK, I'LL COME SEE YOU.
YEAH.
TO HAVE SEX WITH ME?
YOU ARE A COMPLETE FOOL!

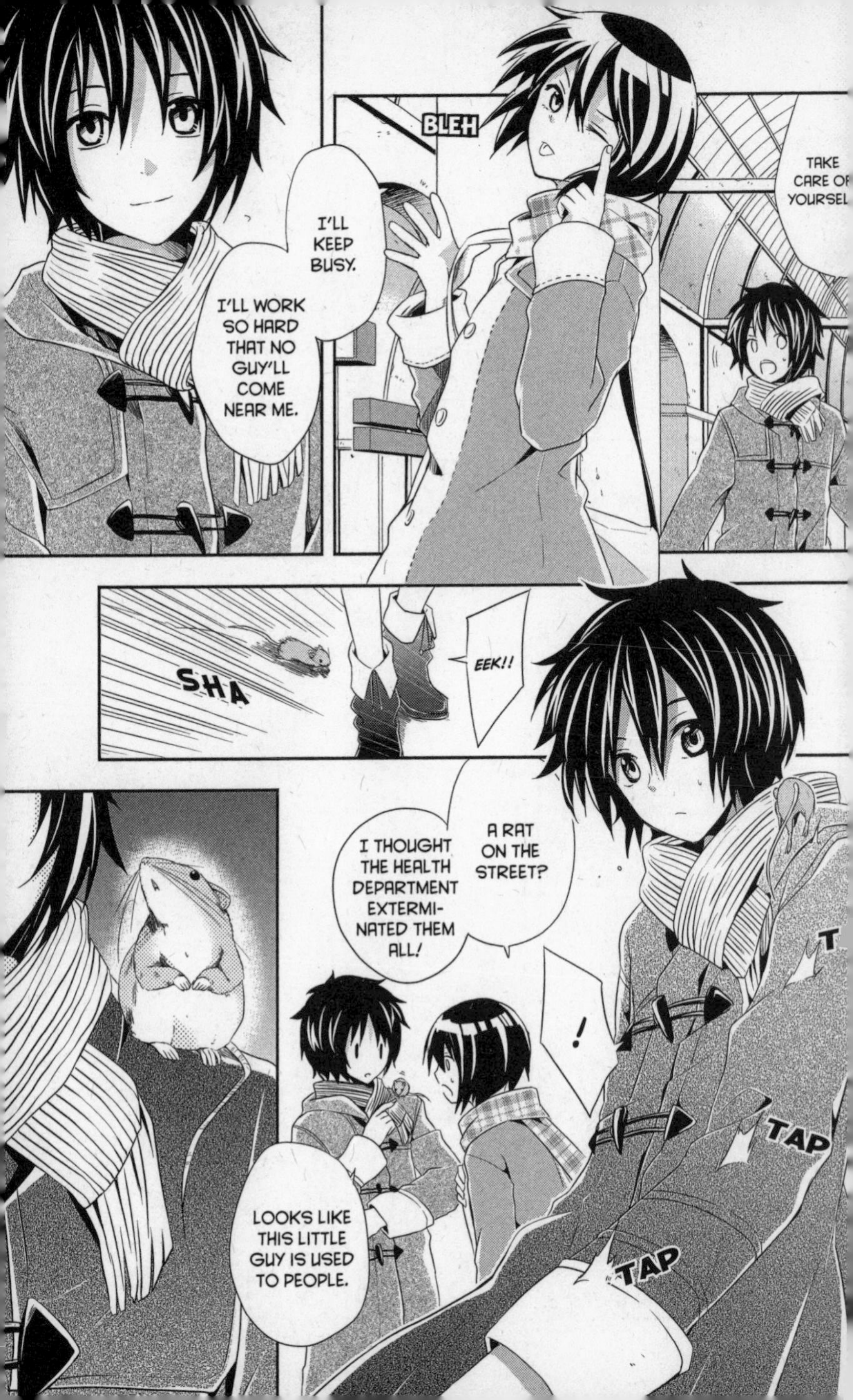
TAKE CARE OF YOURSEL
BLEH
I'LL KEEP BUSY.
I'LL WORK SO HARD THAT NO GUY'LL COME NEAR ME.
EEK!!
SHA
A RAT ON THE STREET?
I THOUGHT THE HEALTH DEPARTMENT EXTERMI-NATED THEM ALL!
!
T
TAP
TAP
LOOKS LIKE THIS LITTLE GUY IS USED TO PEOPLE.

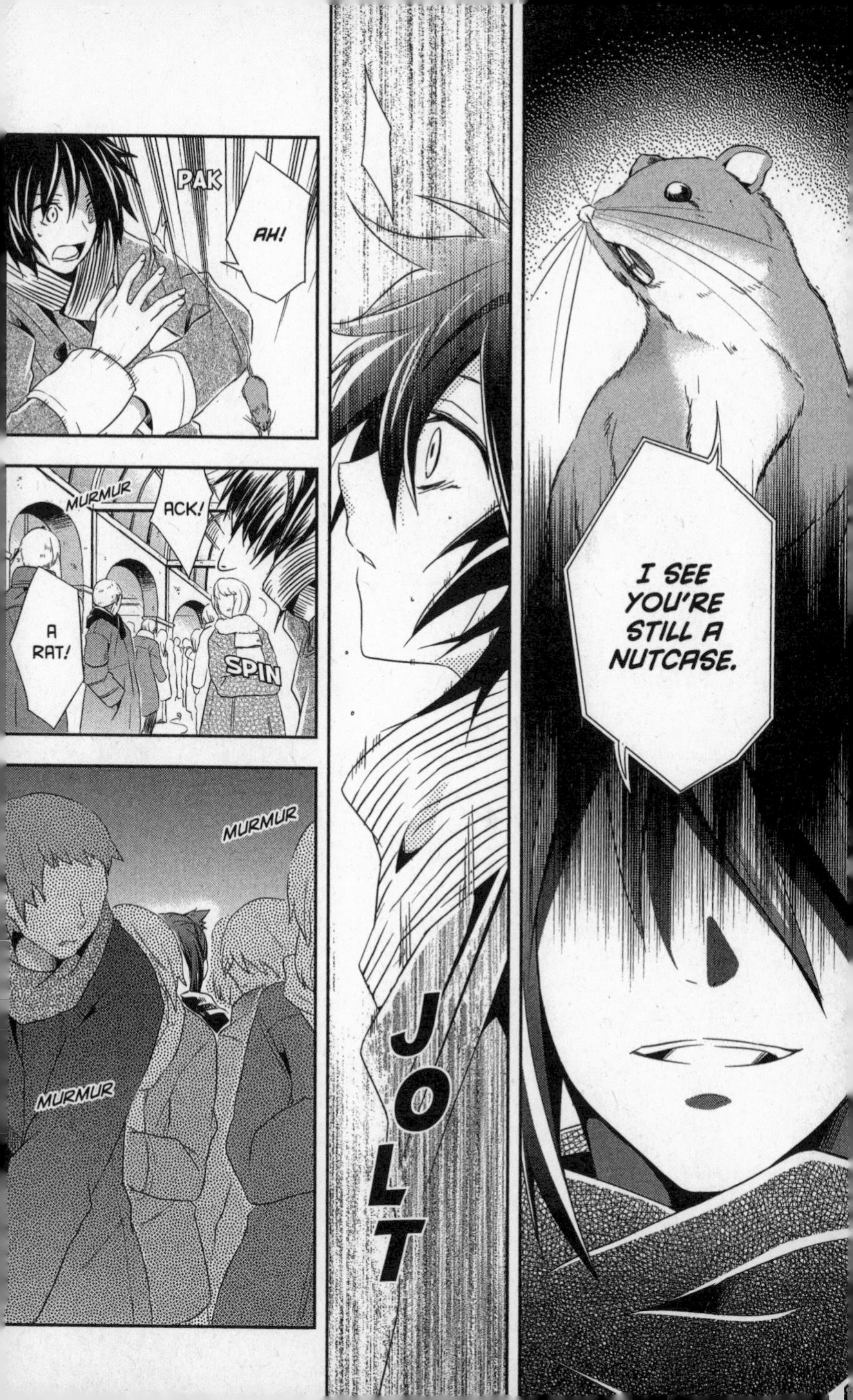
I SEE YOU'RE STILL A NUTCASE.
JOLT
AH!
PAK
ACK!
MURMUR
A RAT!
SPIN
MURMUR
MURMUR

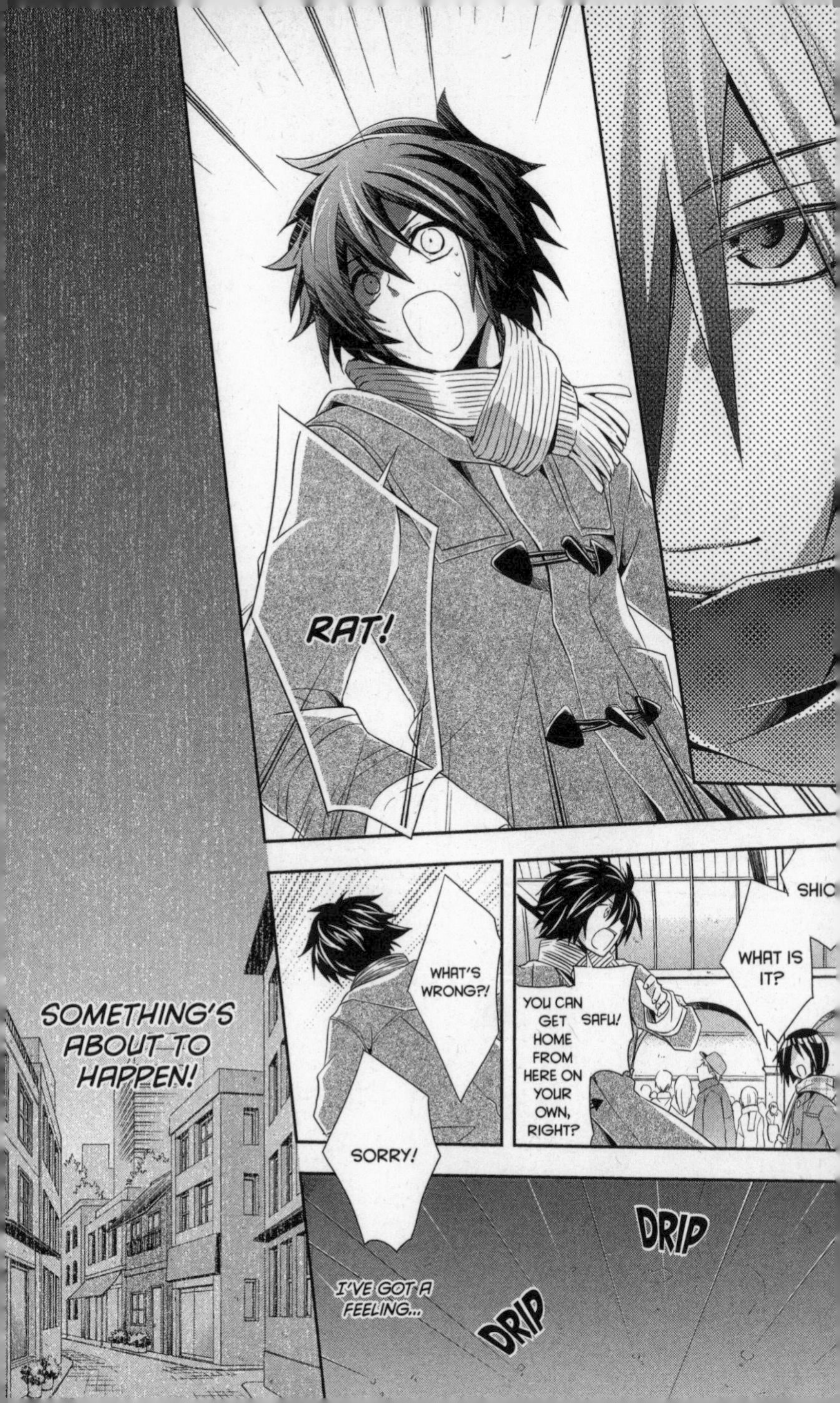

RAT!
SHIC
WHAT IS IT?
SAFU!
YOU CAN GET HOME FROM HERE ON YOUR OWN, RIGHT?
WHAT'S WRONG?!
SORRY!
DRIP
DRIP
I'VE GOT A FEELING...
SOMETHING'S ABOUT TO HAPPEN!

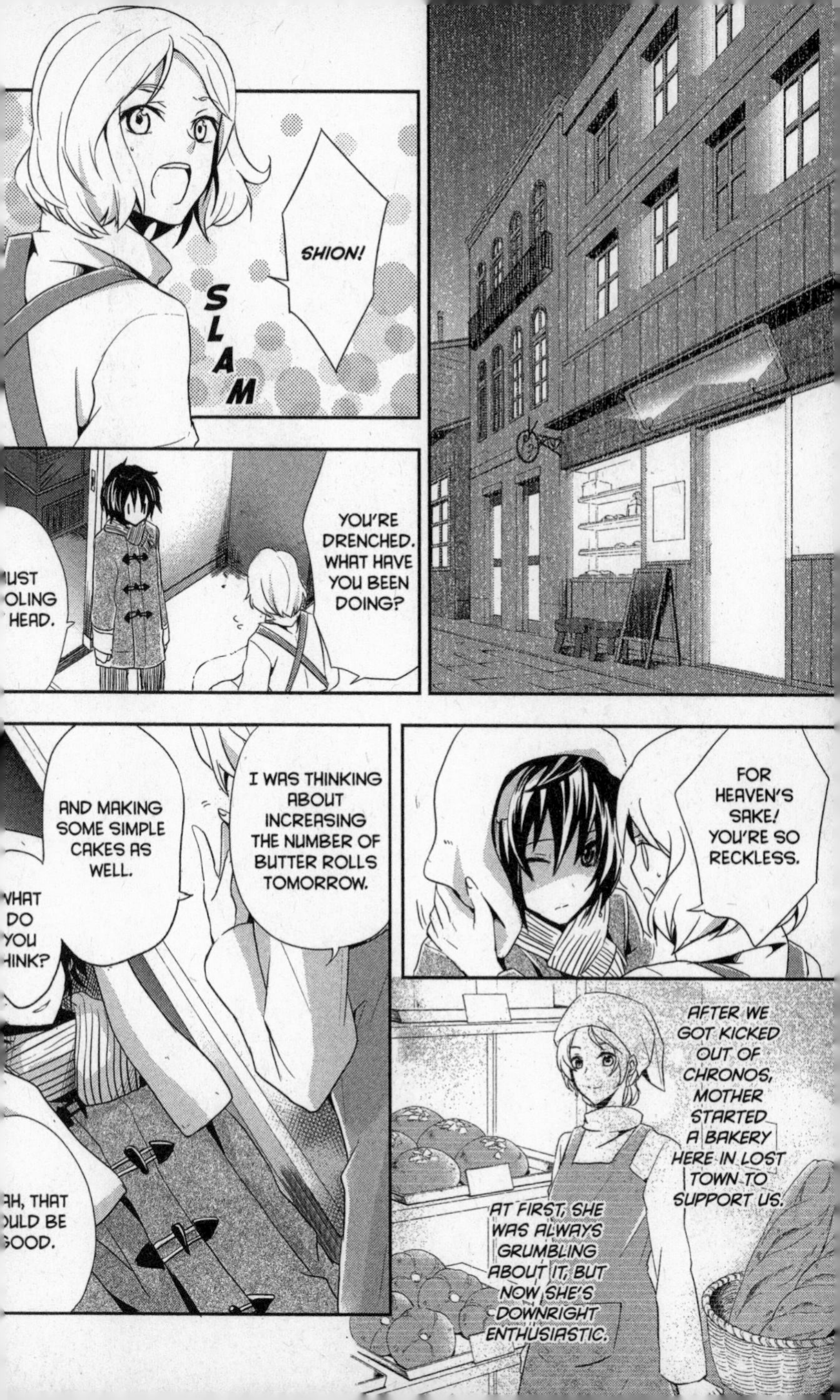
SHION!
SLAM
YOU'RE DRENCHED. WHAT HAVE YOU BEEN DOING?
UST OLING HEAD.
FOR HEAVEN'S SAKE! YOU'RE SO RECKLESS.
AFTER WE GOT KICKED OUT OF CHRONOS, MOTHER STARTED A BAKERY HERE IN LOST TOWN TO SUPPORT US.
AT FIRST, SHE WAS ALWAYS GRUMBLING ABOUT IT, BUT NOW SHE'S DOWNRIGHT ENTHUSIASTIC.
I WAS THINKING ABOUT INCREASING THE NUMBER OF BUTTER ROLLS TOMORROW.
AND MAKING SOME SIMPLE CAKES AS WELL.
VHAT DO YOU HINK?
AH, THAT OULD BE GOOD.

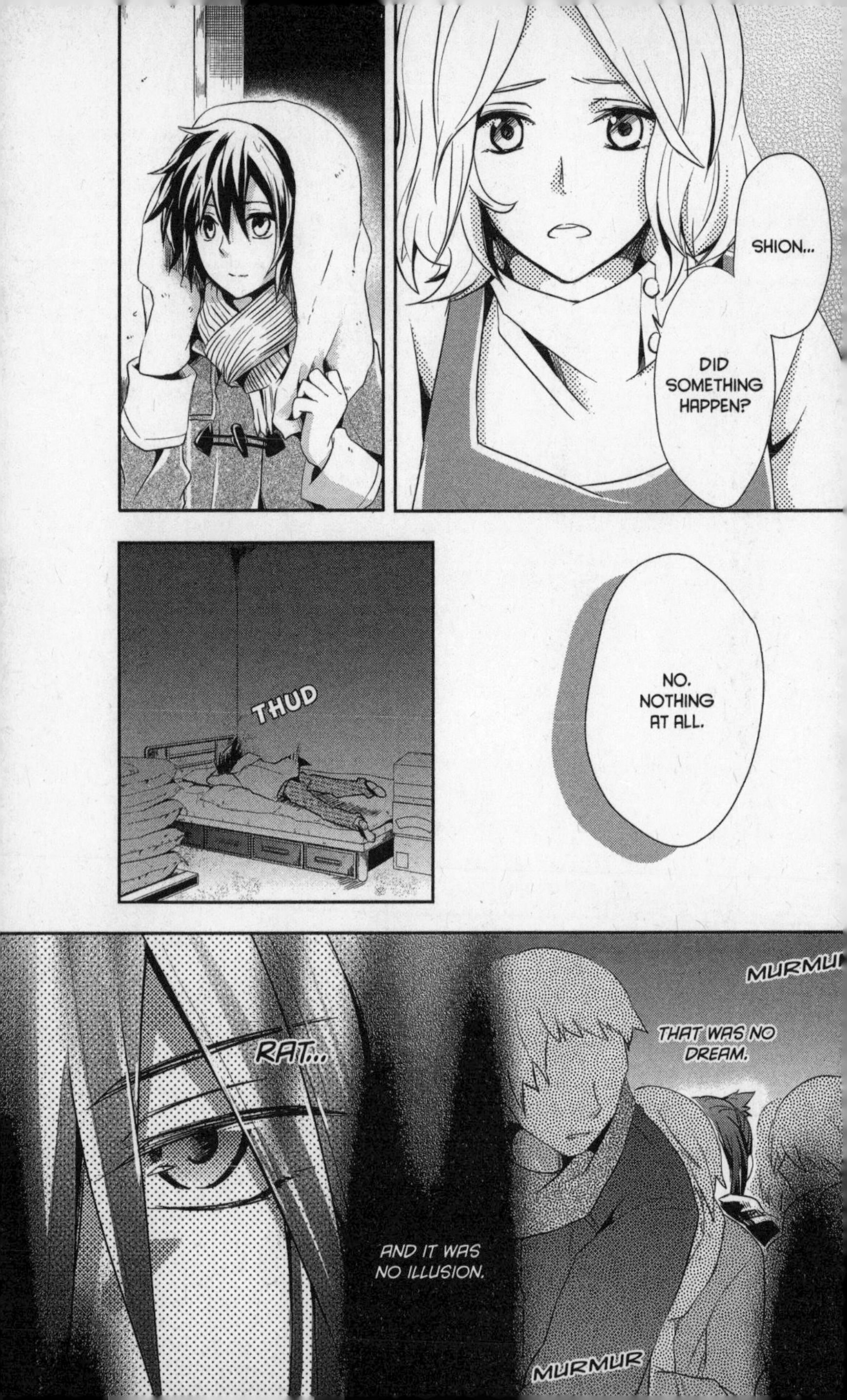
SHION...
DID SOMETHING HAPPEN?
NO. NOTHING AT ALL.
THUD
MURMU
THAT WAS NO DREAM.
RAT...
AND IT WAS NO ILLUSION.
MURMUR

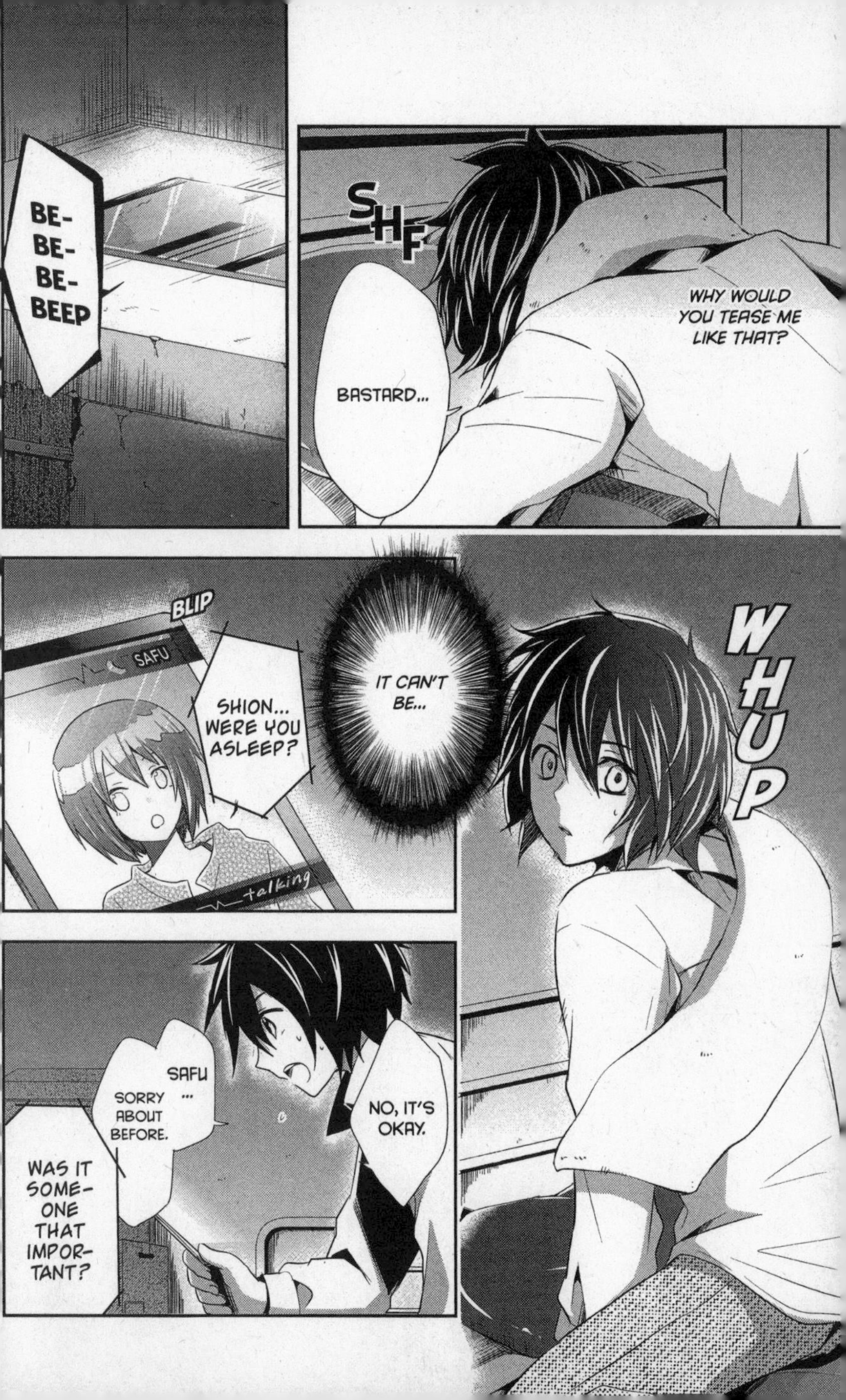
WHY WOULD YOU TEASE ME LIKE THAT?
SHF
BASTARD...
BE-BE-BE-BEEP
WHUP
IT CAN'T BE...
BLIP
SAFU
SHION... WERE YOU ASLEEP?
talking
NO, IT'S OKAY.
SAFU ...
SORRY ABOUT BEFORE.
WAS IT SOME-ONE THAT IMPOR-TANT?

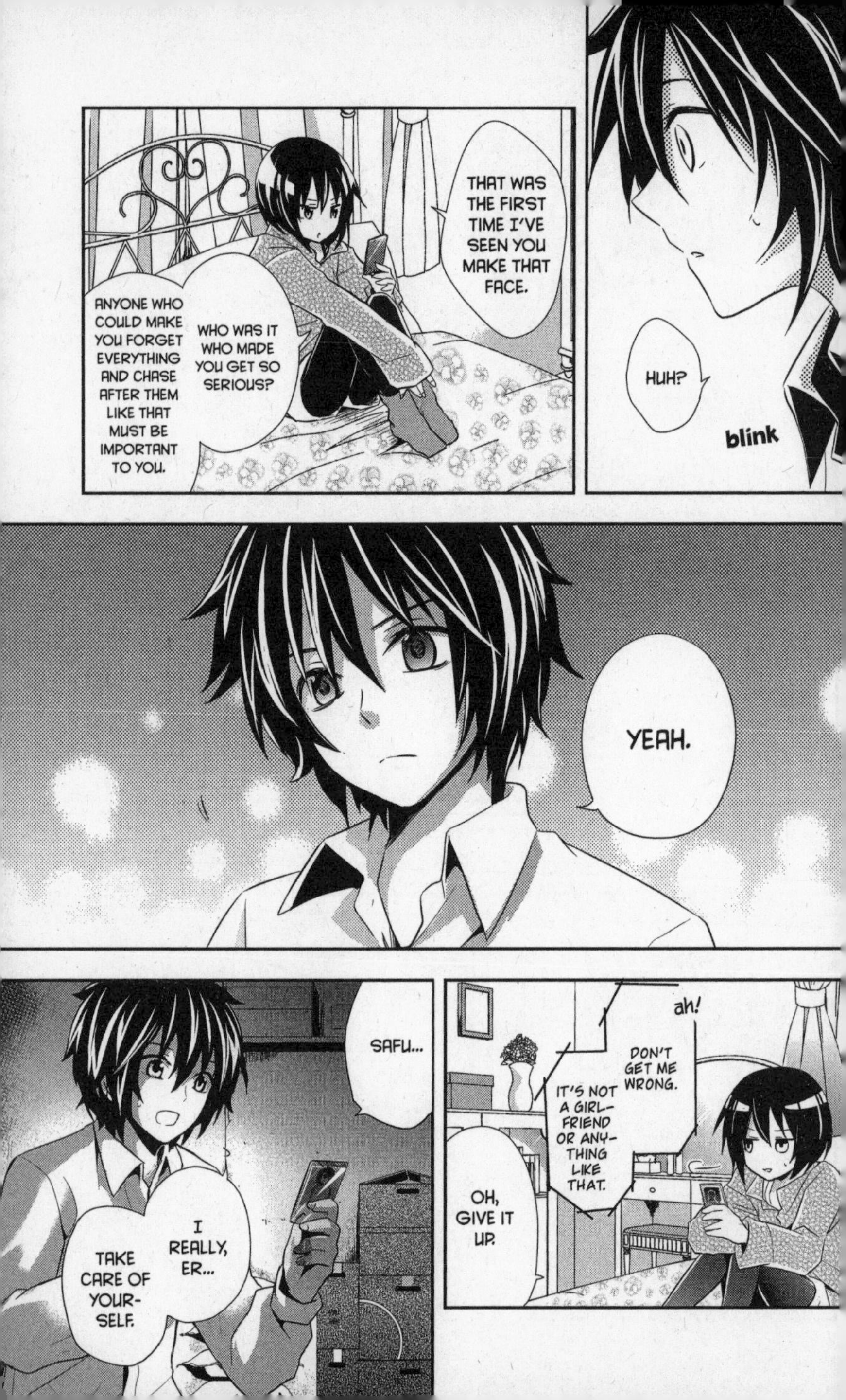
HUH?
blink
THAT WAS THE FIRST TIME I'VE SEEN YOU MAKE THAT FACE.
WHO WAS IT WHO MADE YOU GET SO SERIOUS?
ANYONE WHO COULD MAKE YOU FORGET EVERYTHING AND CHASE AFTER THEM LIKE THAT MUST BE IMPORTANT TO YOU.
YEAH.
ah!
DON'T GET ME WRONG.
IT'S NOT A GIRL-FRIEND OR ANY-THING LIKE THAT.
OH, GIVE IT UP.
SAFU...
I REALLY, ER...
TAKE CARE OF YOUR-SELF.

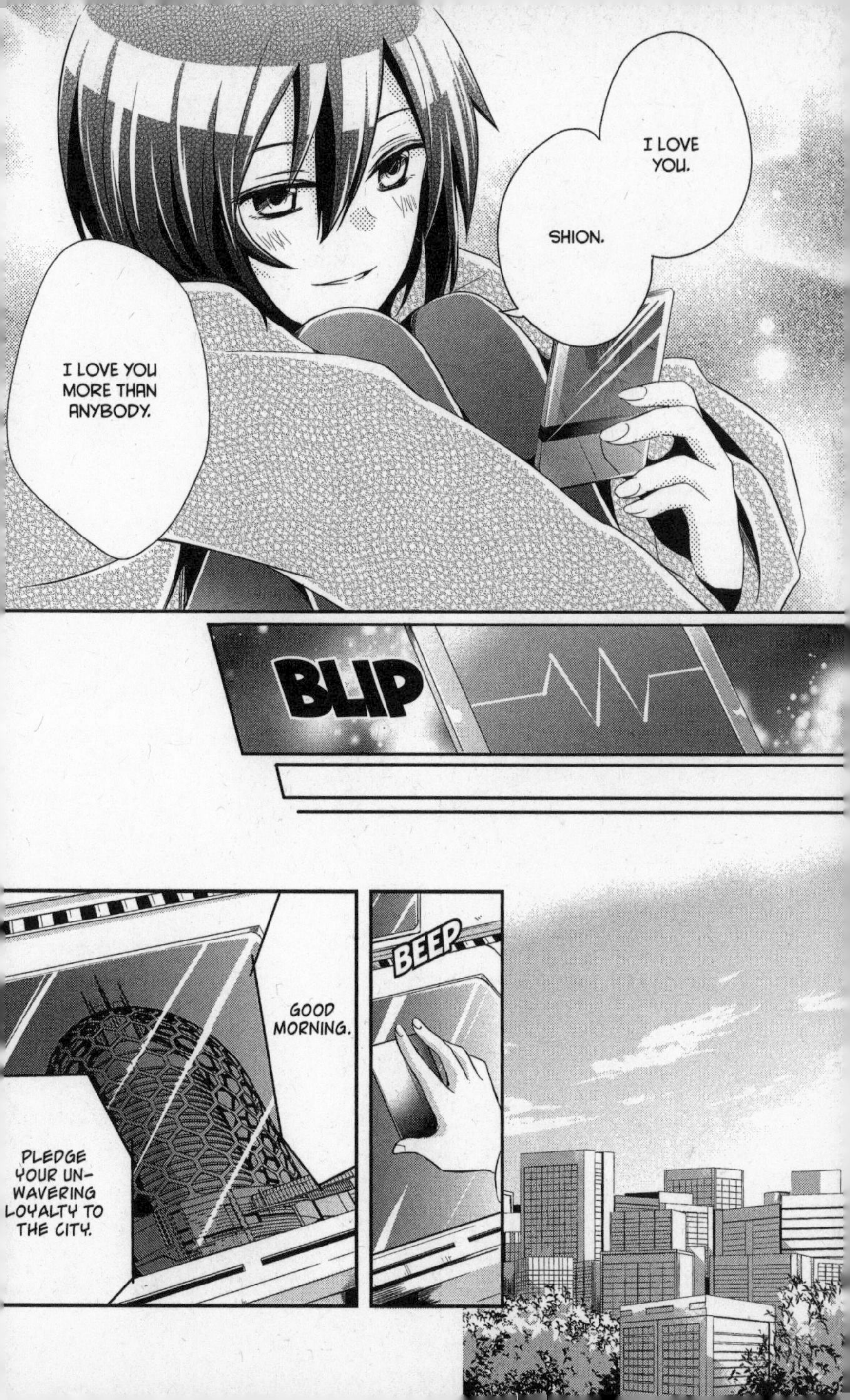

I LOVE YOU.
SHION.
I LOVE YOU MORE THAN ANYBODY.
BLIP
BEEP
GOOD MORNING.
PLEDGE YOUR UN-WAVERING LOYALTY TO THE CITY.

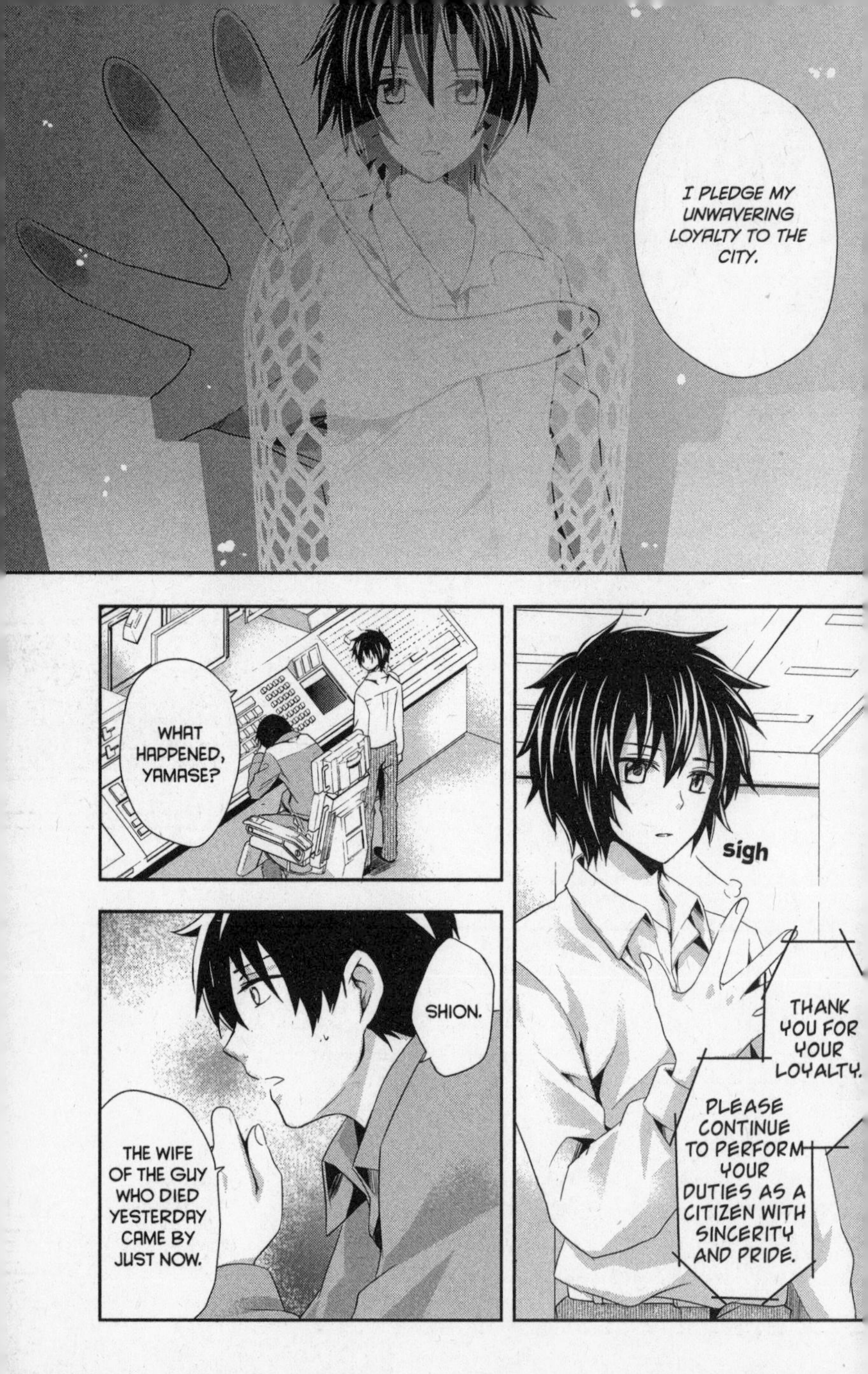
I PLEDGE MY UNWAVERING LOYALTY TO THE CITY.
sigh
THANK YOU FOR YOUR LOYALTY.
PLEASE CONTINUE TO PERFORM YOUR DUTIES AS A CITIZEN WITH SINCERITY AND PRIDE.
WHAT HAPPENED, YAMASE?
SHION.
THE WIFE OF THE GUY WHO DIED YESTERDAY CAME BY JUST NOW.

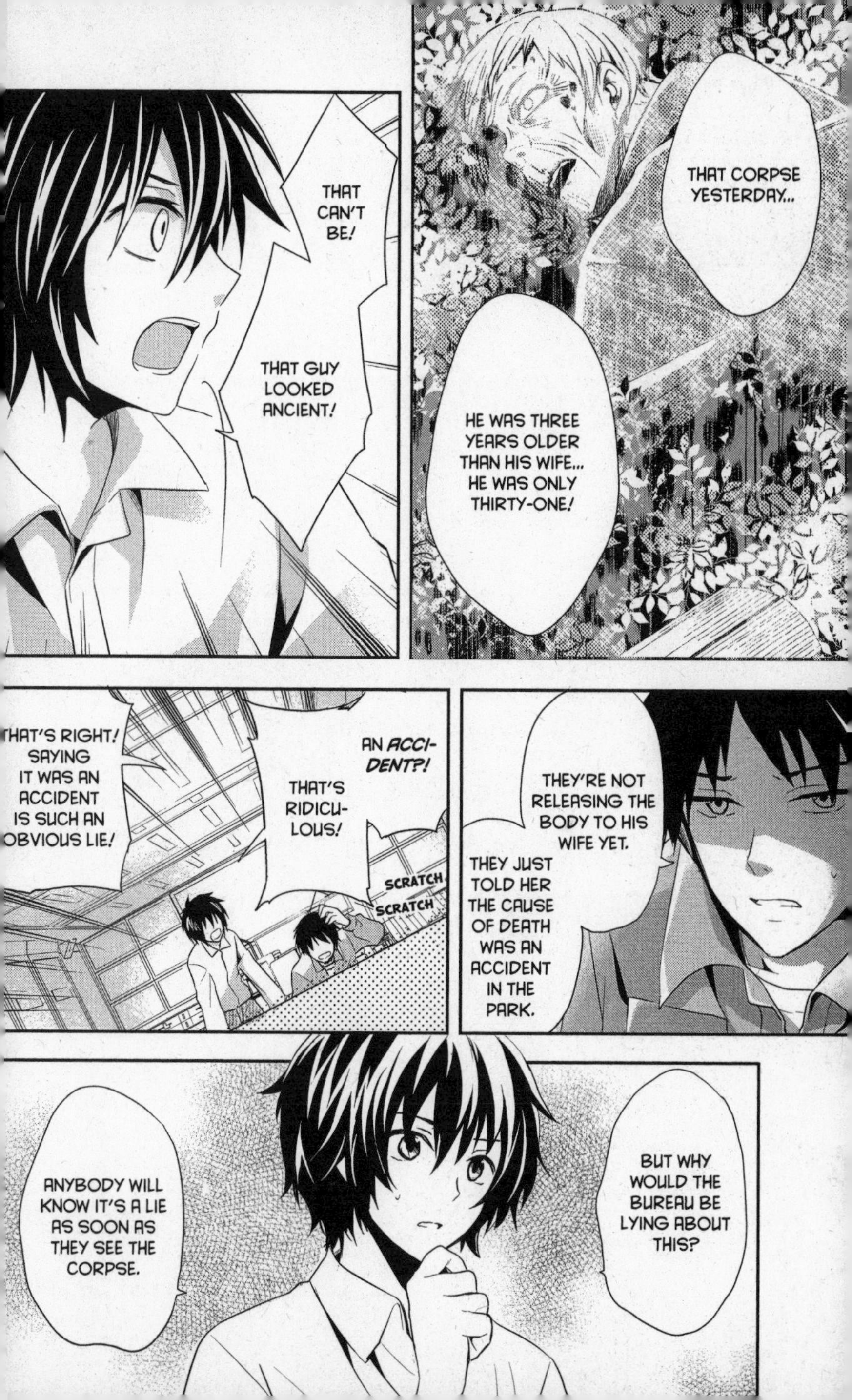
THAT CORPSE YESTERDAY...
HE WAS THREE YEARS OLDER THAN HIS WIFE... HE WAS ONLY THIRTY-ONE!
THAT CAN'T BE!
THAT GUY LOOKED ANCIENT!
THEY'RE NOT RELEASING THE BODY TO HIS WIFE YET.
THEY JUST TOLD HER THE CAUSE OF DEATH WAS AN ACCIDENT IN THE PARK.
AN *ACCI-DENT?!*
THAT'S RIDICU-LOUS!
SCRATCH
SCRATCH
HAT'S RIGHT! SAYING IT WAS AN ACCIDENT IS SUCH AN OBVIOUS LIE!
BUT WHY WOULD THE BUREAU BE LYING ABOUT THIS?
ANYBODY WILL KNOW IT'S A LIE AS SOON AS THEY SEE THE CORPSE.

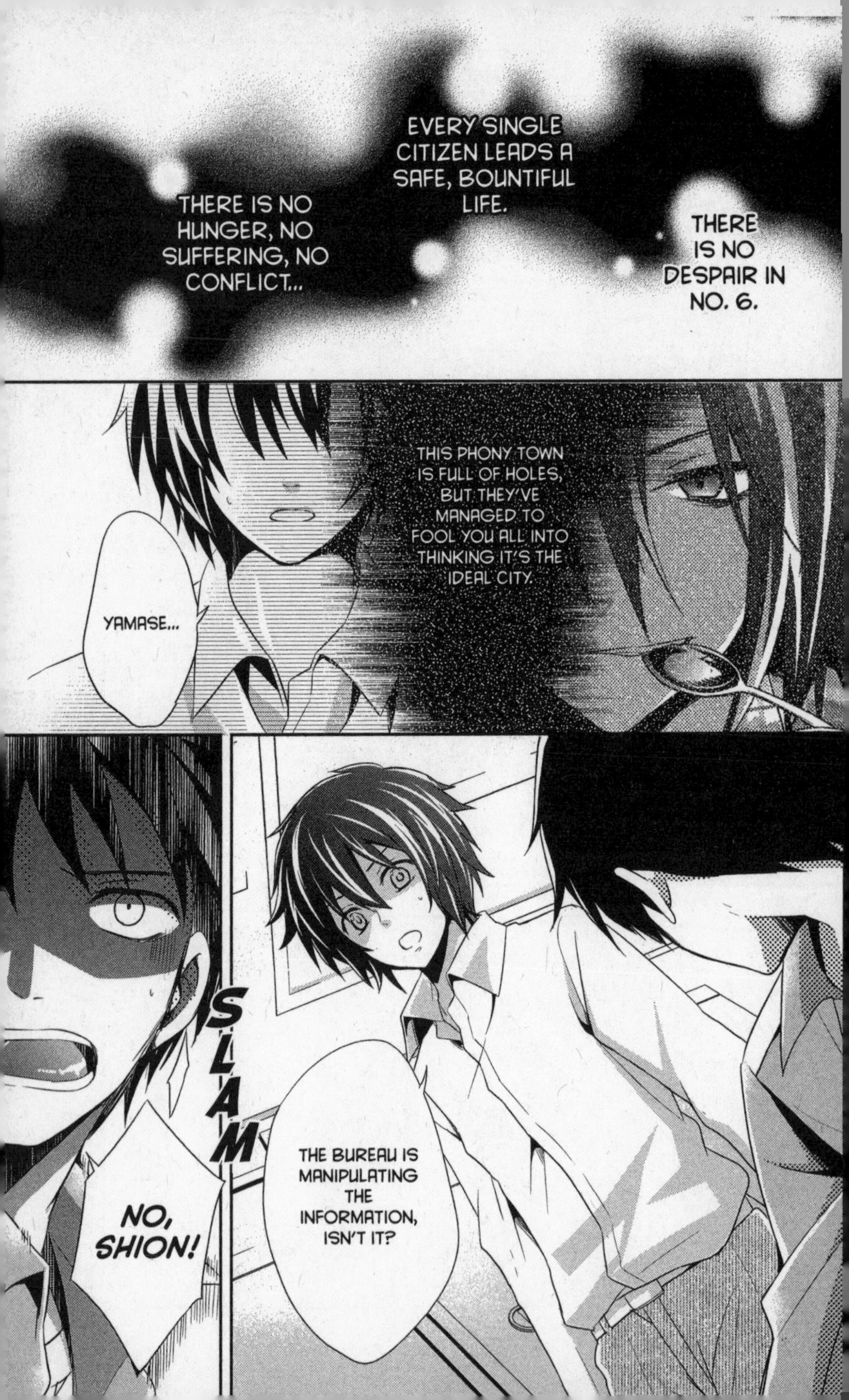
THERE IS NO DESPAIR IN NO. 6.
EVERY SINGLE CITIZEN LEADS A SAFE, BOUNTIFUL LIFE.
THERE IS NO HUNGER, NO SUFFERING, NO CONFLICT...
THIS PHONY TOWN IS FULL OF HOLES, BUT THEY'VE MANAGED TO FOOL YOU ALL INTO THINKING IT'S THE IDEAL CITY.
YAMASE...
THE BUREAU IS MANIPULATING THE INFORMATION, ISN'T IT?
SLAM
NO, SHION!

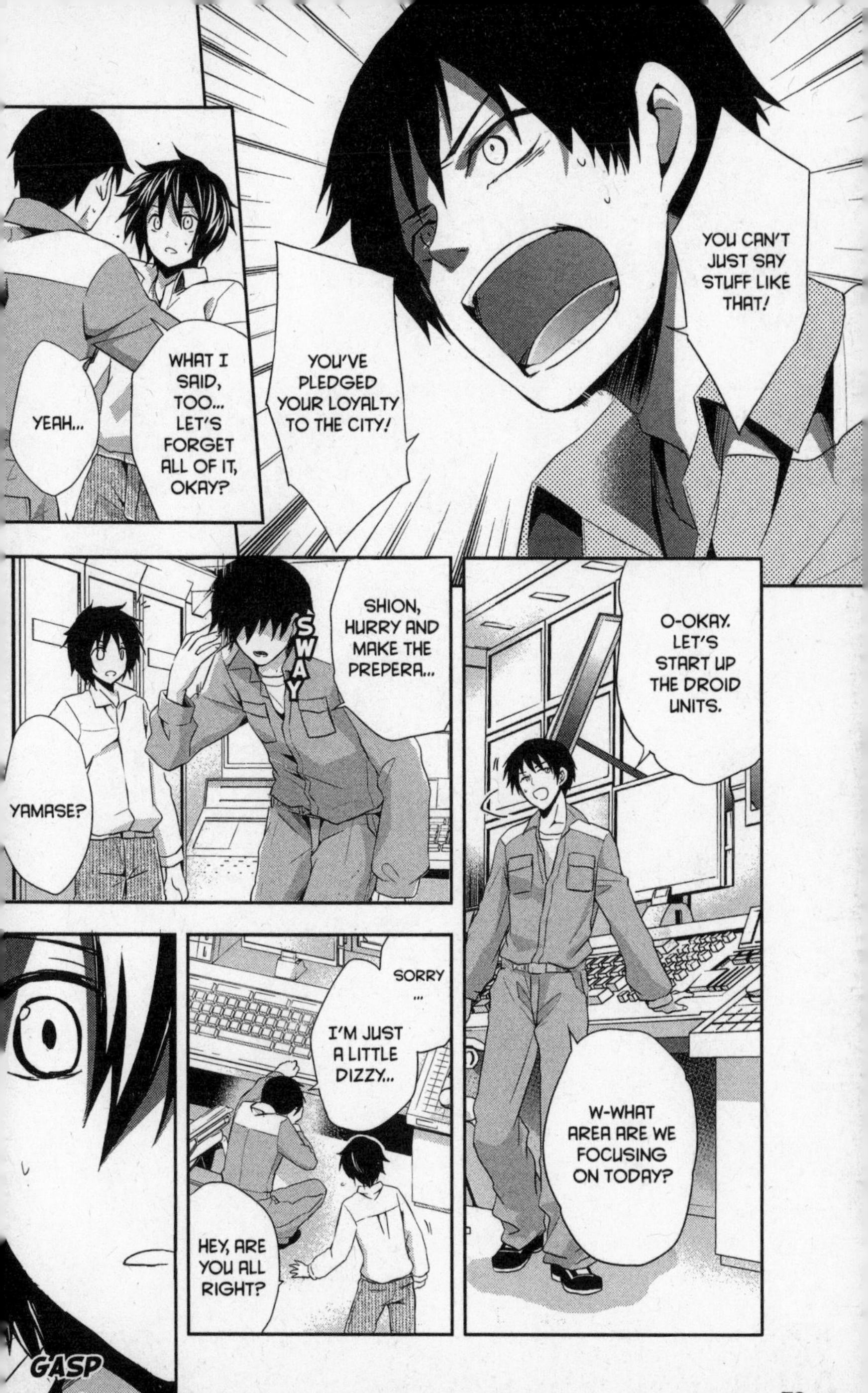
YOU CAN'T JUST SAY STUFF LIKE THAT!
YOU'VE PLEDGED YOUR LOYALTY TO THE CITY!
WHAT I SAID, TOO... LET'S FORGET ALL OF IT, OKAY?
YEAH...
O-OKAY. LET'S START UP THE DROID UNITS.
W-WHAT AREA ARE WE FOCUSING ON TODAY?
SHION, HURRY AND MAKE THE PREPERA...
SWAY
YAMASE?
SORRY ...
I'M JUST A LITTLE DIZZY...
HEY, ARE YOU ALL RIGHT?
GASP

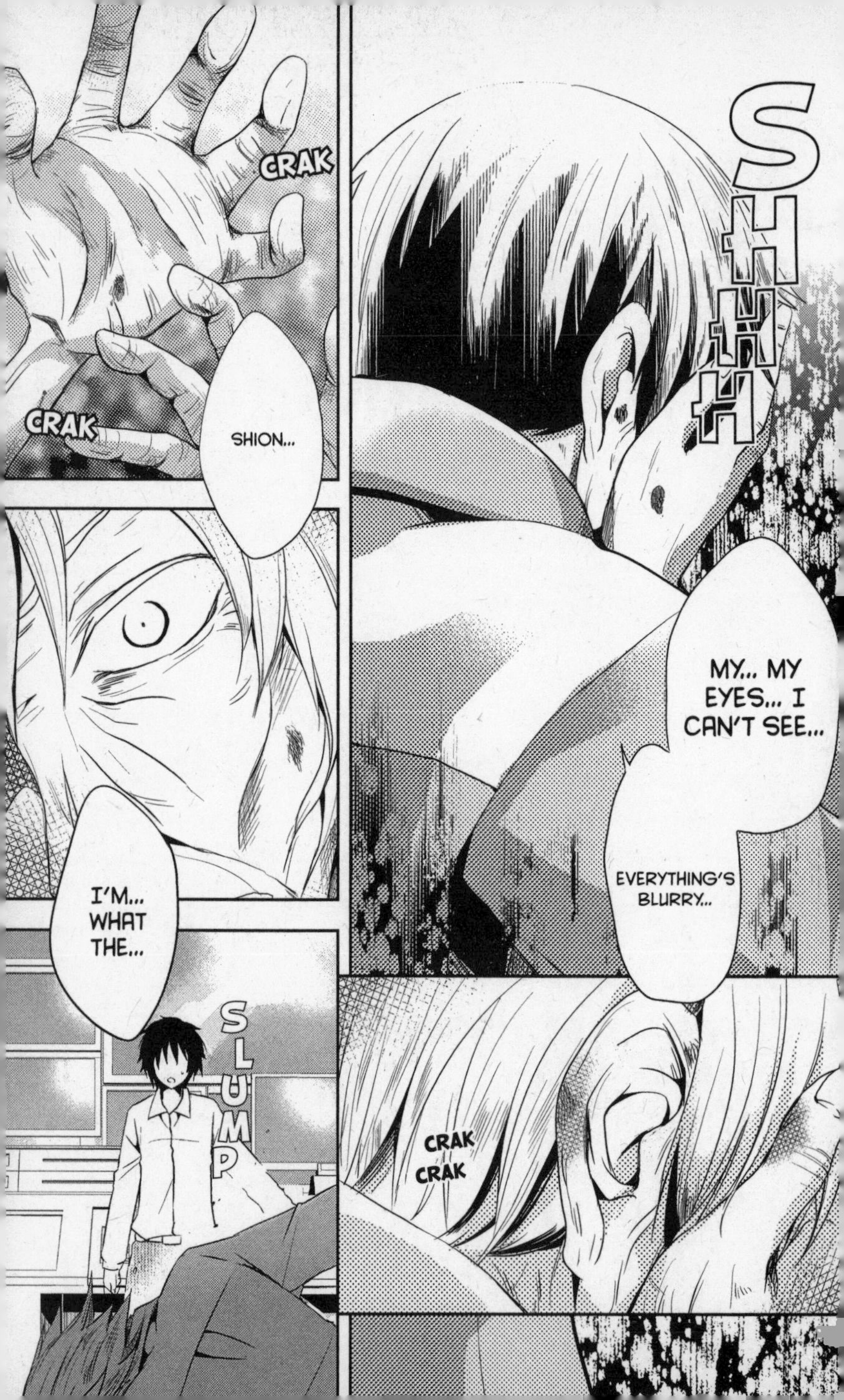
SHHHHH
MY... MY EYES... I CAN'T SEE...
EVERYTHING'S BLURRY...
CRAK
CRAK
SHION...
I'M... WHAT THE...
SLUMP
CRAK CRAK

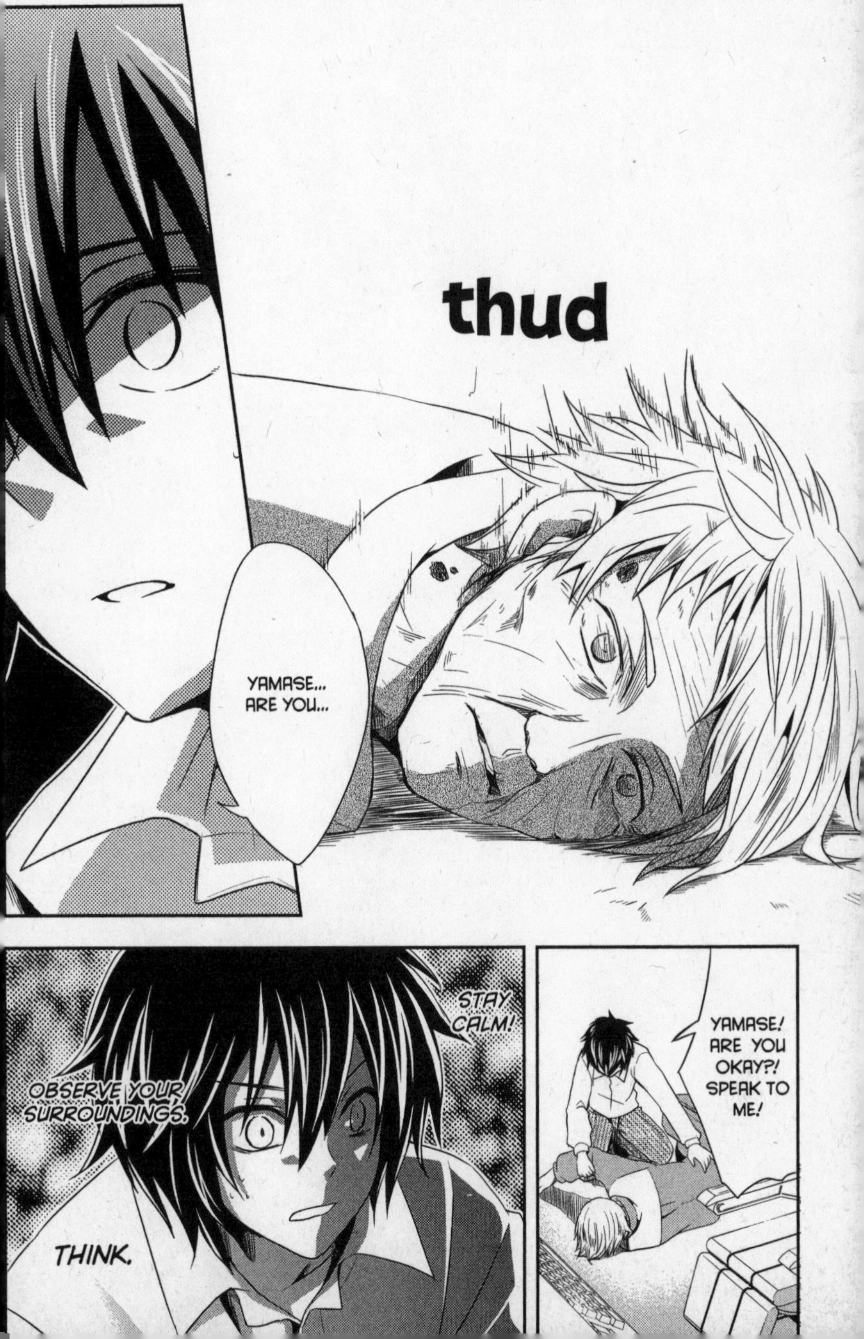
thud
YAMASE... ARE YOU...
YAMASE! ARE YOU OKAY?! SPEAK TO ME!
STAY CALM!
OBSERVE YOUR SURROUNDINGS.
THINK.

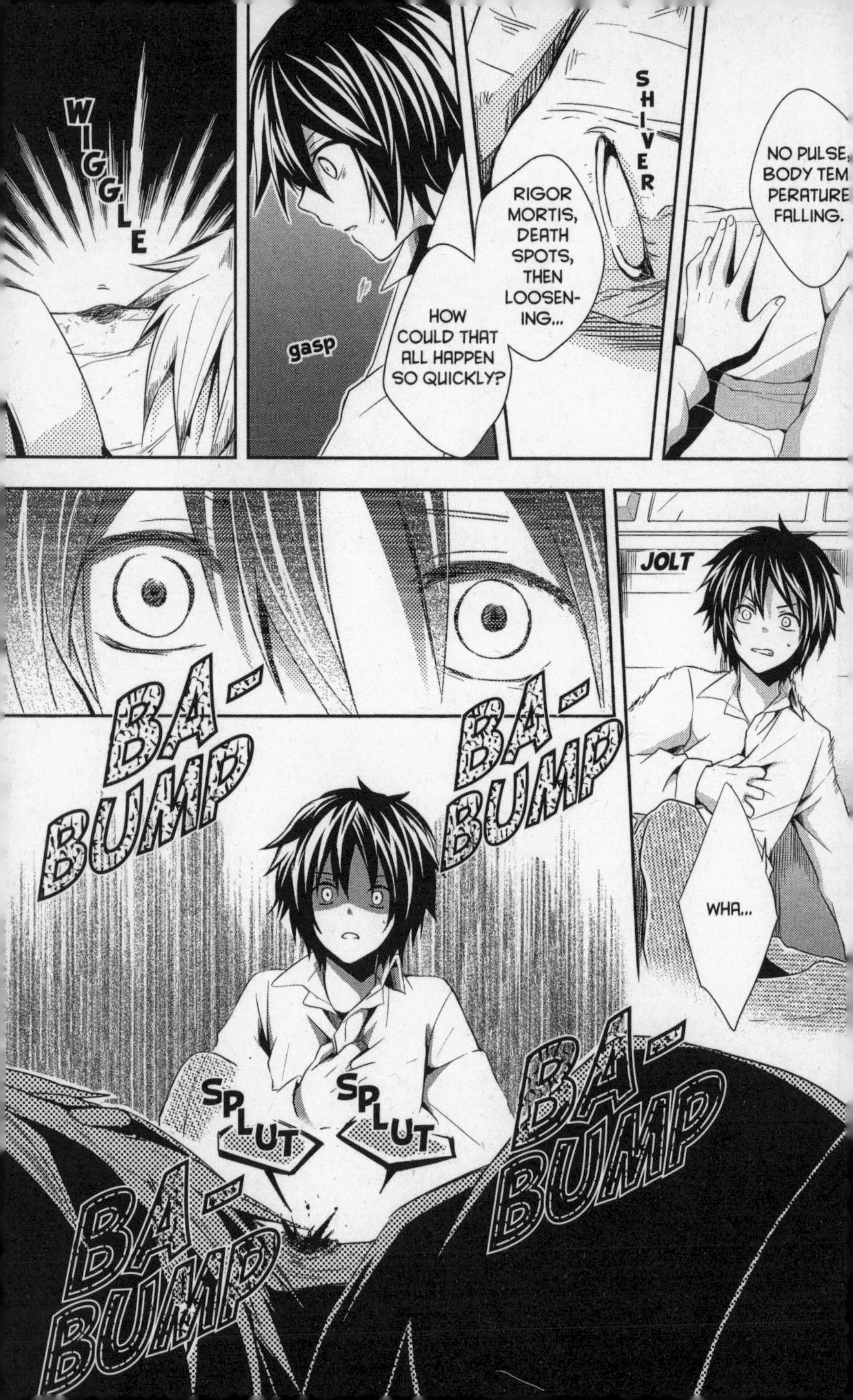
NO PULSE, BODY TEM PERATURE FALLING.
SHIVER
RIGOR MORTIS, DEATH SPOTS, THEN LOOSENING...
HOW COULD THAT ALL HAPPEN SO QUICKLY?
gasp
WIGGLE
JOLT
WHA...
BA-BUMP
BA-BUMP
SPLUT
SPLUT
BA-BUMP
BA-BUMP

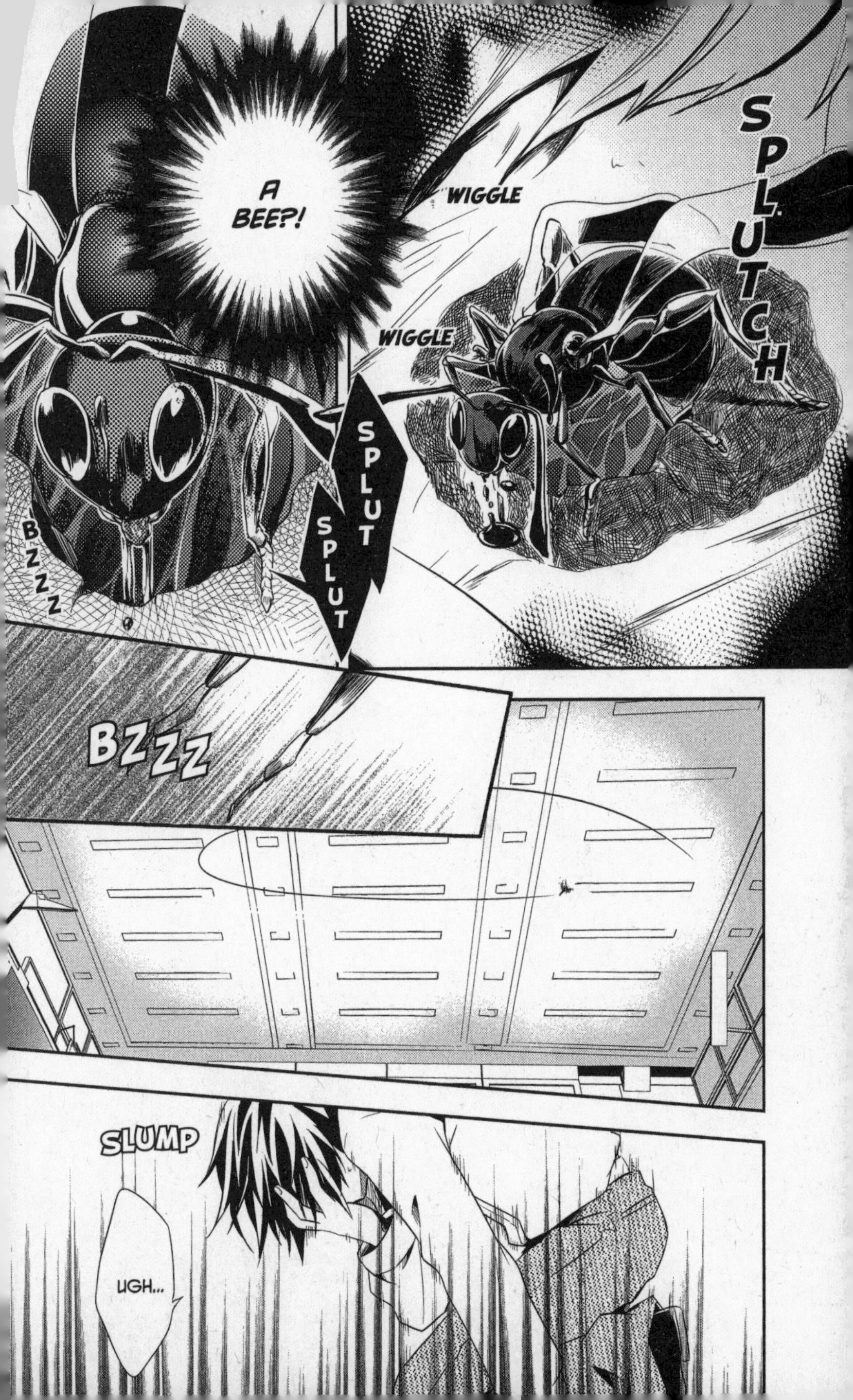
SPLUTCH
WIGGLE
A BEE?!
WIGGLE
SPLUT
SPLUT
BZZZ
BZZZ
SLUMP
UGH...

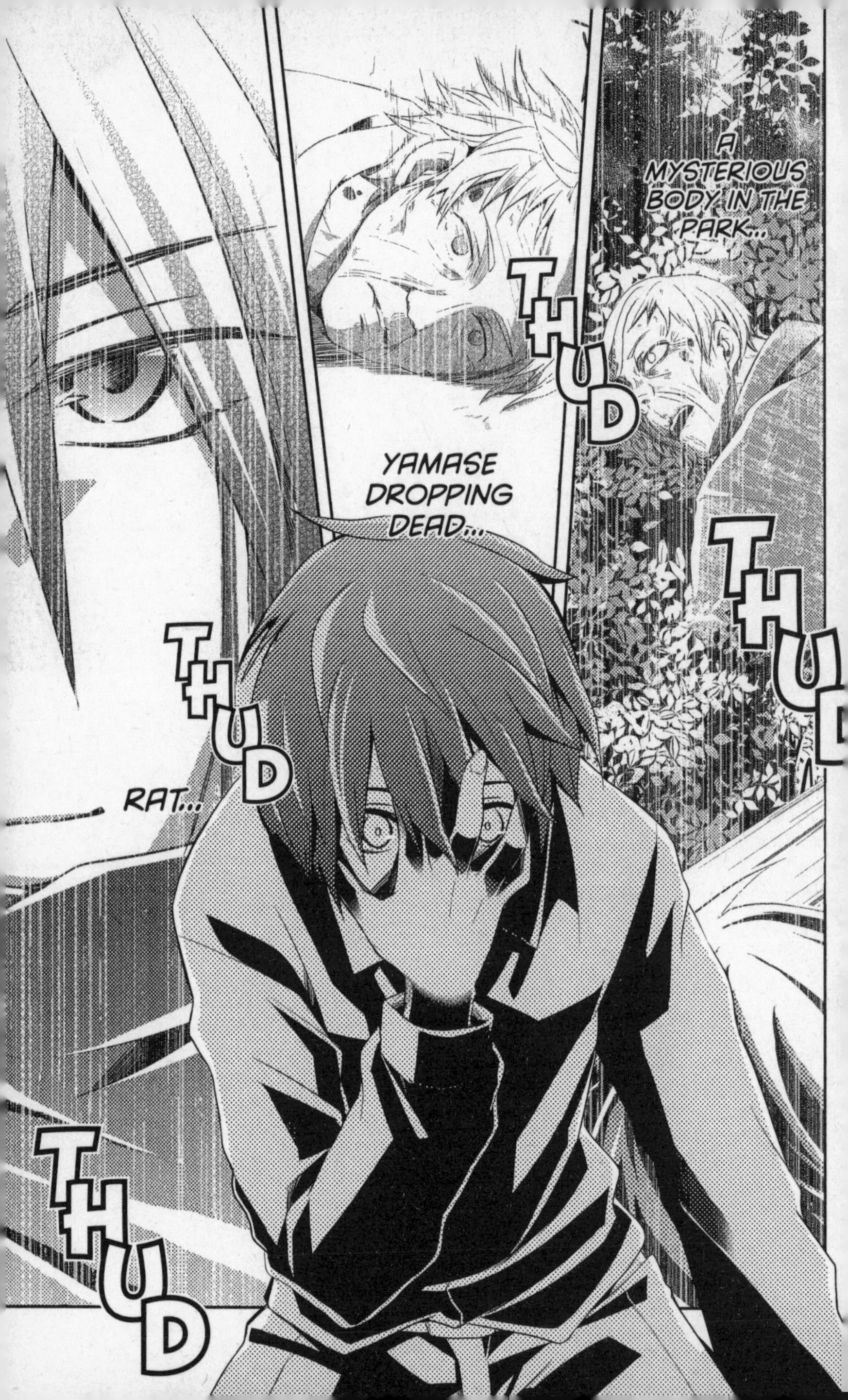
A MYSTERIOUS BODY IN THE PARK...
THUD
THUD
YAMASE DROPPING DEAD...
THUD
RAT...
THUD

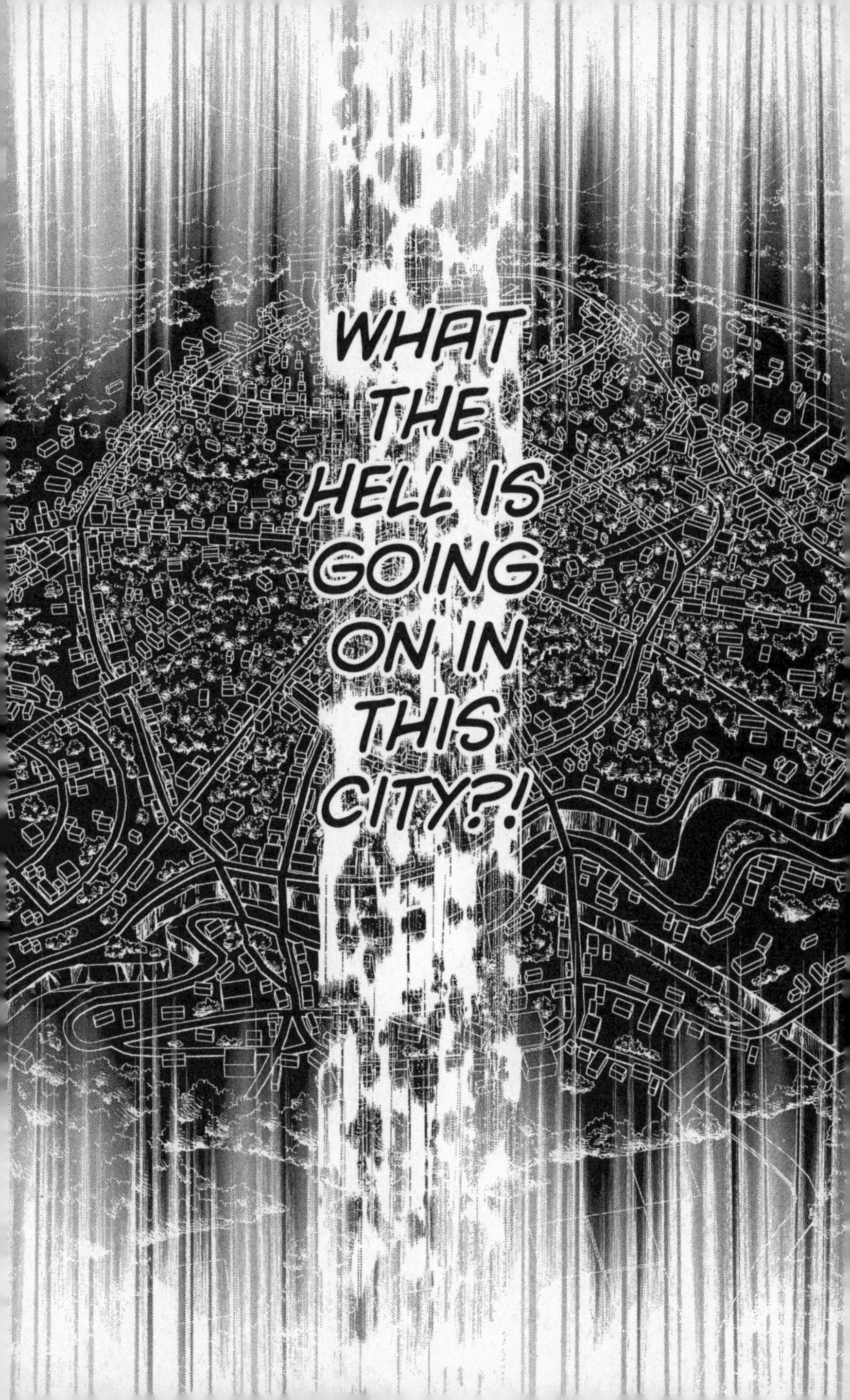
WHAT THE HELL IS GOING ON IN THIS CITY?!

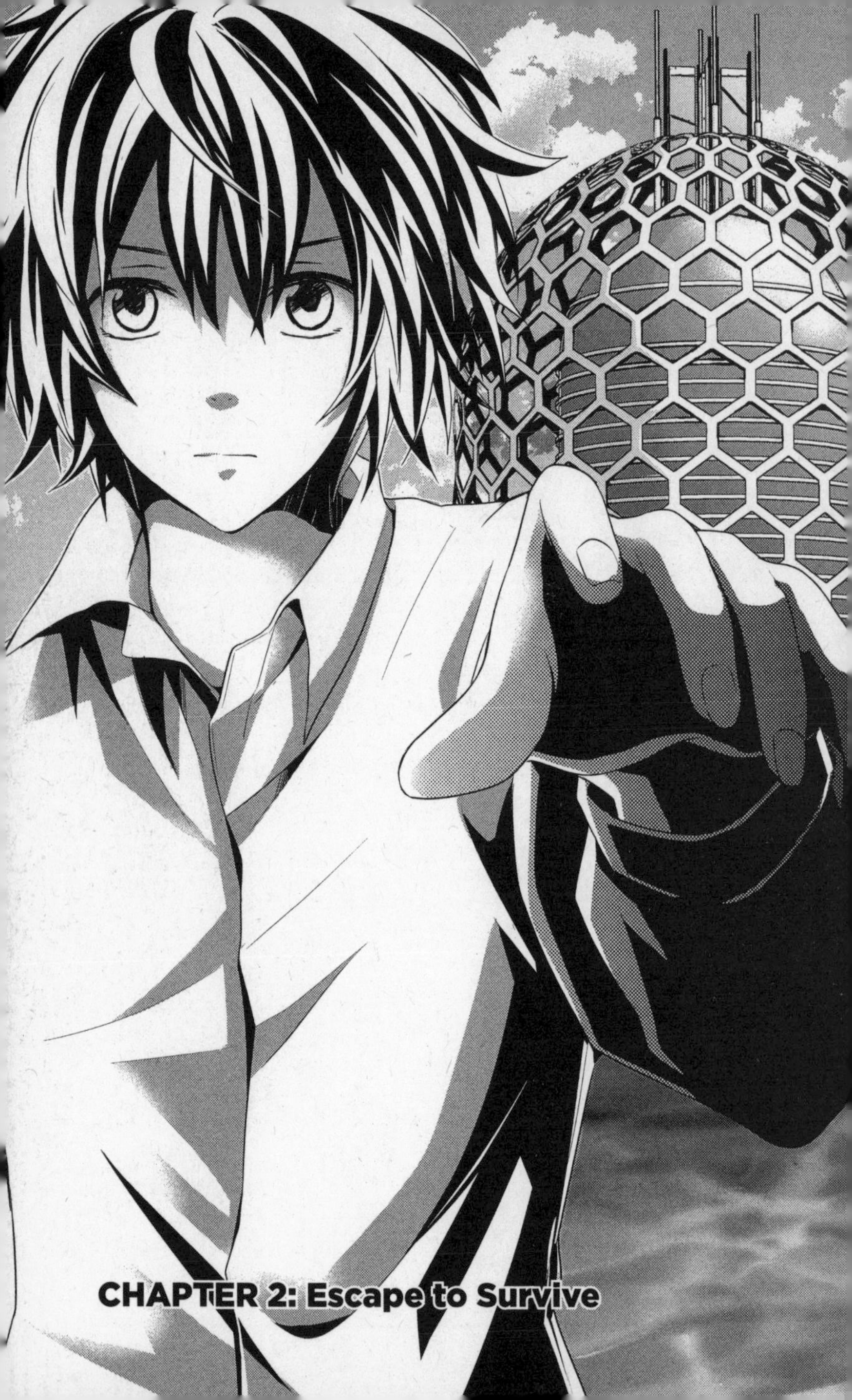
CHAPTER 2: Escape to Survive

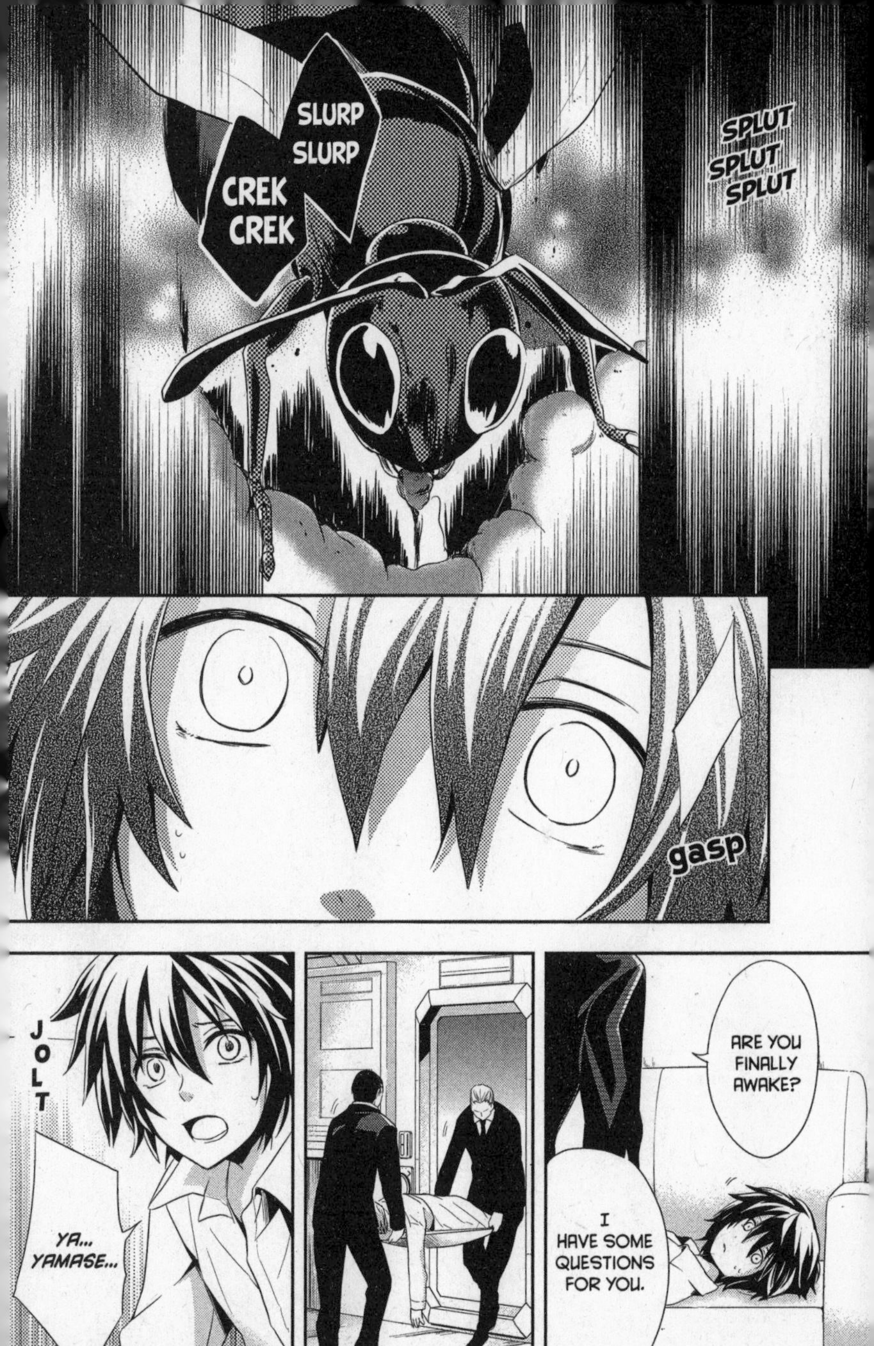
SPLUT SPLUT SPLUT
SLURP SLURP
CREK CREK
gasp
ARE YOU FINALLY AWAKE?
I HAVE SOME QUESTIONS FOR YOU.
JOLT
YA... YAMASE...

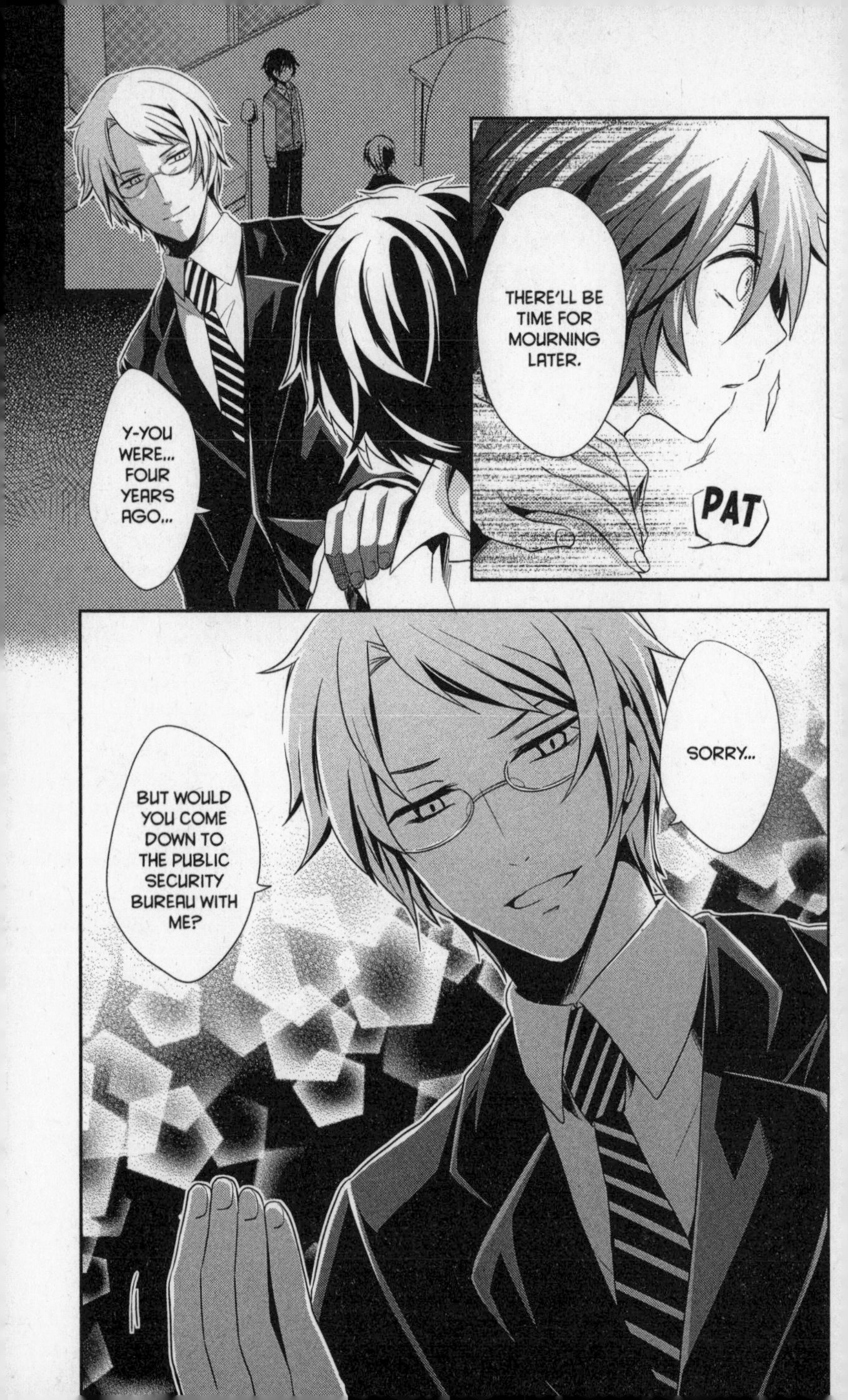
THERE'LL BE TIME FOR MOURNING LATER.
PAT
Y-YOU WERE... FOUR YEARS AGO...
SORRY...
BUT WOULD YOU COME DOWN TO THE PUBLIC SECURITY BUREAU WITH ME?

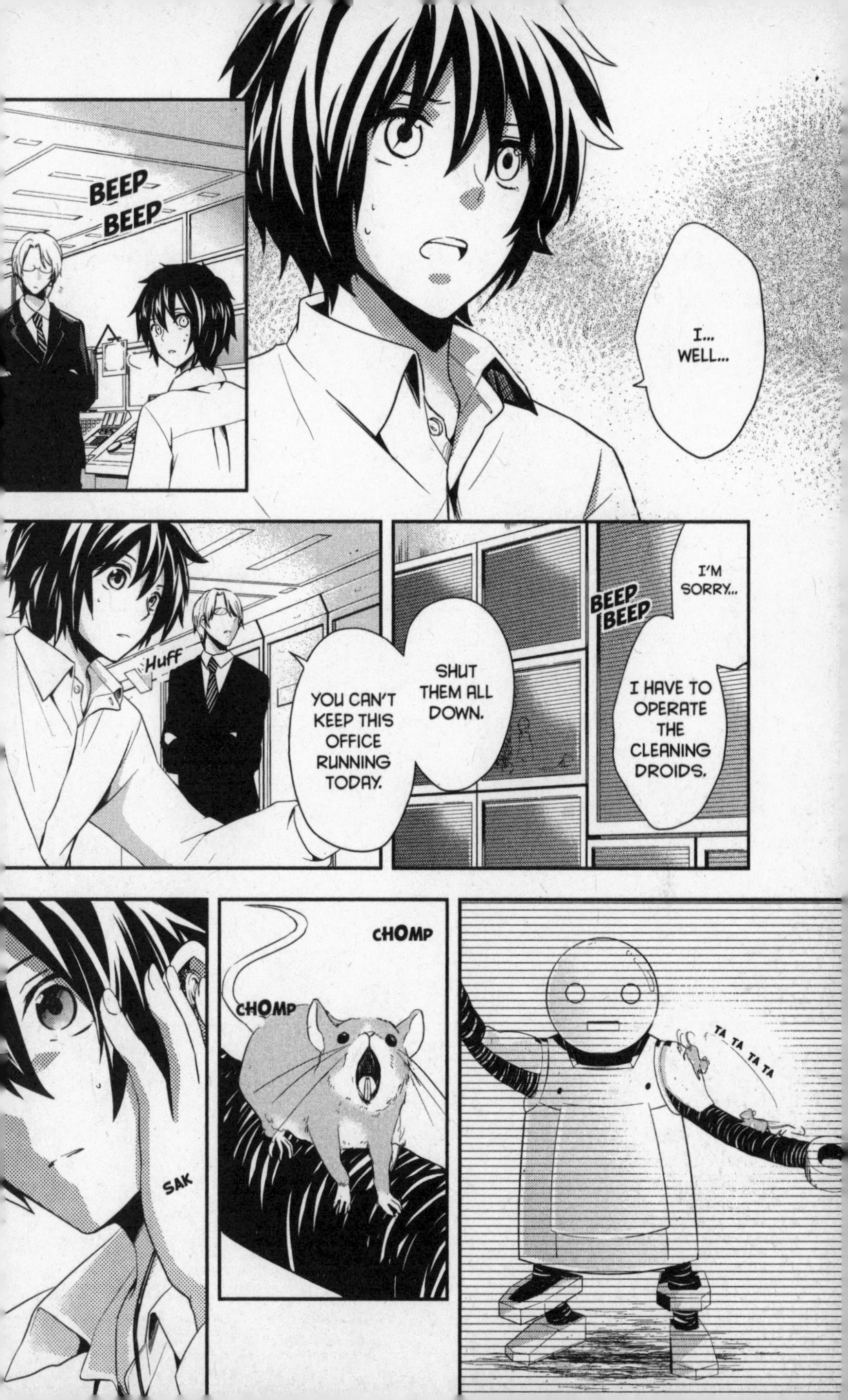
I... WELL...
BEEP BEEP
I'M SORRY...
BEEP BEEP
I HAVE TO OPERATE THE CLEANING DROIDS.
SHUT THEM ALL DOWN.
YOU CAN'T KEEP THIS OFFICE RUNNING TODAY.
Huff
TA TA TA TA
CHOMP
CHOMP
SAK

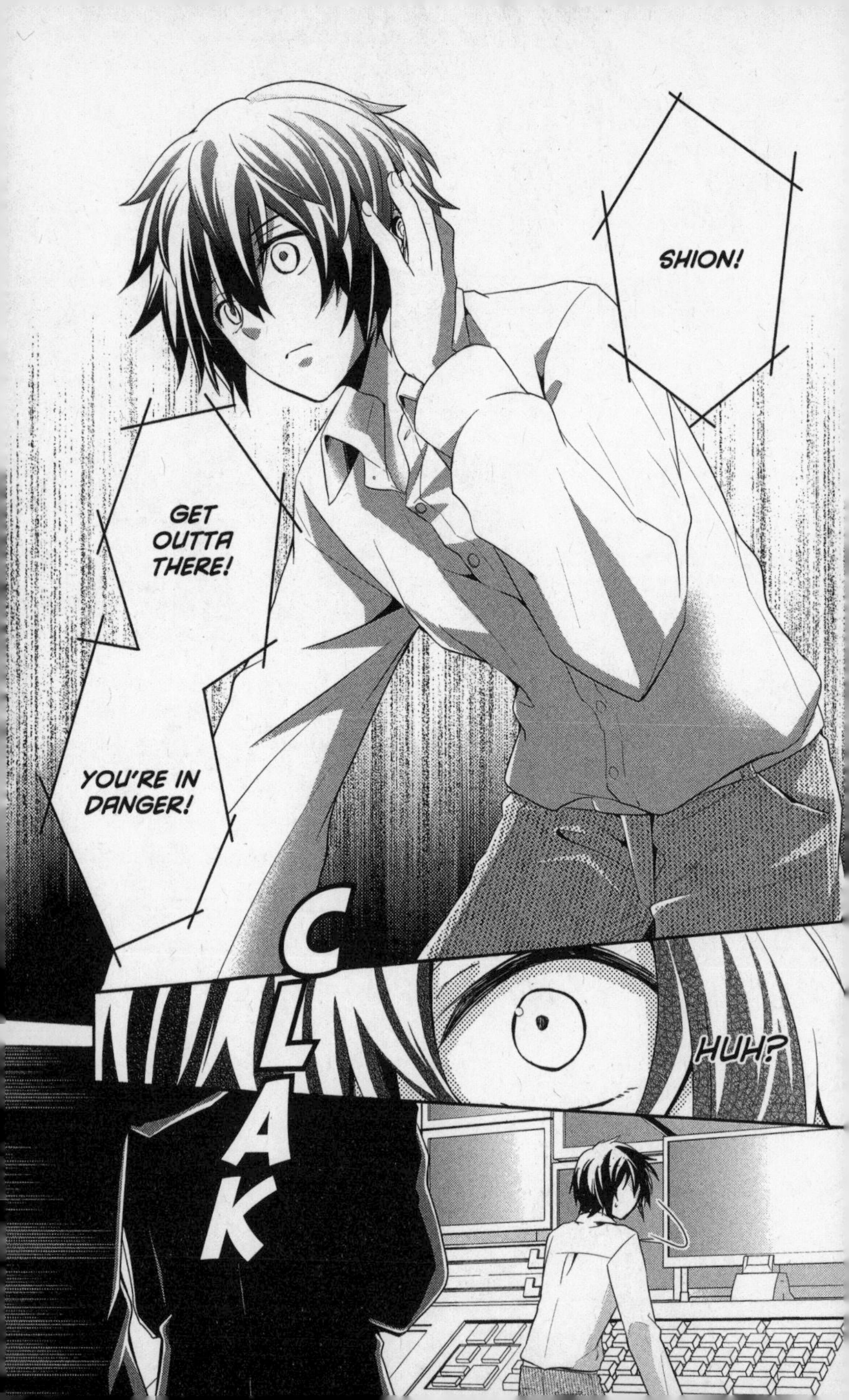
SHION!
GET OUTTA THERE!
YOU'RE IN DANGER!
CLAK
HUH?

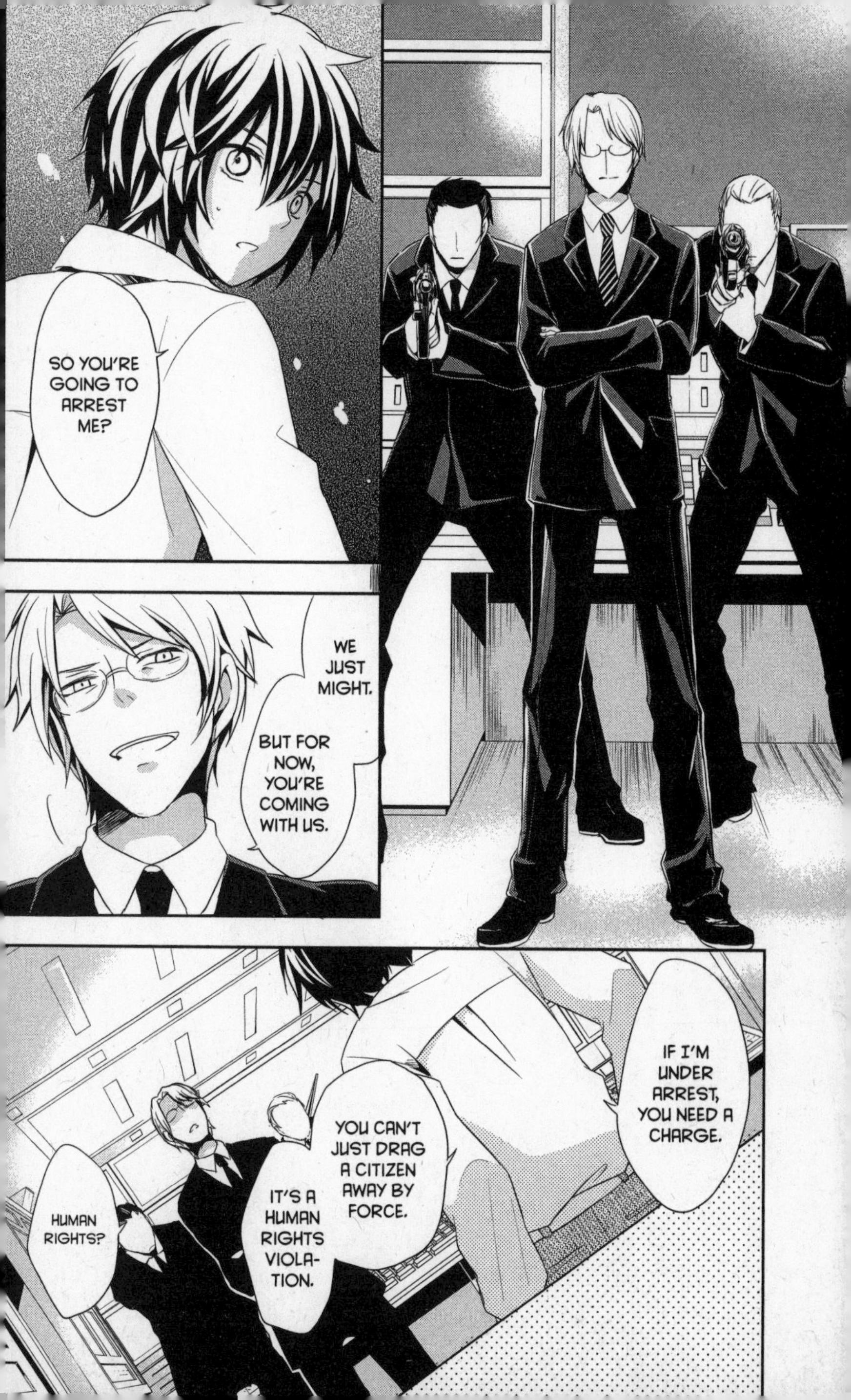
SO YOU'RE GOING TO ARREST ME?
WE JUST MIGHT.
BUT FOR NOW, YOU'RE COMING WITH US.
IF I'M UNDER ARREST, YOU NEED A CHARGE.
YOU CAN'T JUST DRAG A CITIZEN AWAY BY FORCE.
IT'S A HUMAN RIGHTS VIOLA-TION.
HUMAN RIGHTS?

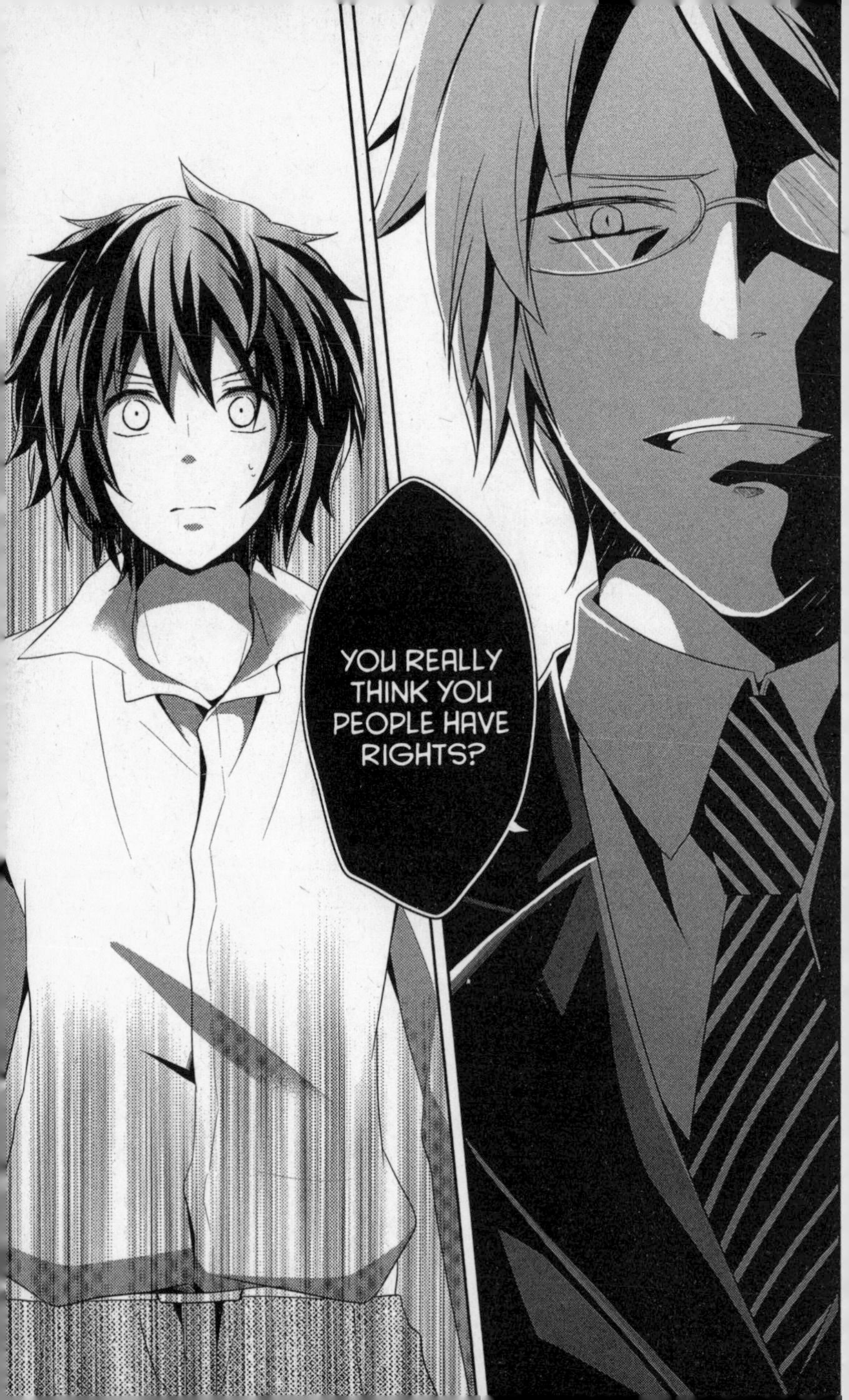
YOU REALLY THINK YOU PEOPLE HAVE RIGHTS?

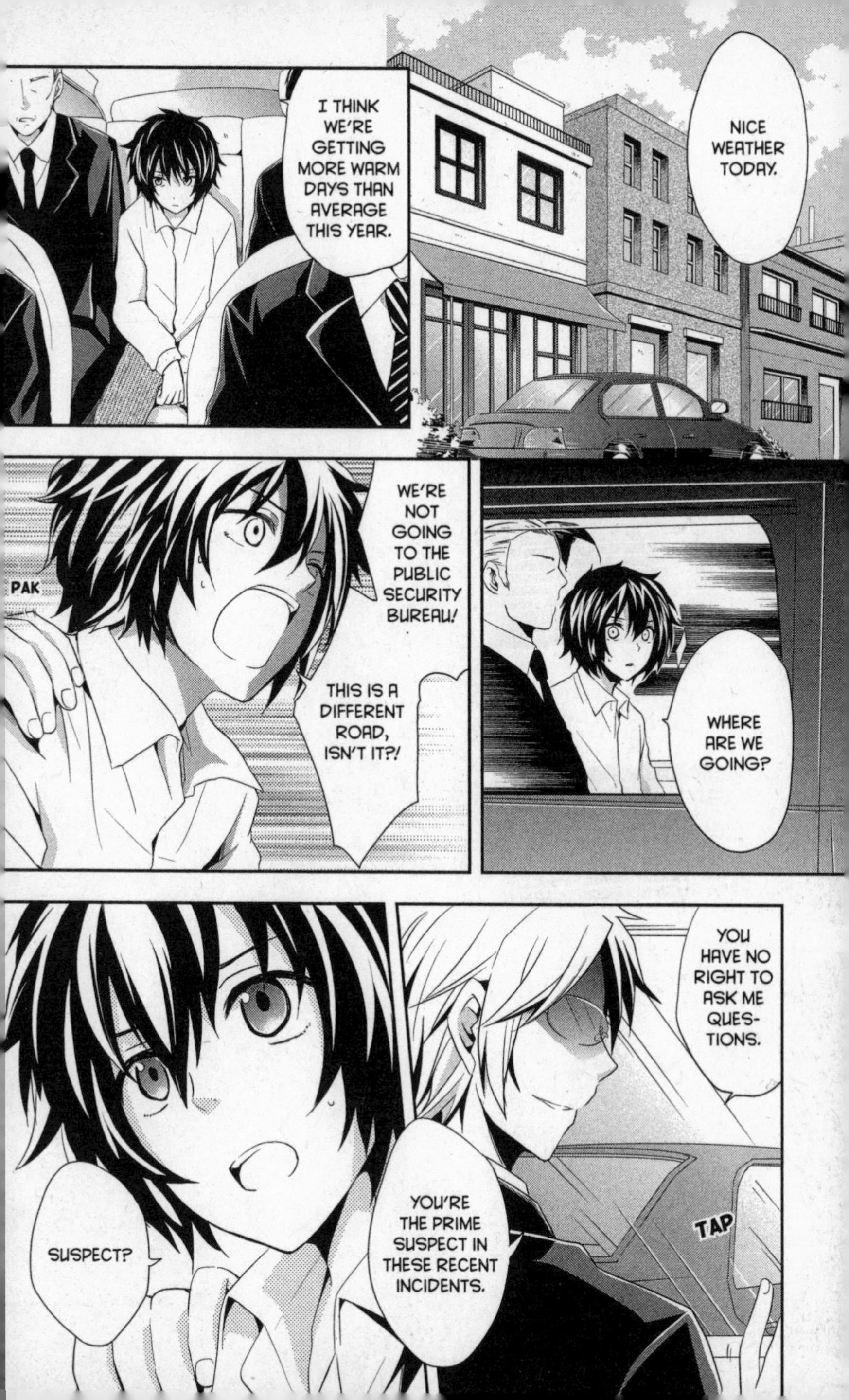
NICE WEATHER TODAY.
I THINK WE'RE GETTING MORE WARM DAYS THAN AVERAGE THIS YEAR.
WHERE ARE WE GOING?
WE'RE NOT GOING TO THE PUBLIC SECURITY BUREAU!
PAK
THIS IS A DIFFERENT ROAD, ISN'T IT?!
YOU HAVE NO RIGHT TO ASK ME QUES-TIONS.
TAP
YOU'RE THE PRIME SUSPECT IN THESE RECENT INCIDENTS.
SUSPECT?

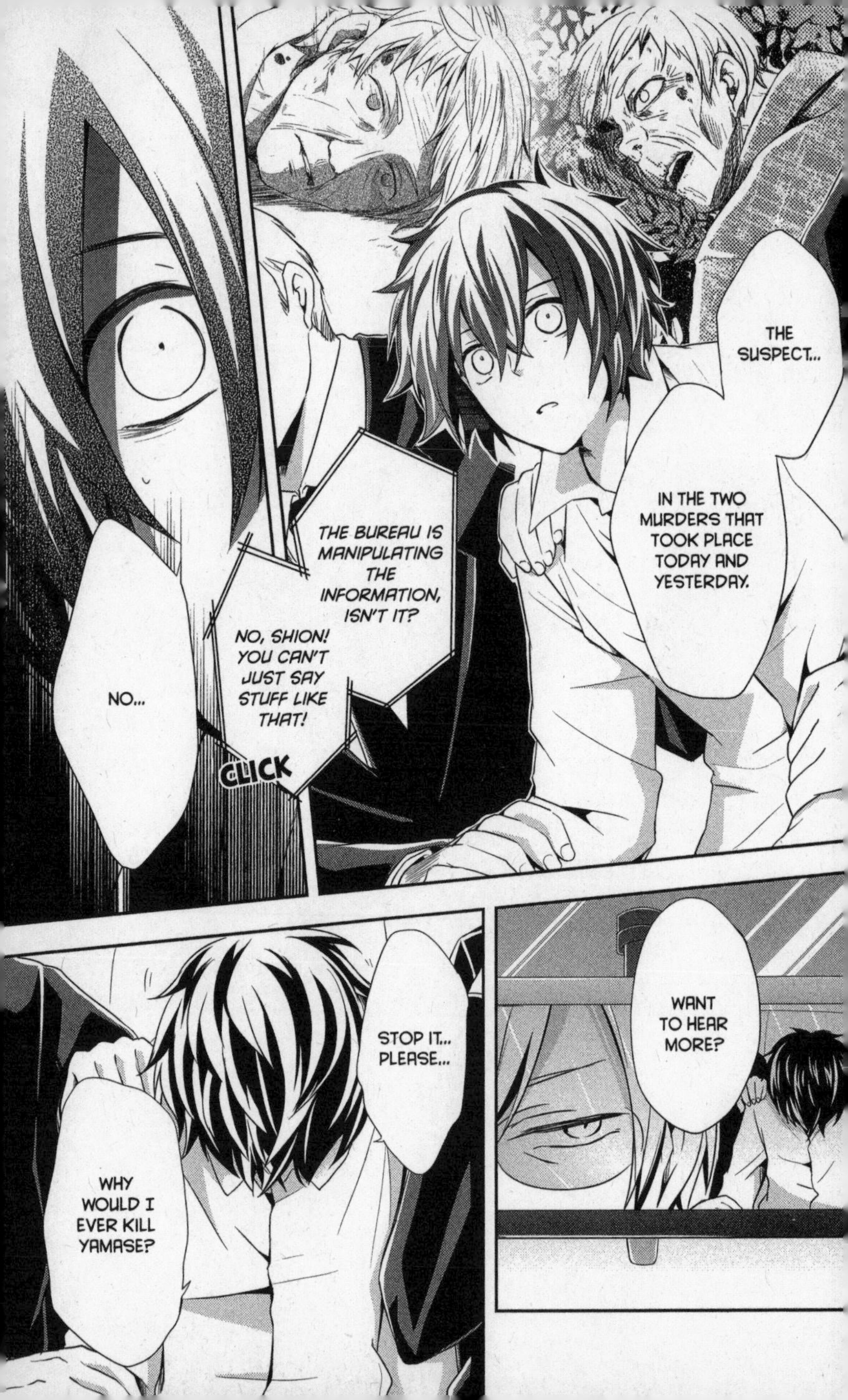
THE SUSPECT...
IN THE TWO MURDERS THAT TOOK PLACE TODAY AND YESTERDAY.
THE BUREAU IS MANIPULATING THE INFORMATION, ISN'T IT?
NO, SHION! YOU CAN'T JUST SAY STUFF LIKE THAT!
CLICK
NO...
WANT TO HEAR MORE?
STOP IT... PLEASE...
WHY WOULD I EVER KILL YAMASE?

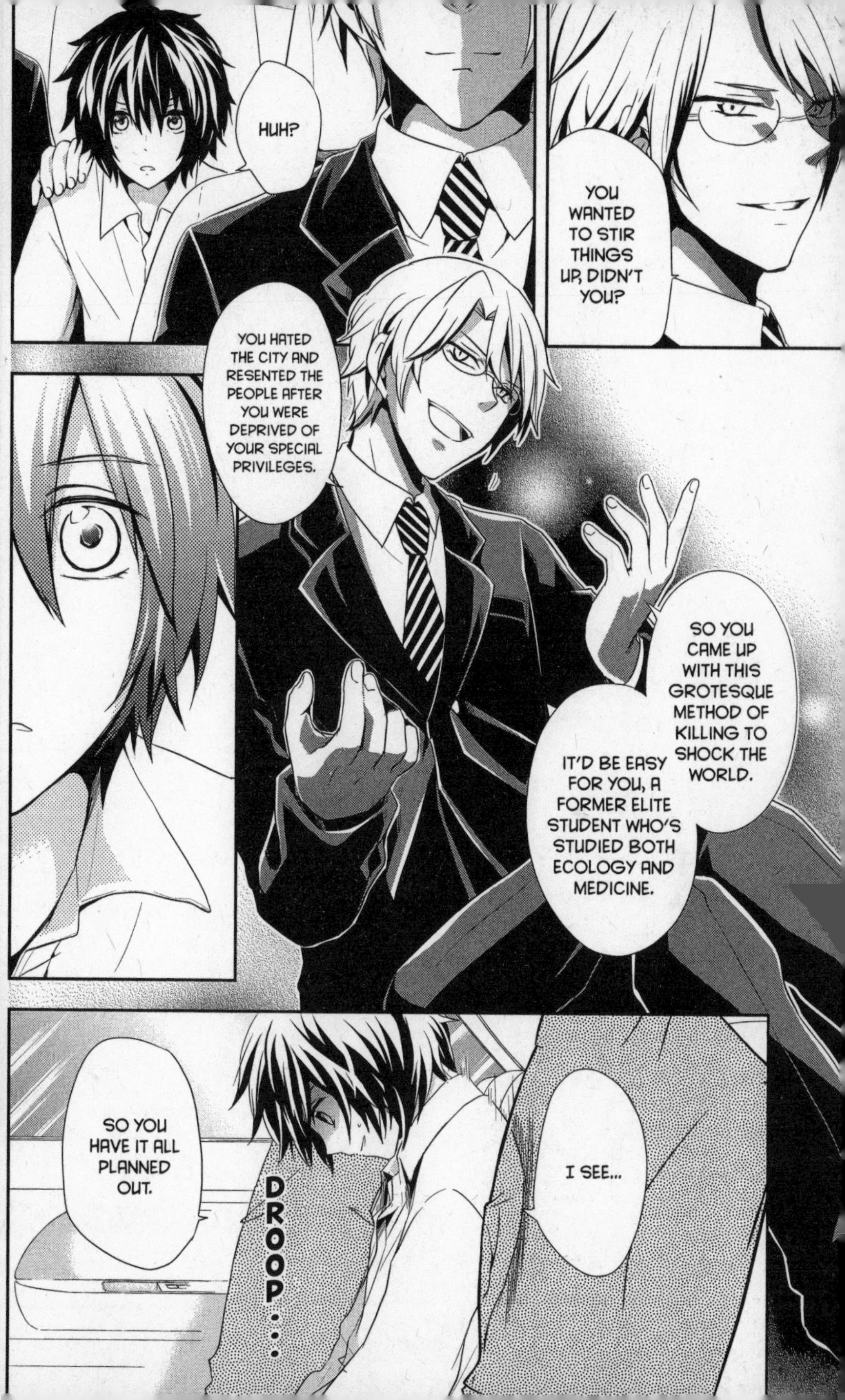
YOU WANTED TO STIR THINGS UP, DIDN'T YOU?
HUH?
YOU HATED THE CITY AND RESENTED THE PEOPLE AFTER YOU WERE DEPRIVED OF YOUR SPECIAL PRIVILEGES.
SO YOU CAME UP WITH THIS GROTESQUE METHOD OF KILLING TO SHOCK THE WORLD.
IT'D BE EASY FOR YOU, A FORMER ELITE STUDENT WHO'S STUDIED BOTH ECOLOGY AND MEDICINE.
I SEE...
DROOP...
SO YOU HAVE IT ALL PLANNED OUT.

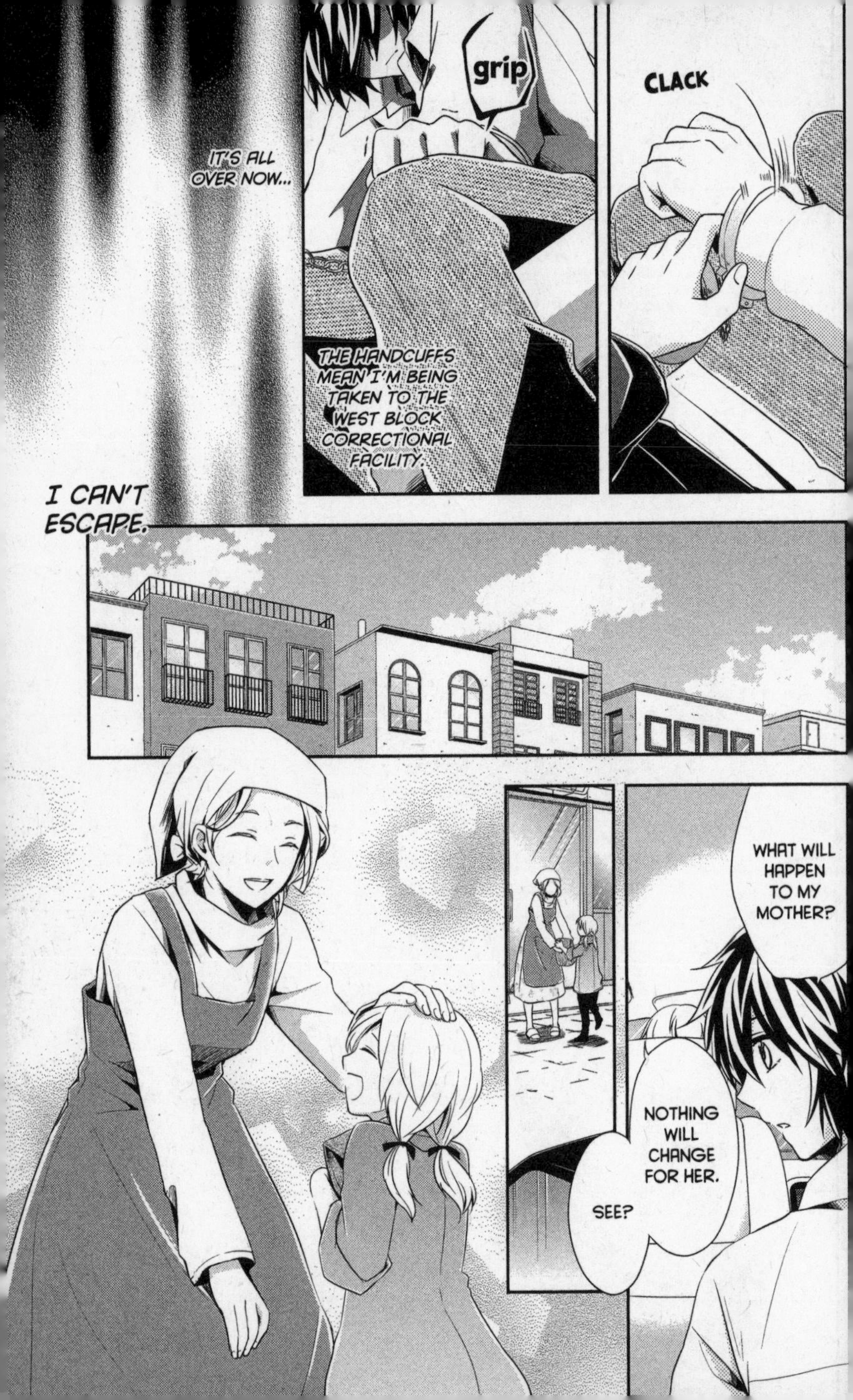
CLACK
grip
THE HANDCUFFS MEAN I'M BEING TAKEN TO THE WEST BLOCK CORRECTIONAL FACILITY.
IT'S ALL OVER NOW...
I CAN'T ESCAPE.
WHAT WILL HAPPEN TO MY MOTHER?
NOTHING WILL CHANGE FOR HER.
SEE?

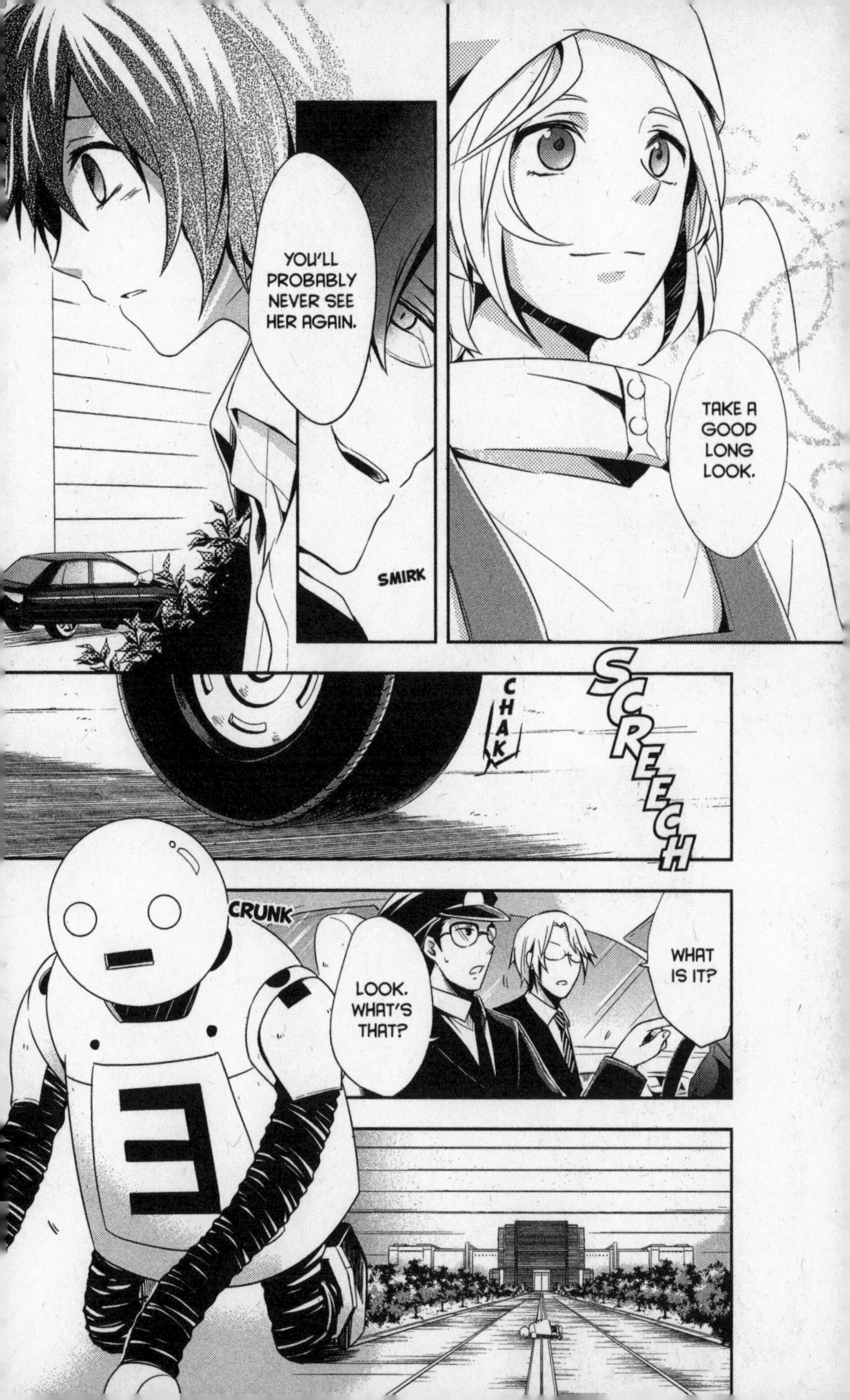

TAKE A GOOD LONG LOOK.
YOU'LL PROBABLY NEVER SEE HER AGAIN.
SMIRK
SCREECH
CHAK
WHAT IS IT?
LOOK. WHAT'S THAT?
CRUNK

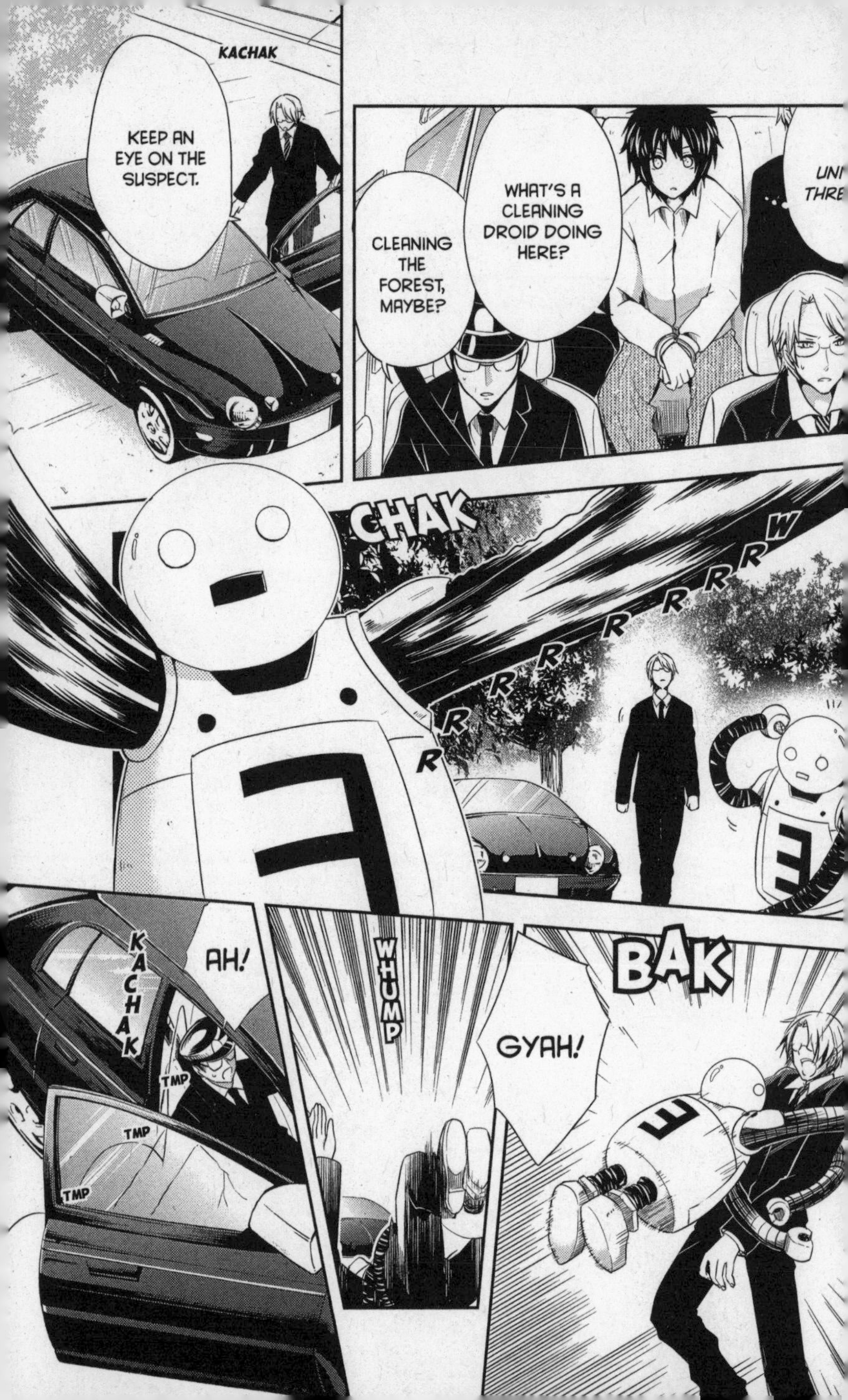
UNI THRE
WHAT'S A CLEANING DROID DOING HERE?
CLEANING THE FOREST, MAYBE?
KACHAK
KEEP AN EYE ON THE SUSPECT.
CHAK
RRRRRRRRRRW
BAK
GYAH!
WHUMP
KACHAK
AH!
TMP
TMP
TMP

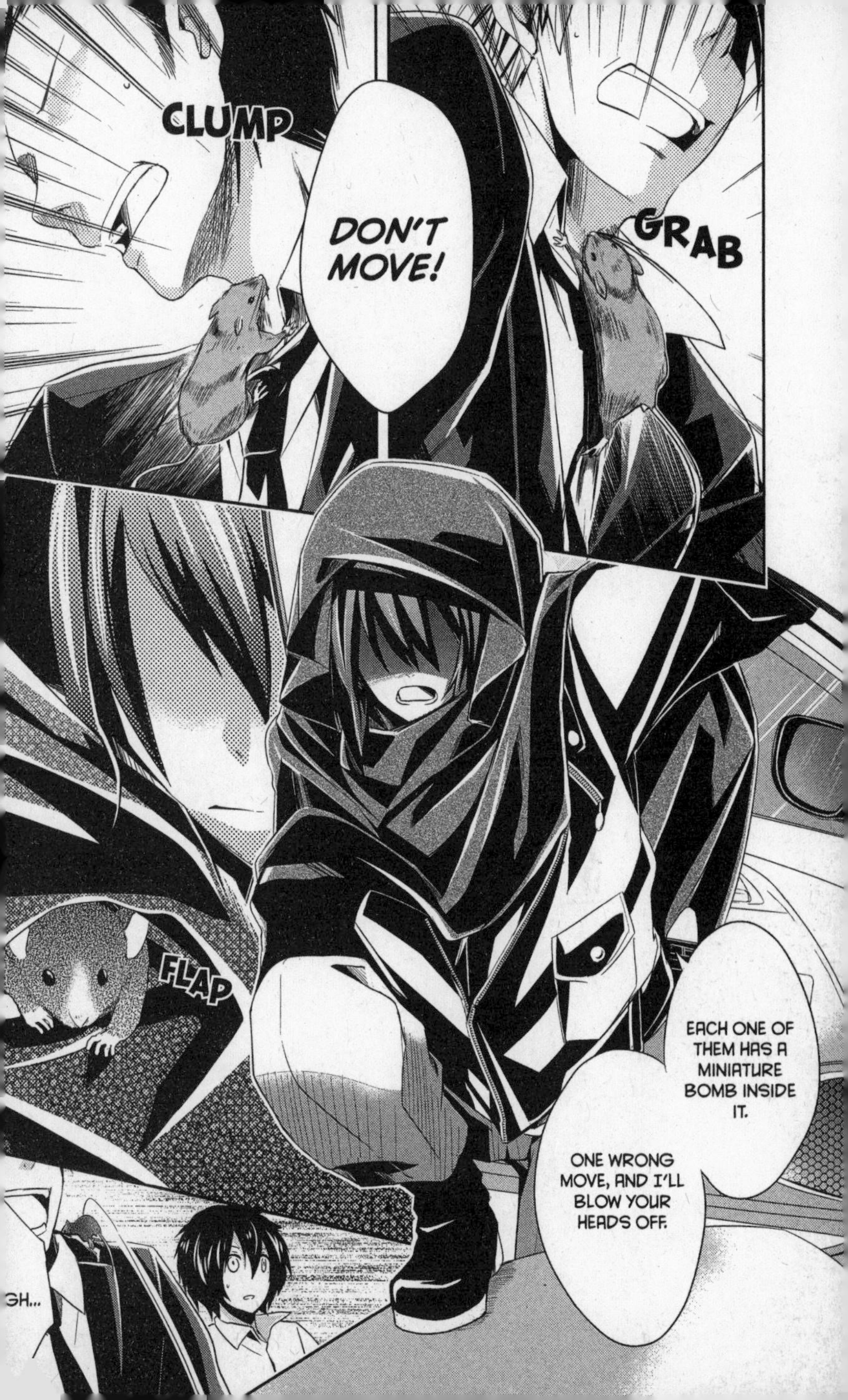
GRAB
DON'T MOVE!
CLUMP
EACH ONE OF THEM HAS A MINIATURE BOMB INSIDE IT.
ONE WRONG MOVE, AND I'LL BLOW YOUR HEADS OFF.
FLAP
GH...

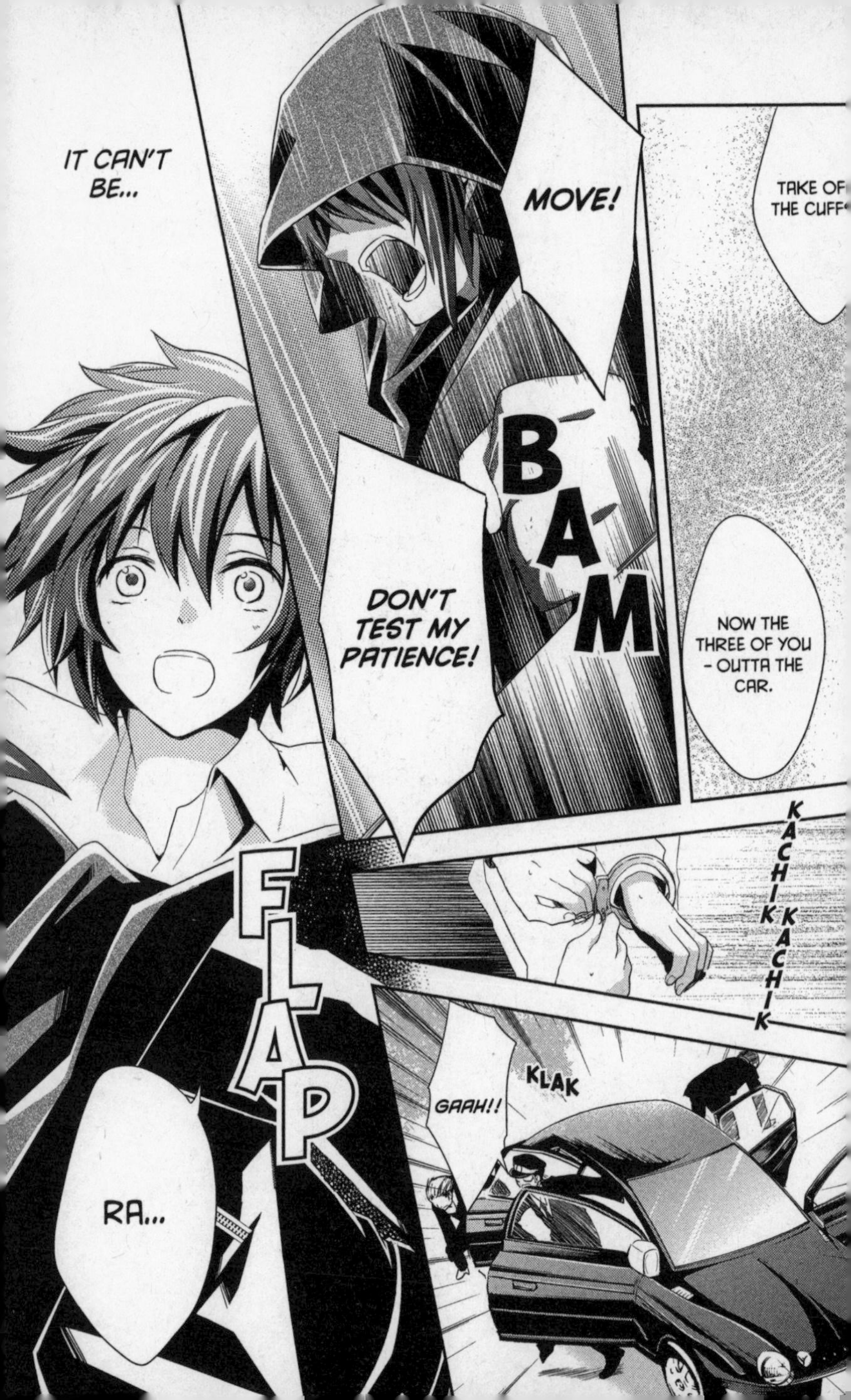
TAKE OF THE CUFF
NOW THE THREE OF YOU - OUTTA THE CAR.
MOVE!
BAM
DON'T TEST MY PATIENCE!
KACHIK KACHIK
KACHIK
KLAK
GAAH!!
IT CAN'T BE...
FLAP
RA...

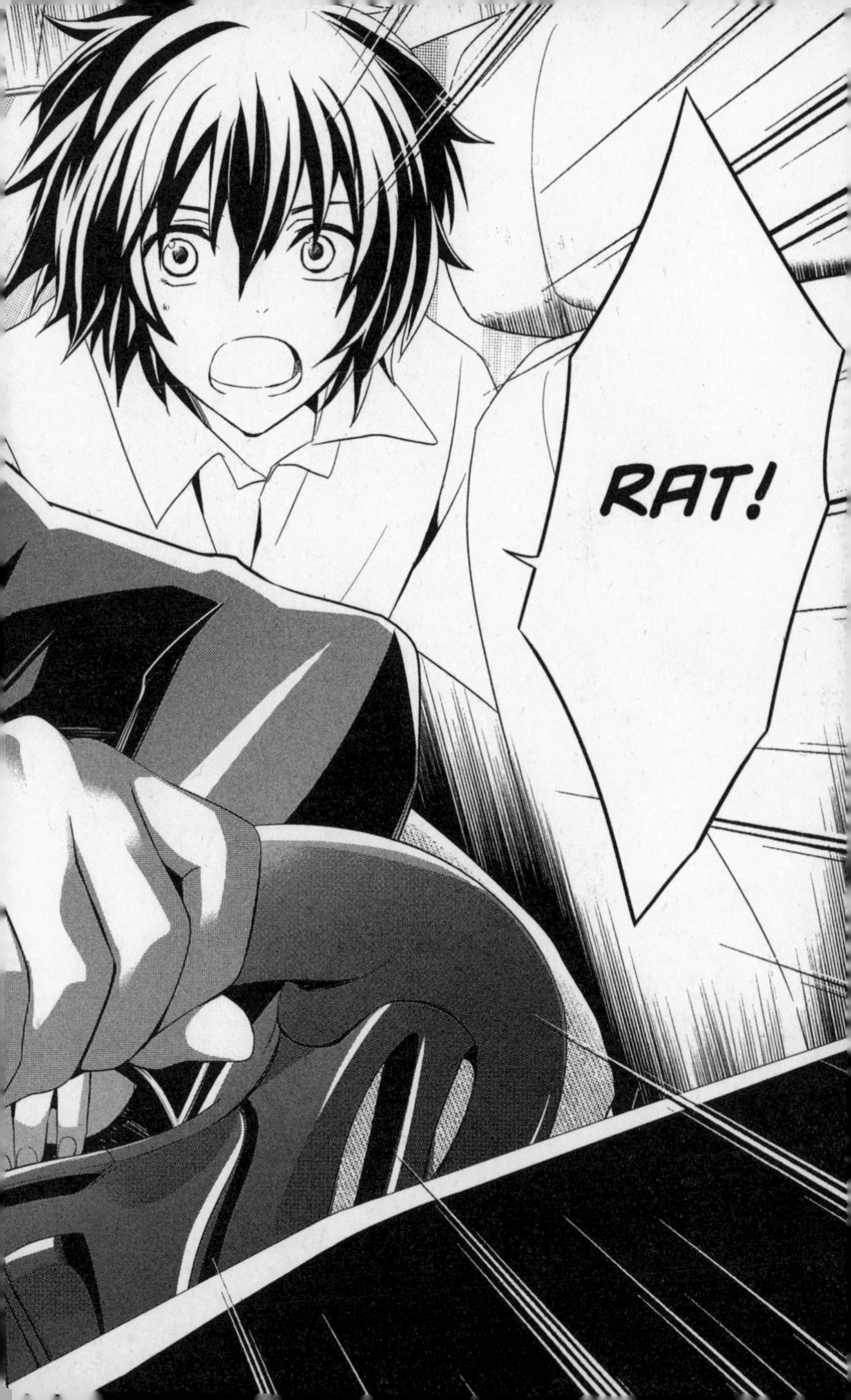
RAT!

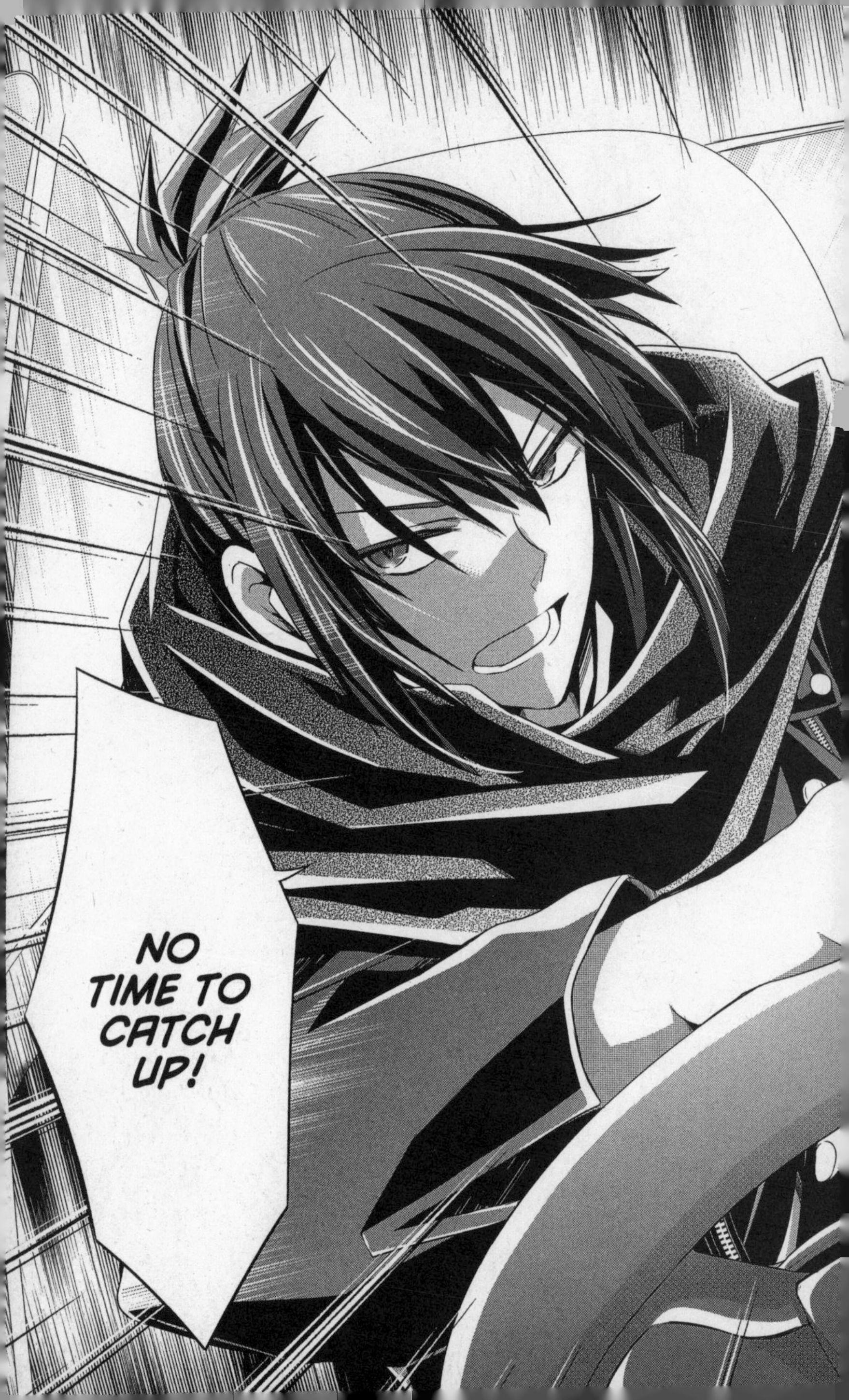
NO TIME TO CATCH UP!

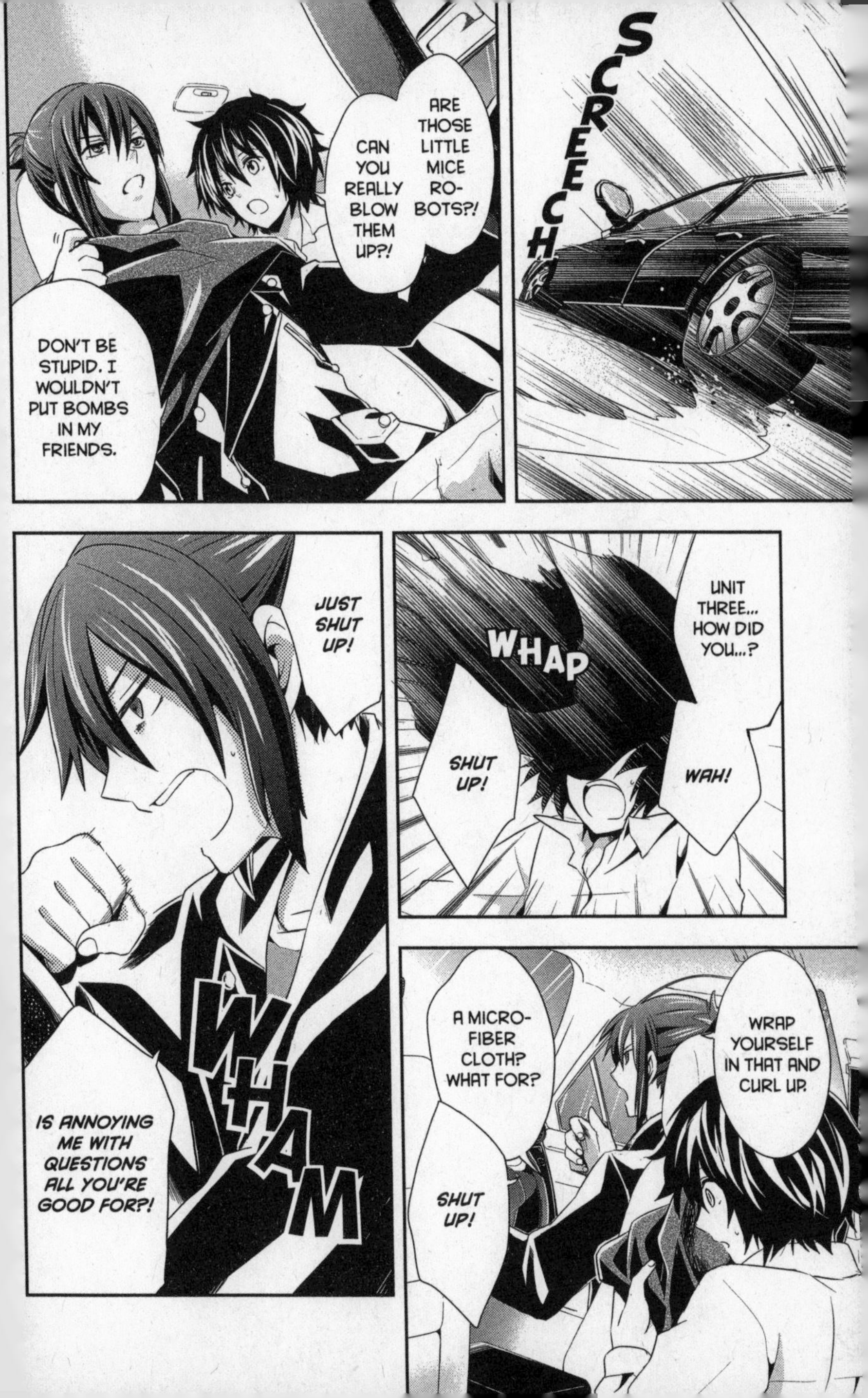
SCREECH
ARE THOSE LITTLE MICE RO-BOTS?! CAN YOU REALLY BLOW THEM UP?!
DON'T BE STUPID. I WOULDN'T PUT BOMBS IN MY FRIENDS.
UNIT THREE... HOW DID YOU...?
WHAP
WAH!
SHUT UP!
WRAP YOURSELF IN THAT AND CURL UP.
A MICRO-FIBER CLOTH? WHAT FOR?
SHUT UP!
JUST SHUT UP!
WHAM
IS ANNOYING ME WITH QUESTIONS ALL YOU'RE GOOD FOR?!

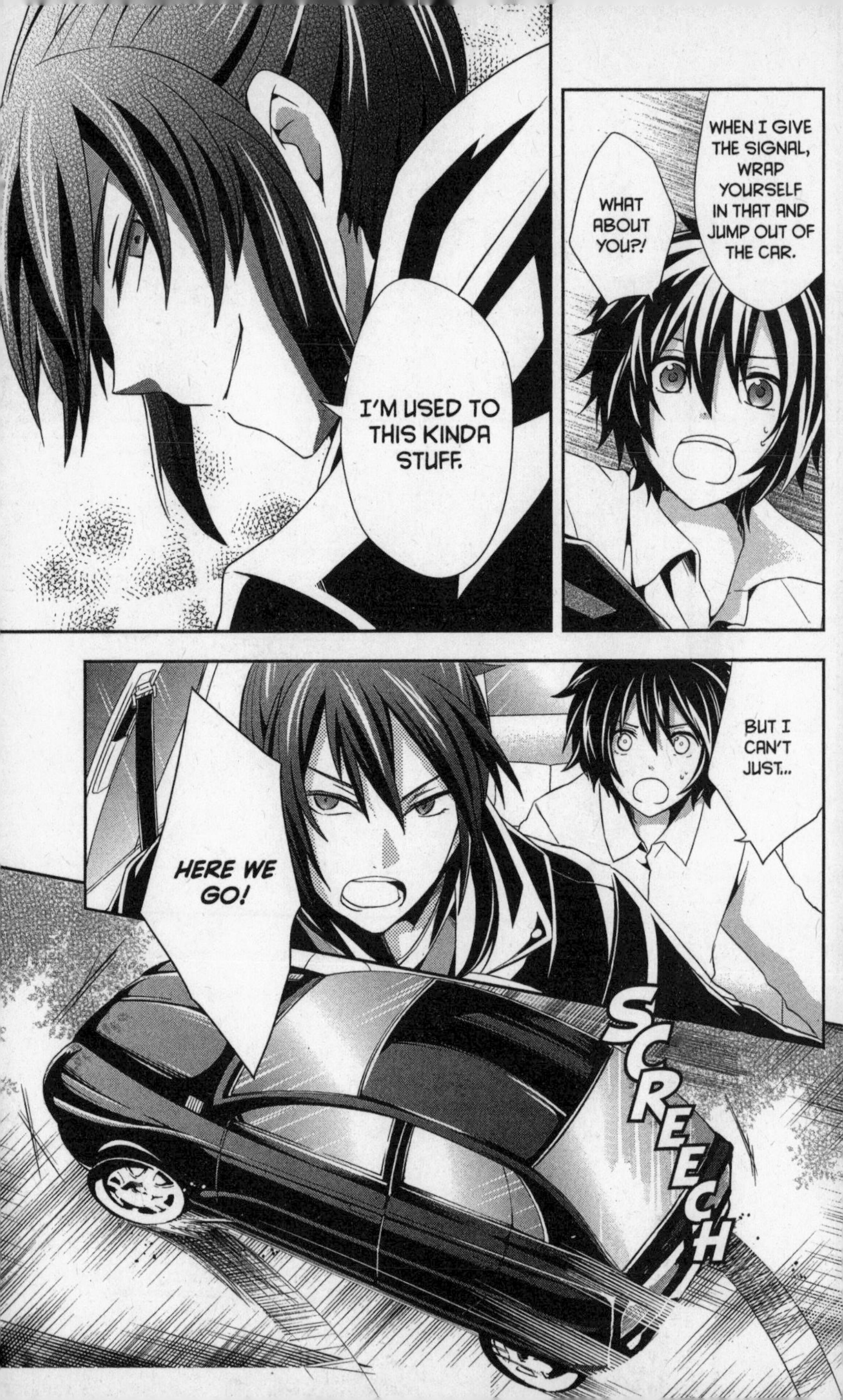
WHEN I GIVE THE SIGNAL, WRAP YOURSELF IN THAT AND JUMP OUT OF THE CAR.
WHAT ABOUT YOU?!
I'M USED TO THIS KINDA STUFF.
BUT I CAN'T JUST...
HERE WE GO!
SCREECH

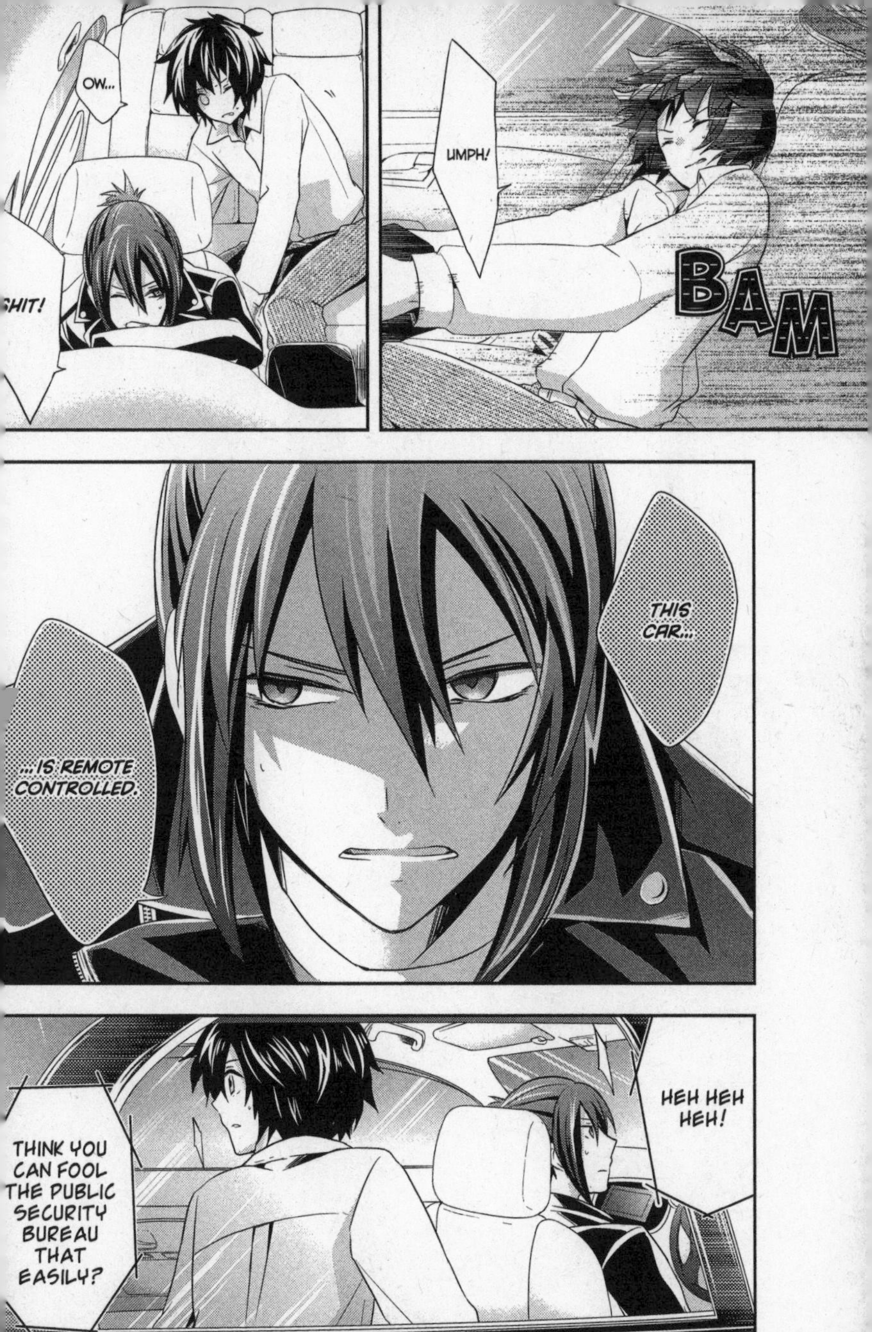
UMPH!
BAM
OW...
SHIT!
THIS CAR...
...IS REMOTE CONTROLLED.
HEH HEH HEH!
THINK YOU CAN FOOL THE PUBLIC SECURITY BUREAU THAT EASILY?

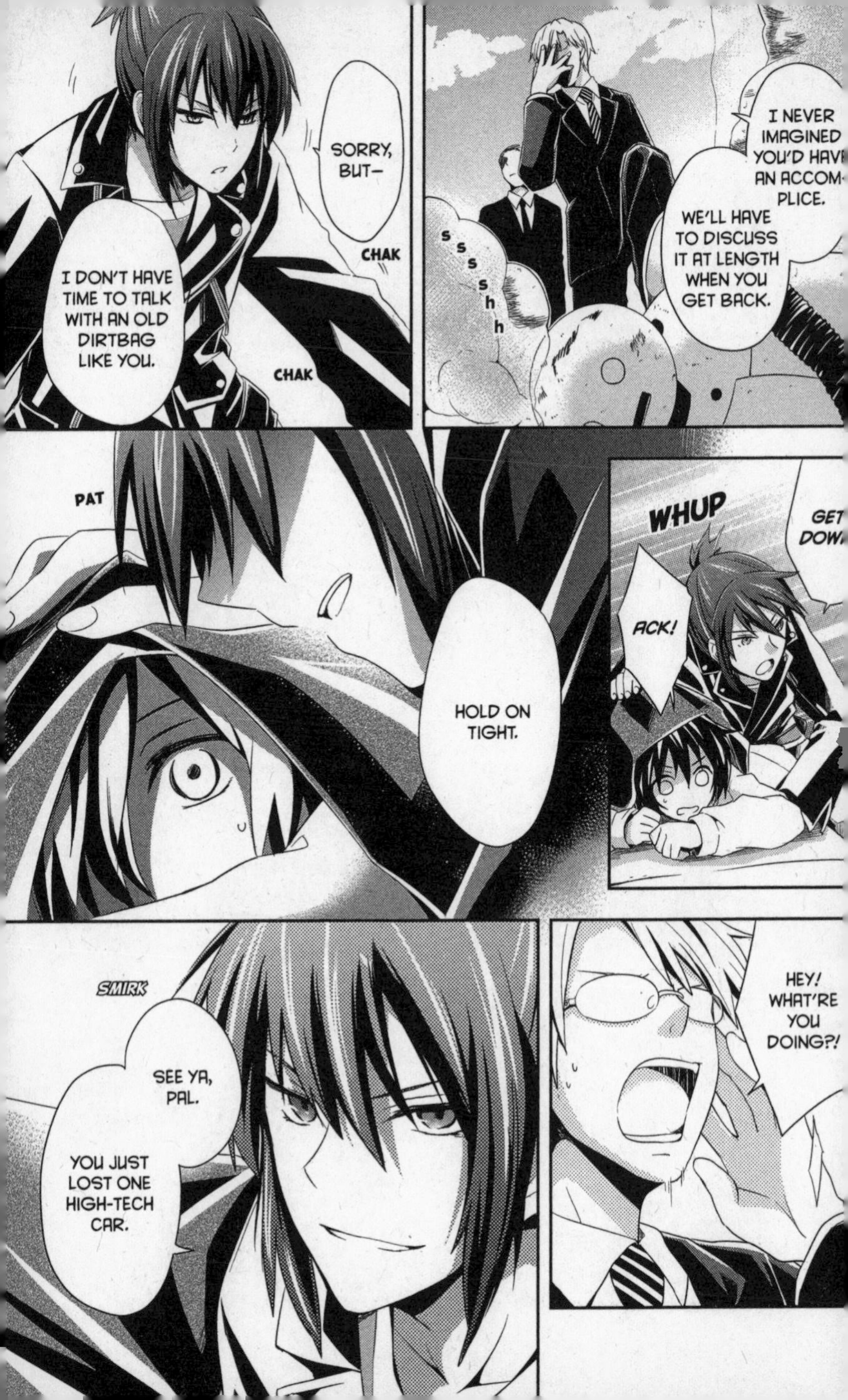
I NEVER IMAGINED YOU'D HAV AN ACCOM-PLICE.
WE'LL HAVE TO DISCUSS IT AT LENGTH WHEN YOU GET BACK.
sssshh
SORRY, BUT—
CHAK
I DON'T HAVE TIME TO TALK WITH AN OLD DIRTBAG LIKE YOU.
CHAK
WHUP
GET DOW
ACK!
PAT
HOLD ON TIGHT.
HEY! WHAT'RE YOU DOING?!
SMIRK
SEE YA, PAL.
YOU JUST LOST ONE HIGH-TECH CAR.

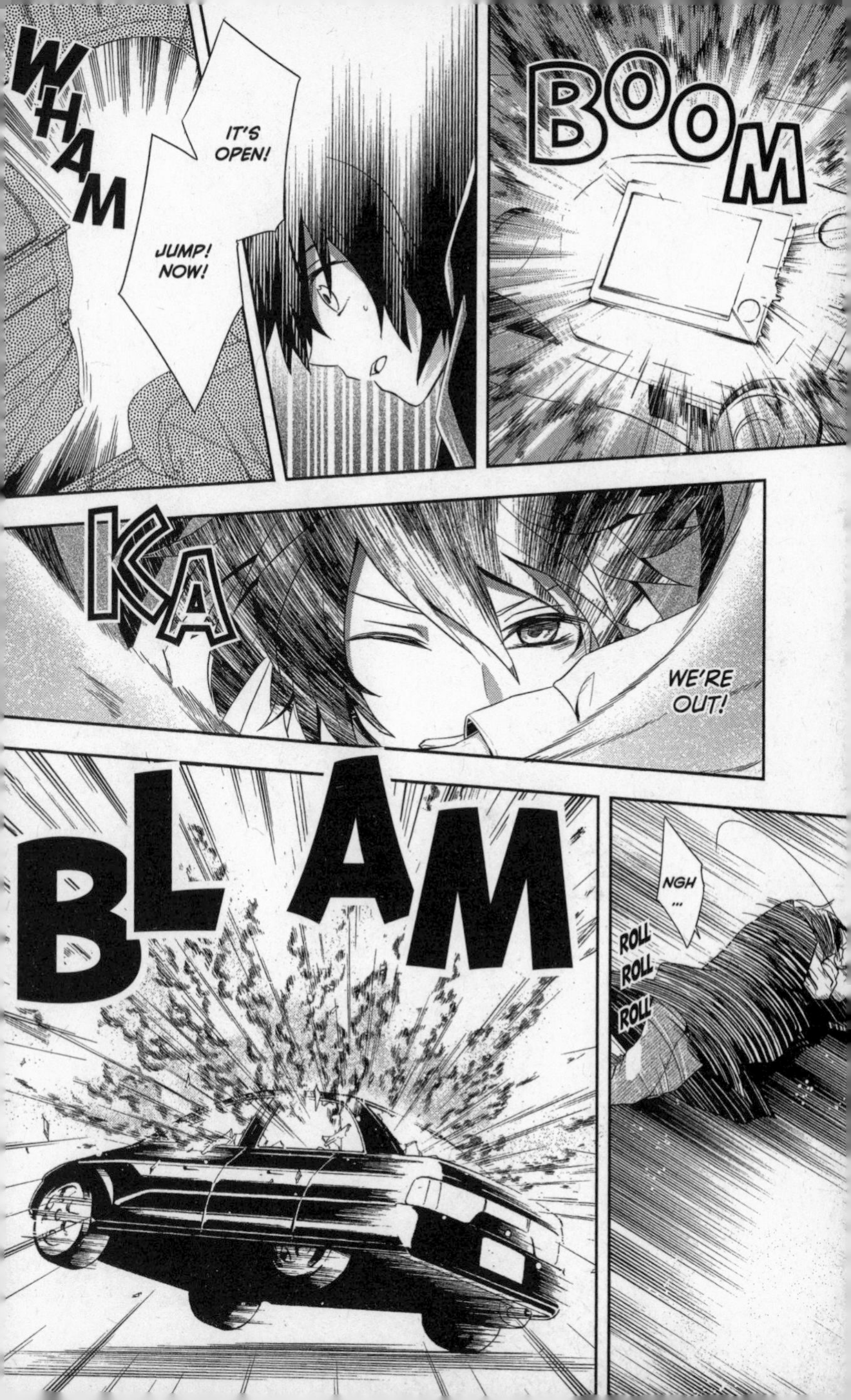
BOOM
IT'S OPEN!
JUMP! NOW!
WHAM
WE'RE OUT!
KA
NGH ...
ROLL ROLL ROLL
BLAM

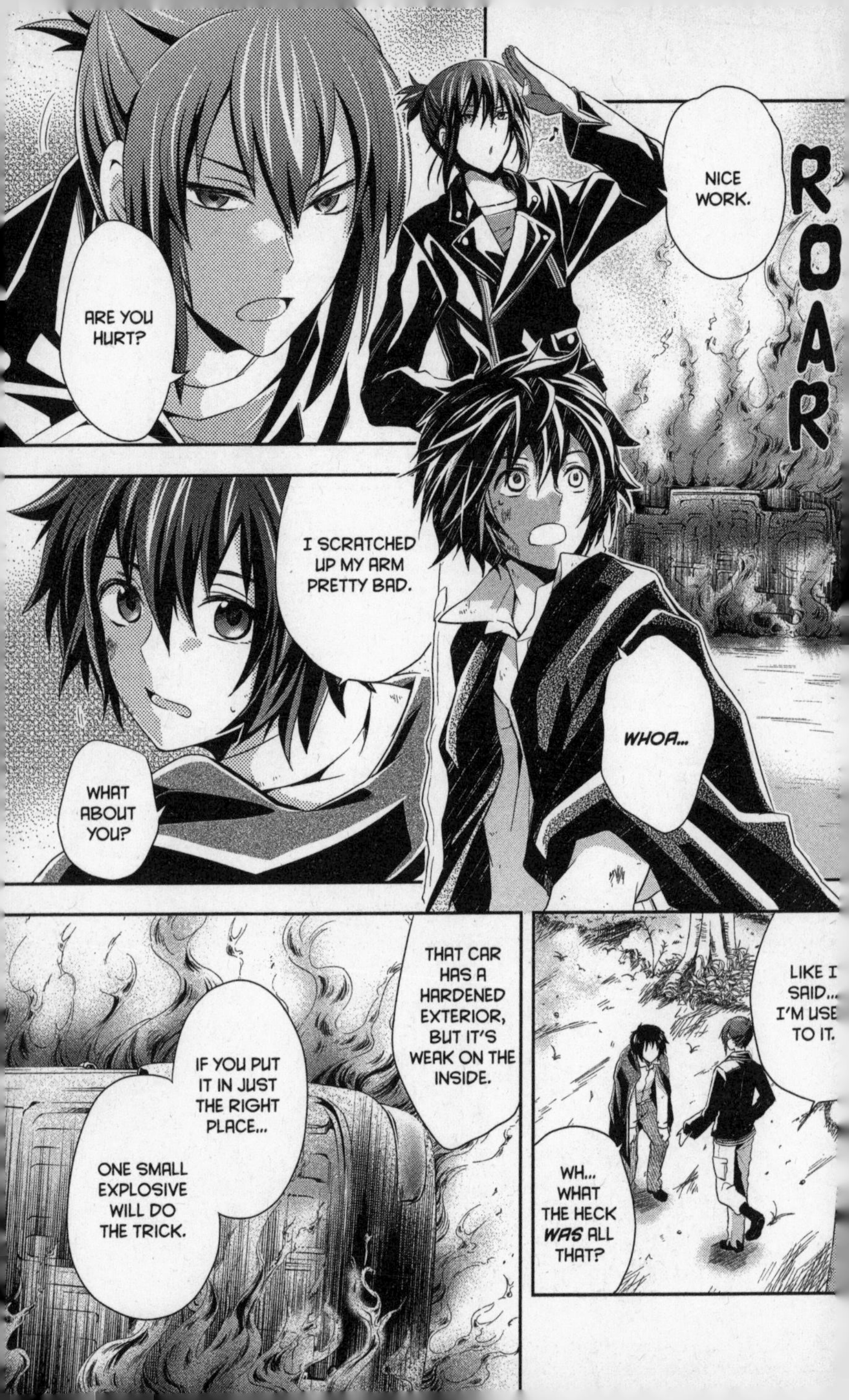
NICE WORK.
ROAR
ARE YOU HURT?
WHOA...
I SCRATCHED UP MY ARM PRETTY BAD.
WHAT ABOUT YOU?
LIKE I SAID... I'M USE TO IT.
WH... WHAT THE HECK *WAS* ALL THAT?
THAT CAR HAS A HARDENED EXTERIOR, BUT IT'S WEAK ON THE INSIDE.
IF YOU PUT IT IN JUST THE RIGHT PLACE...
ONE SMALL EXPLOSIVE WILL DO THE TRICK.

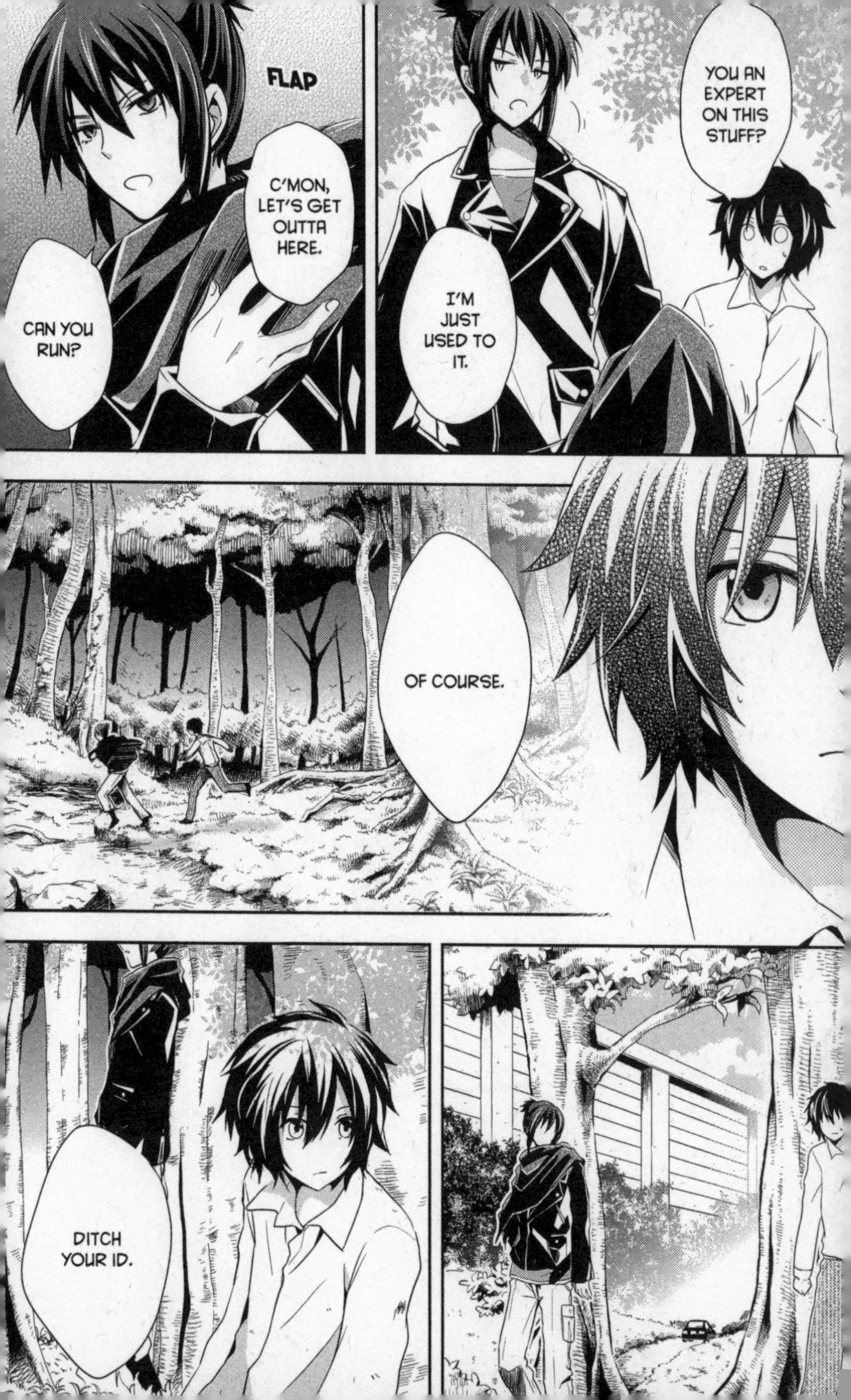
YOU AN EXPERT ON THIS STUFF?
I'M JUST USED TO IT.
FLAP
C'MON, LET'S GET OUTTA HERE.
CAN YOU RUN?
OF COURSE.
DITCH YOUR ID.

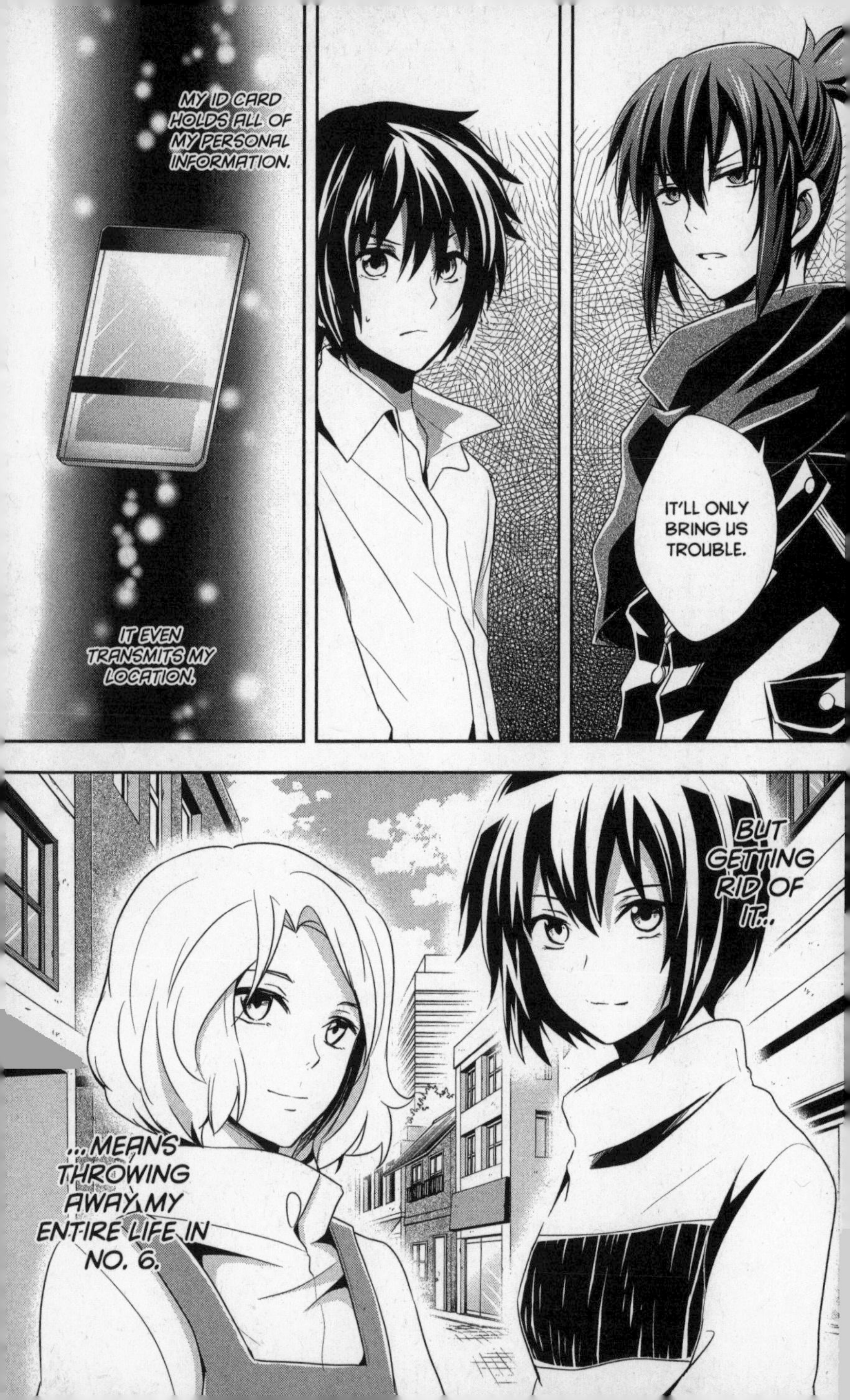
IT'LL ONLY BRING US TROUBLE.
MY ID CARD HOLDS ALL OF MY PERSONAL INFORMATION.
IT EVEN TRANSMITS MY LOCATION.
BUT GETTING RID OF IT...
...MEANS THROWING AWAY MY ENTIRE LIFE IN NO. 6.

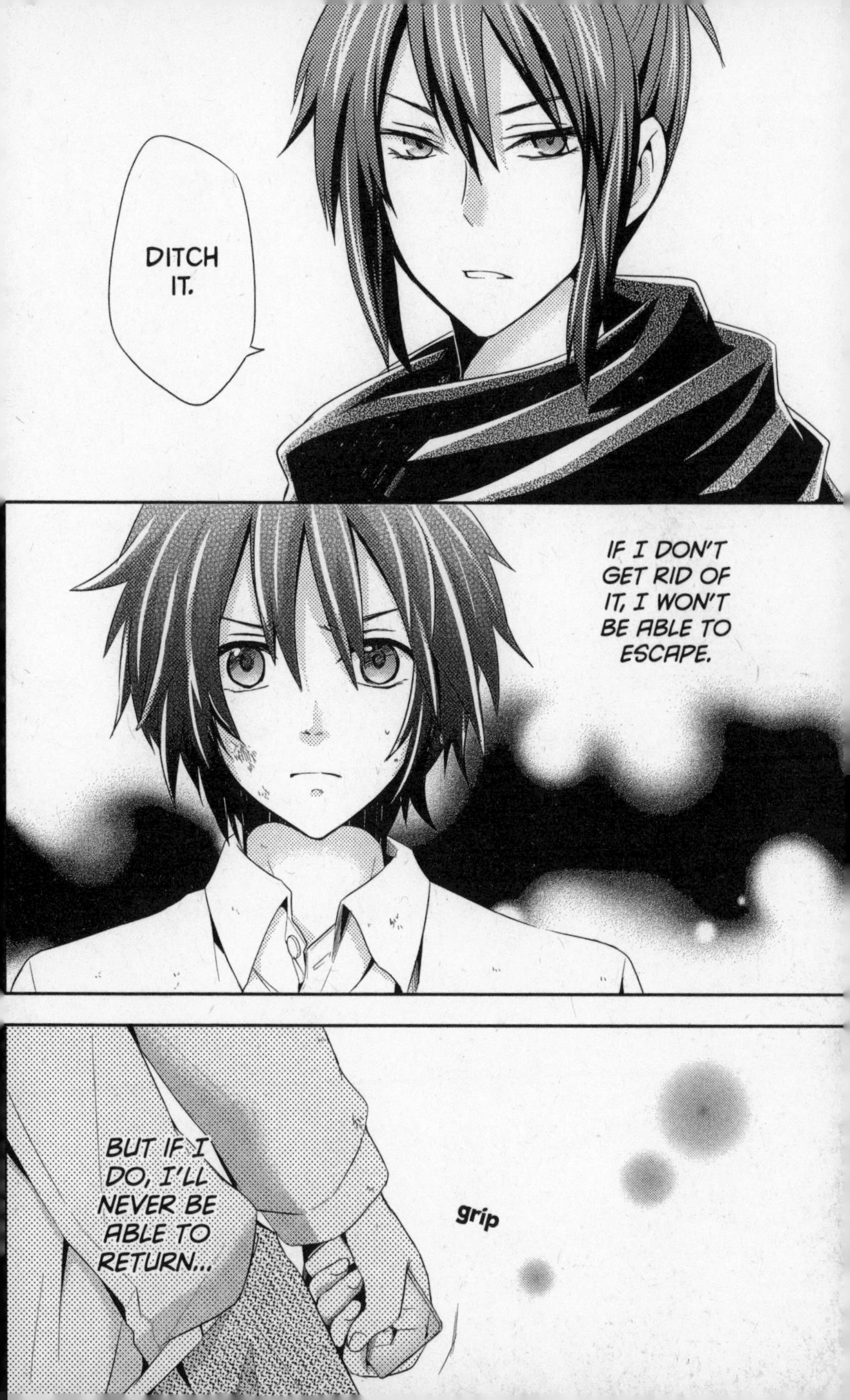
DITCH IT.
IF I DON'T GET RID OF IT, I WON'T BE ABLE TO ESCAPE.
BUT IF I DO, I'LL NEVER BE ABLE TO RETURN...
grip

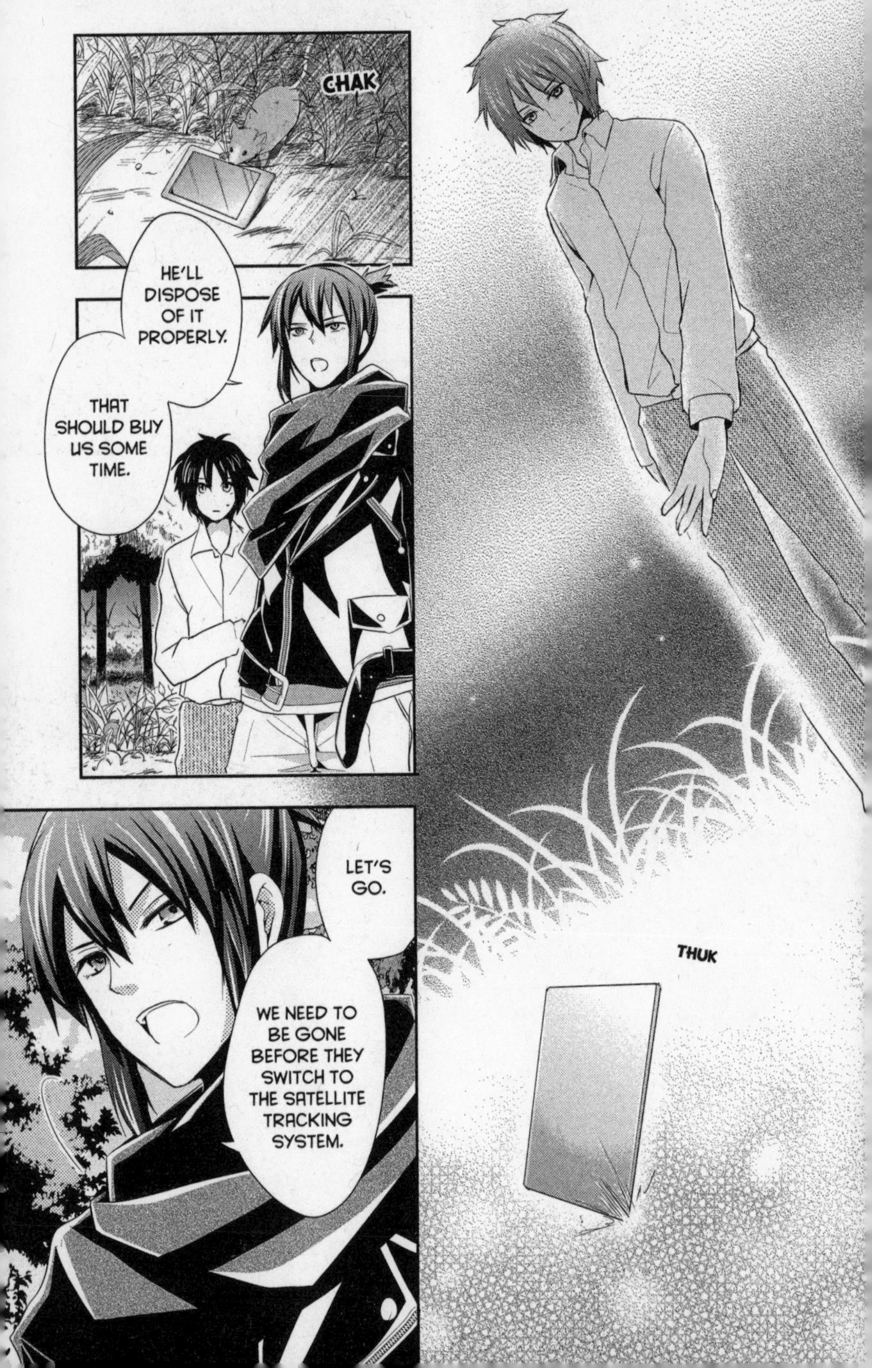
THUK
CHAK
HE'LL DISPOSE OF IT PROPERLY.
THAT SHOULD BUY US SOME TIME.
LET'S GO.
WE NEED TO BE GONE BEFORE THEY SWITCH TO THE SATELLITE TRACKING SYSTEM.

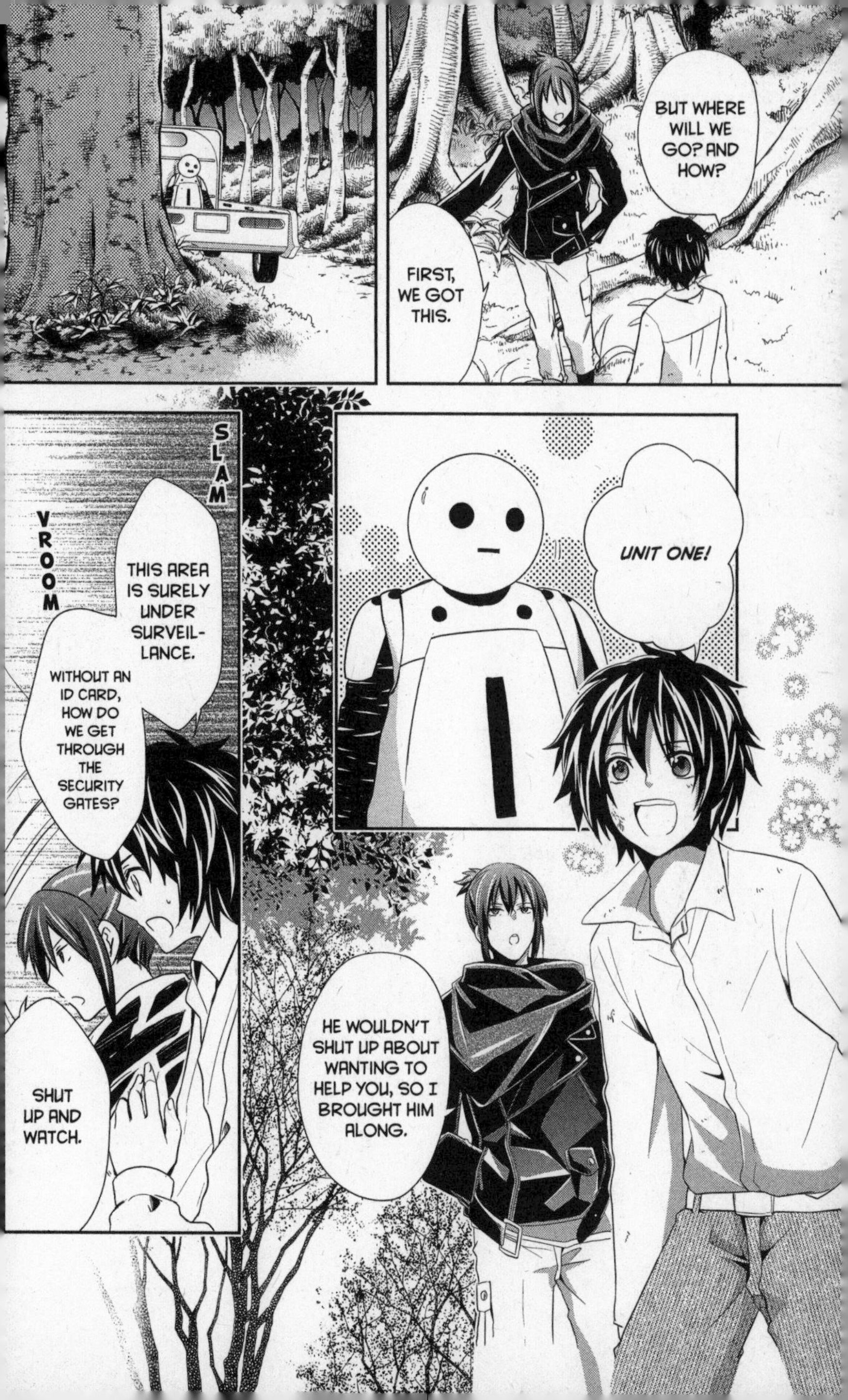
BUT WHERE WILL WE GO? AND HOW?
FIRST, WE GOT THIS.
UNIT ONE!
HE WOULDN'T SHUT UP ABOUT WANTING TO HELP YOU, SO I BROUGHT HIM ALONG.
SLAM
VROOM
THIS AREA IS SURELY UNDER SURVEIL-LANCE.
WITHOUT AN ID CARD, HOW DO WE GET THROUGH THE SECURITY GATES?
SHUT UP AND WATCH.

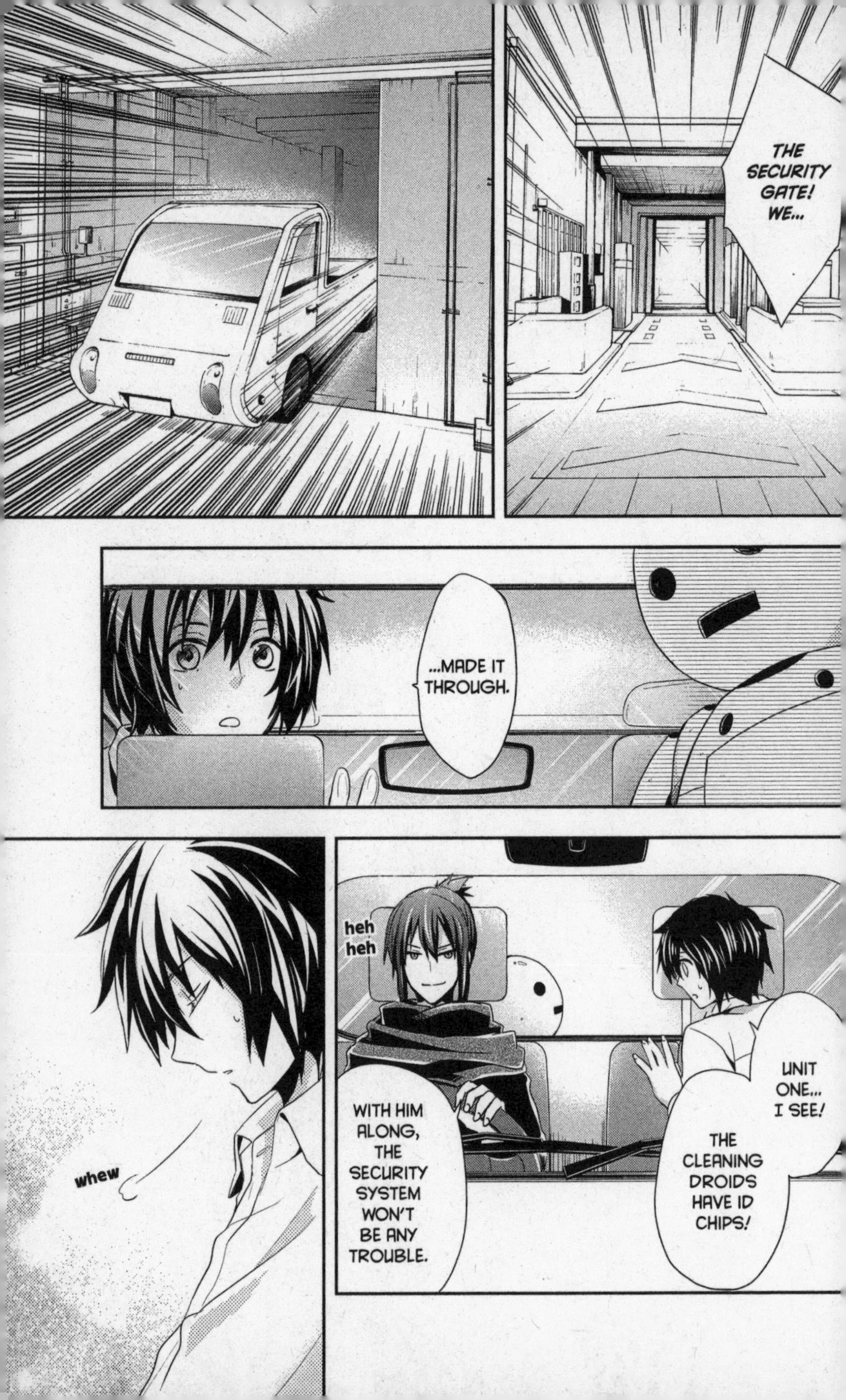
THE SECURITY GATE! WE...
...MADE IT THROUGH.
UNIT ONE... I SEE!
THE CLEANING DROIDS HAVE ID CHIPS!
heh heh
WITH HIM ALONG, THE SECURITY SYSTEM WON'T BE ANY TROUBLE.
whew

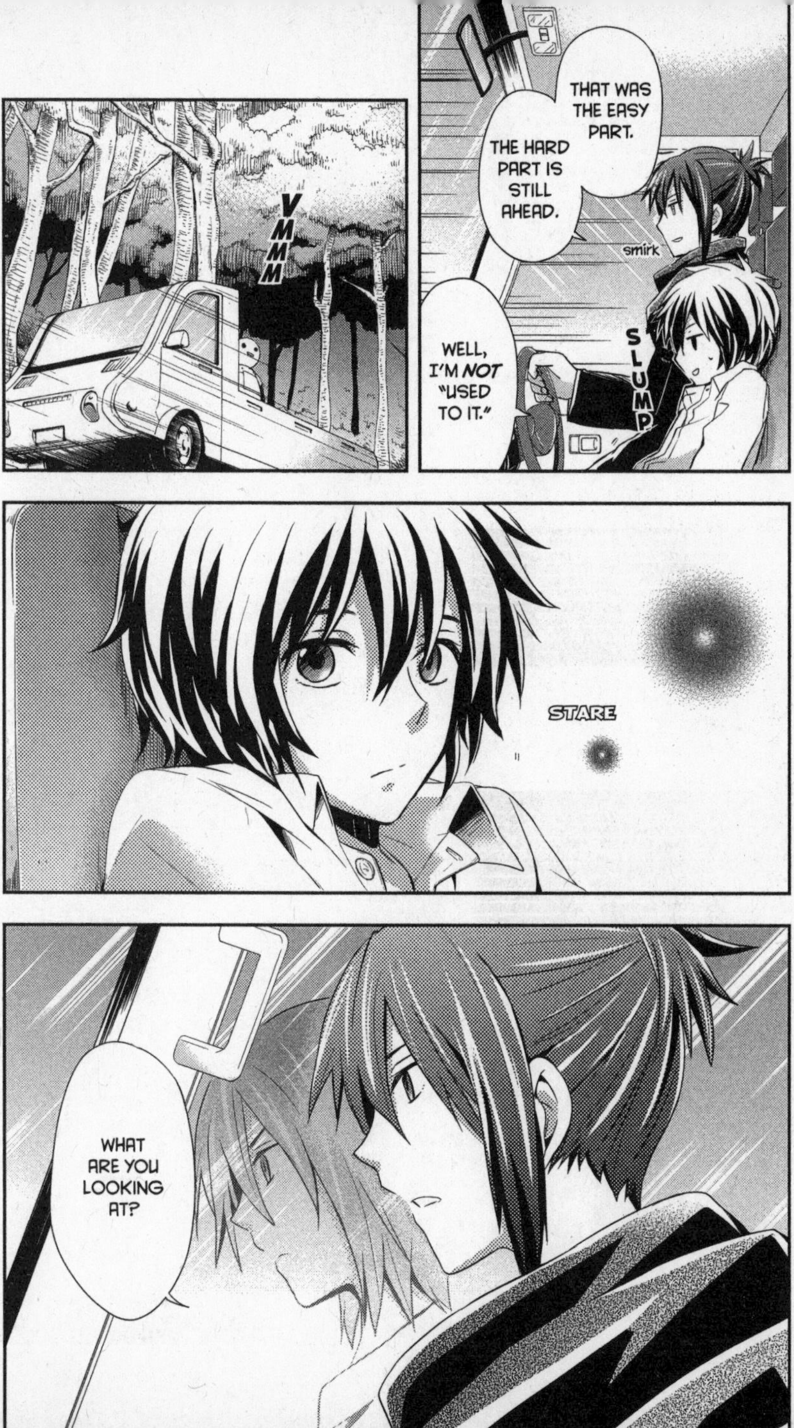
THAT WAS THE EASY PART.
THE HARD PART IS STILL AHEAD.
smirk
WELL, I'M *NOT* "USED TO IT."
SLUMP
VMMM
STARE
WHAT ARE YOU LOOKING AT?

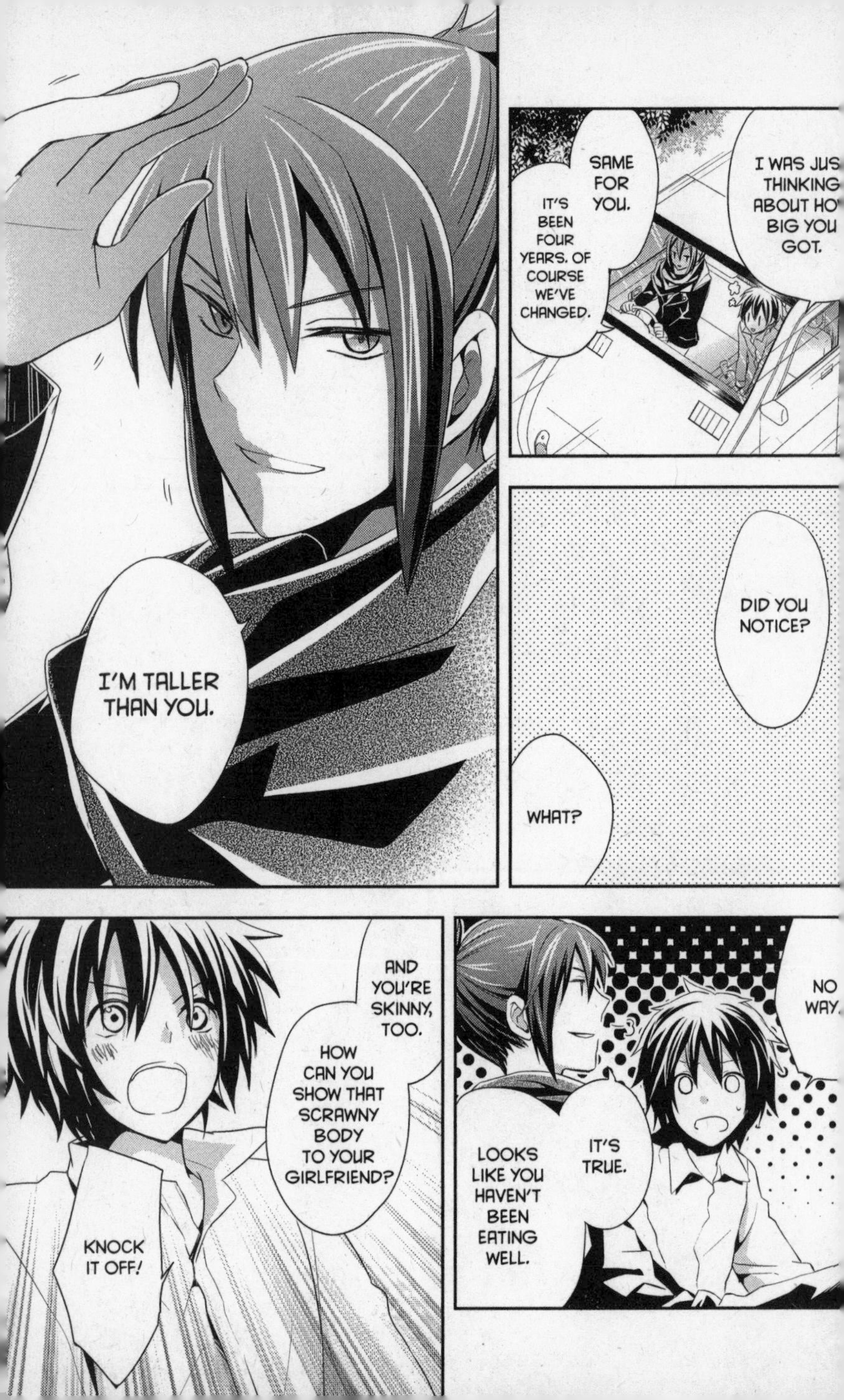

I WAS JUS THINKING ABOUT HO BIG YOU GOT.
SAME FOR YOU.
IT'S BEEN FOUR YEARS. OF COURSE WE'VE CHANGED.
DID YOU NOTICE?
WHAT?
I'M TALLER THAN YOU.
NO WAY.
IT'S TRUE.
LOOKS LIKE YOU HAVEN'T BEEN EATING WELL.
AND YOU'RE SKINNY, TOO.
HOW CAN YOU SHOW THAT SCRAWNY BODY TO YOUR GIRLFRIEND?
KNOCK IT OFF!

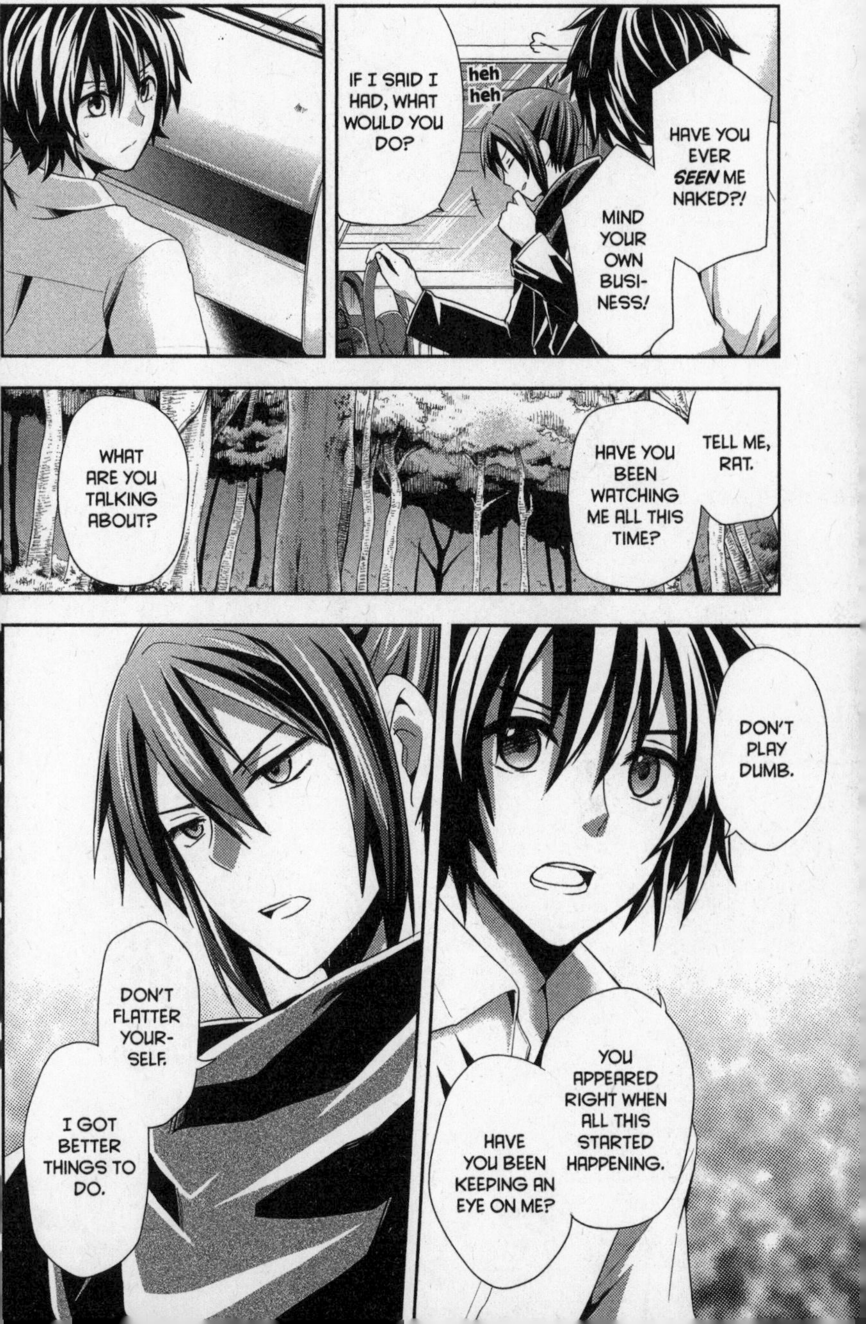
HAVE YOU EVER ***SEEN*** ME NAKED?!
MIND YOUR OWN BUSI-NESS!
heh heh
IF I SAID I HAD, WHAT WOULD YOU DO?
TELL ME, RAT.
HAVE YOU BEEN WATCHING ME ALL THIS TIME?
WHAT ARE YOU TALKING ABOUT?
DON'T PLAY DUMB.
YOU APPEARED RIGHT WHEN ALL THIS STARTED HAPPENING.
HAVE YOU BEEN KEEPING AN EYE ON ME?
DON'T FLATTER YOUR-SELF.
I GOT BETTER THINGS TO DO.

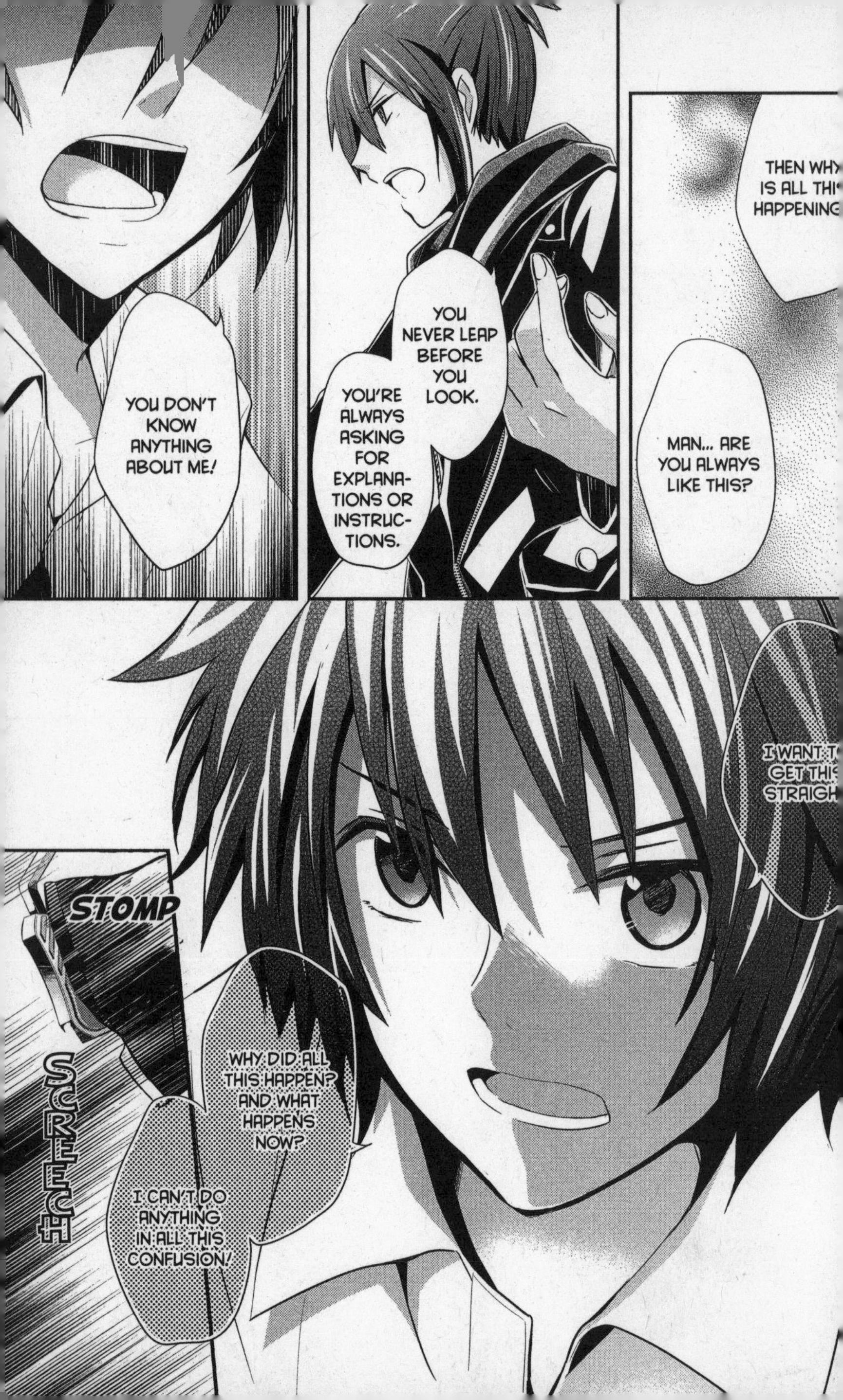
THEN WHY IS ALL THI HAPPENING
MAN... ARE YOU ALWAYS LIKE THIS?
YOU NEVER LEAP BEFORE YOU LOOK.
YOU'RE ALWAYS ASKING FOR EXPLANATIONS OR INSTRUCTIONS.
YOU DON'T KNOW ANYTHING ABOUT ME!
I WANT T GET THIS STRAIGH
WHY DID ALL THIS HAPPEN? AND WHAT HAPPENS NOW?
I CAN'T DO ANYTHING IN ALL THIS CONFUSION!
STOMP
SCREECH

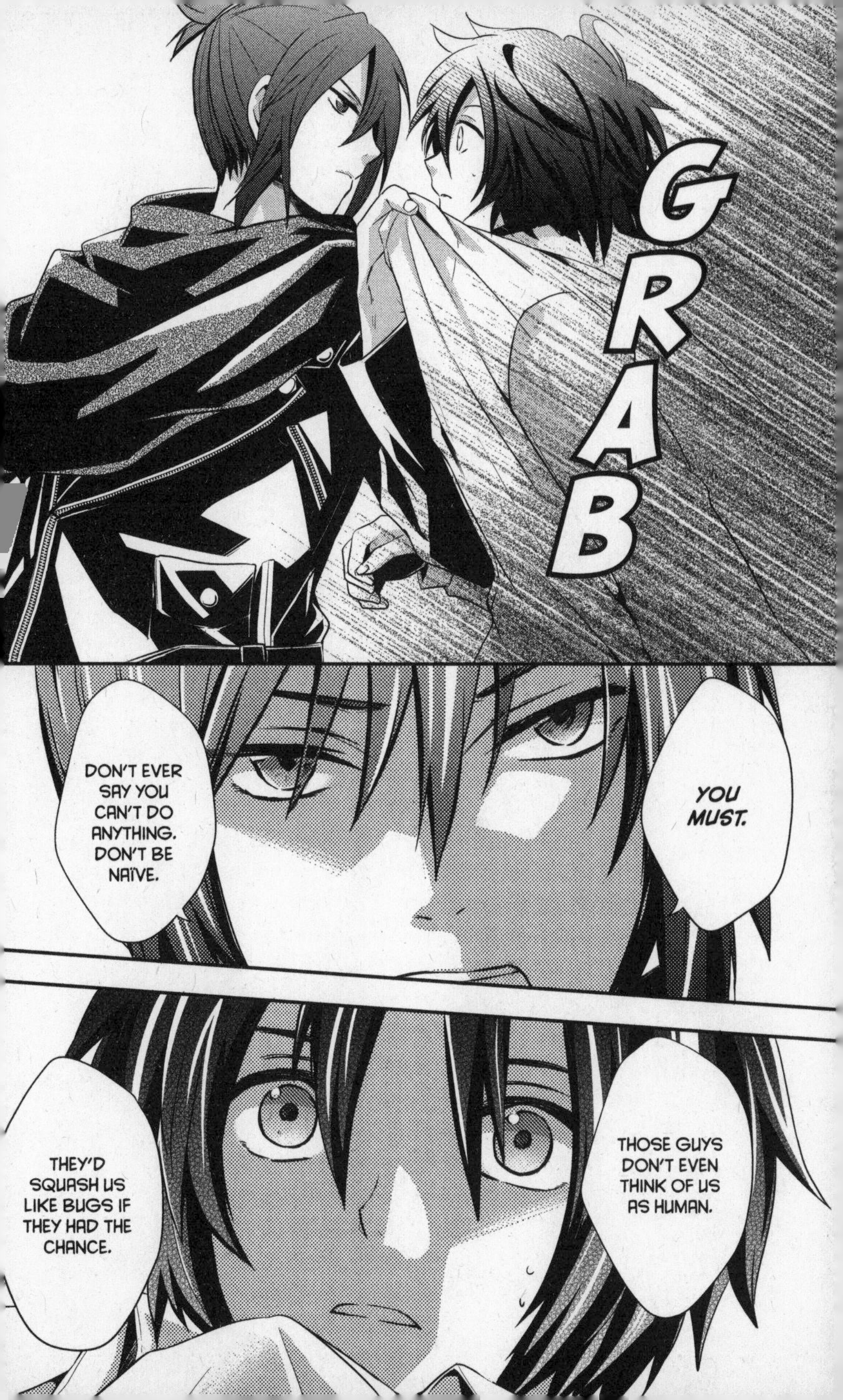
GRAB
YOU MUST.
DON'T EVER SAY YOU CAN'T DO ANYTHING. DON'T BE NAÏVE.
THOSE GUYS DON'T EVEN THINK OF US AS HUMAN.
THEY'D SQUASH US LIKE BUGS IF THEY HAD THE CHANCE.

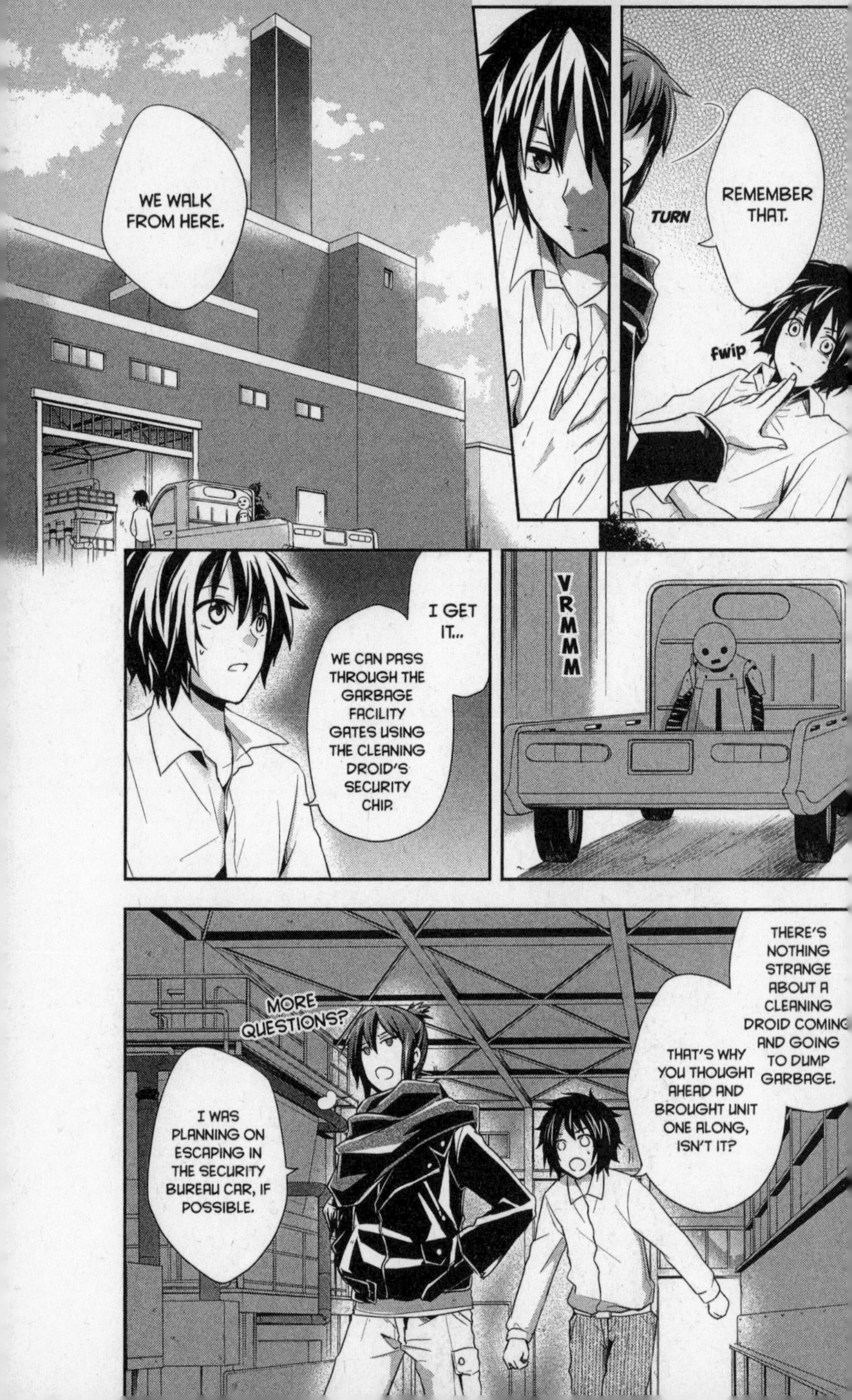
TURN
REMEMBER THAT.
fwip
WE WALK FROM HERE.
VRMMM
I GET IT...
WE CAN PASS THROUGH THE GARBAGE FACILITY GATES USING THE CLEANING DROID'S SECURITY CHIP.
THERE'S NOTHING STRANGE ABOUT A CLEANING DROID COMING AND GOING TO DUMP GARBAGE.
THAT'S WHY YOU THOUGHT AHEAD AND BROUGHT UNIT ONE ALONG, ISN'T IT?
MORE QUESTIONS?
I WAS PLANNING ON ESCAPING IN THE SECURITY BUREAU CAR, IF POSSIBLE.

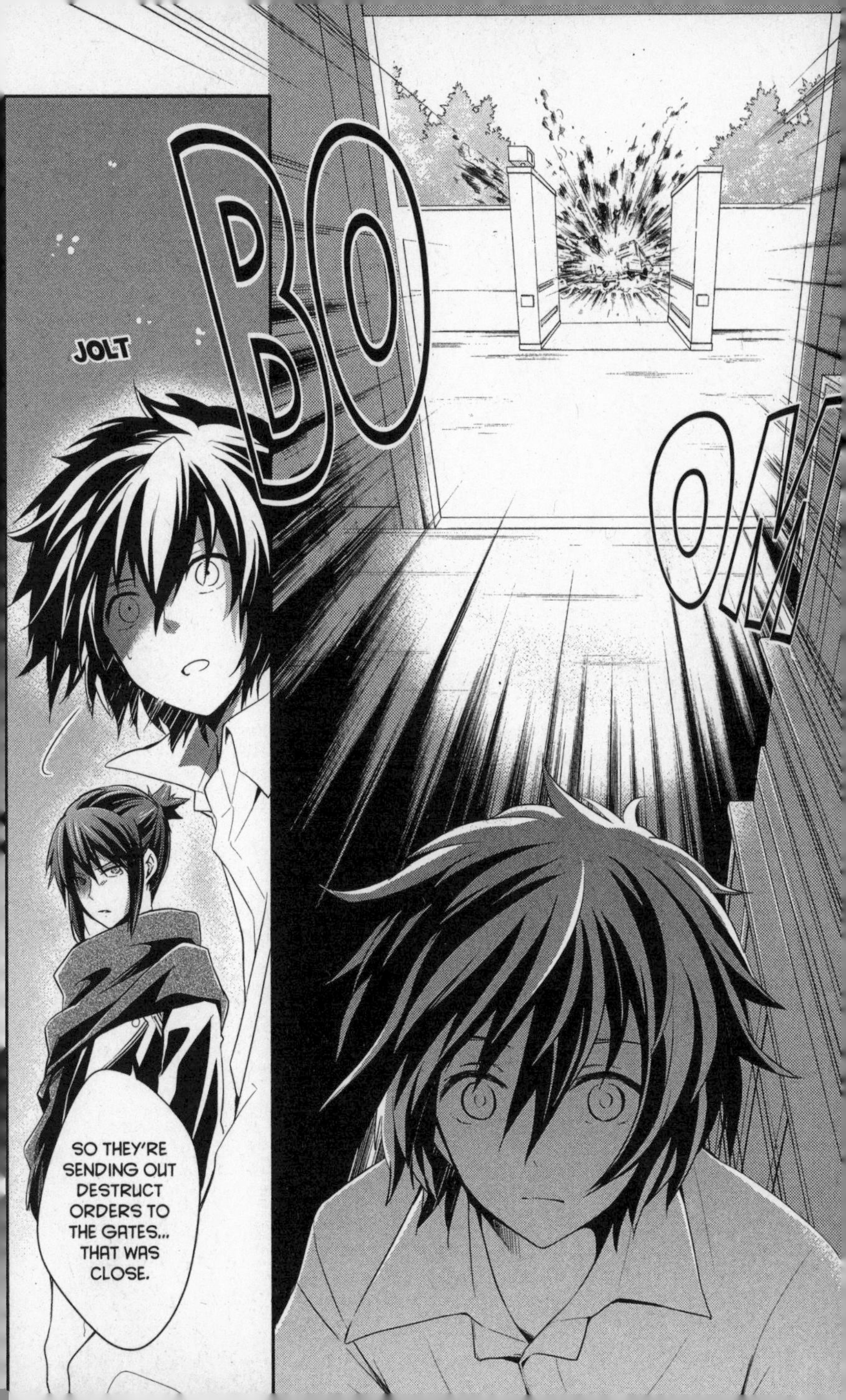
BOOM
JOLT
SO THEY'RE SENDING OUT DESTRUCT ORDERS TO THE GATES... THAT WAS CLOSE.

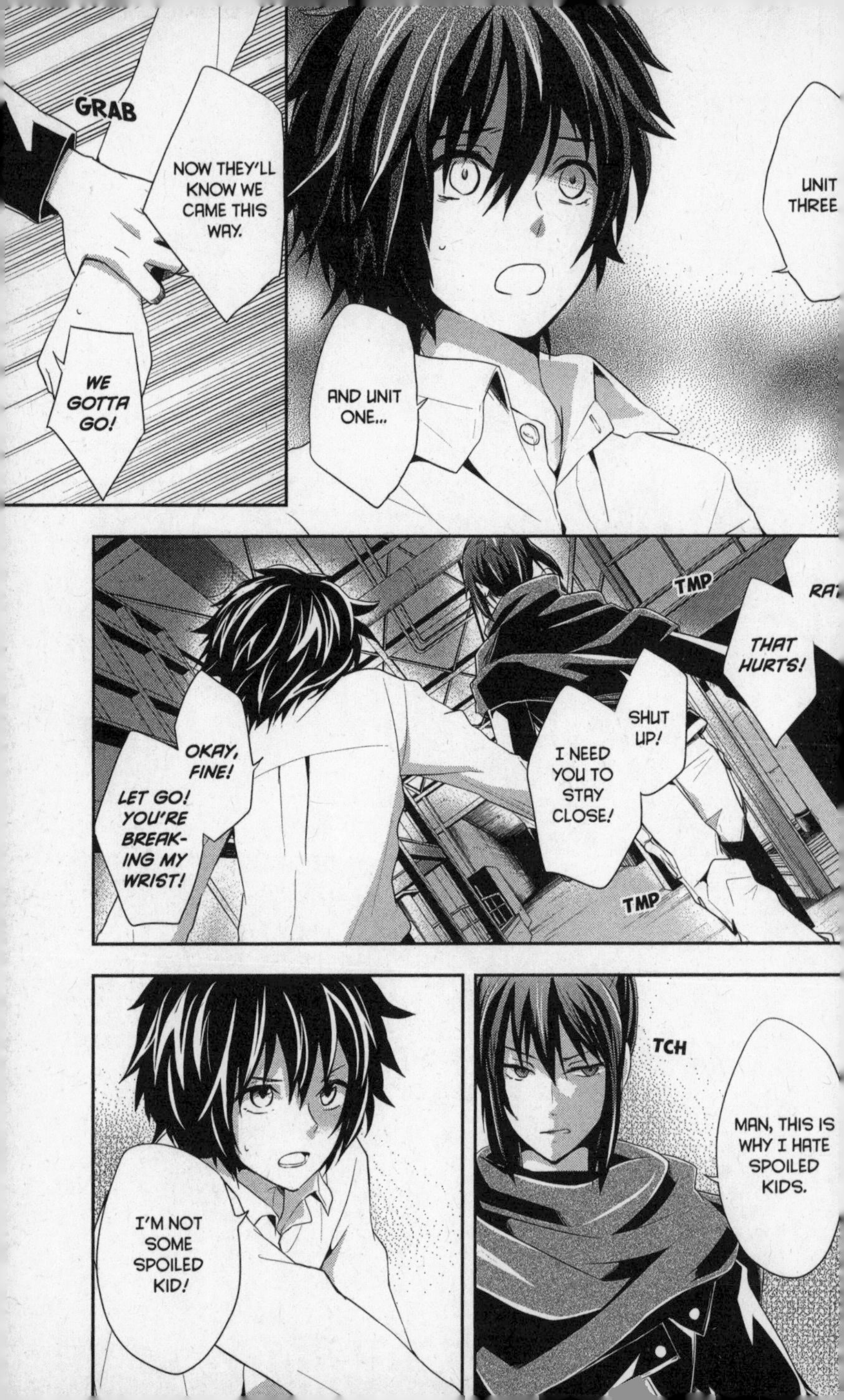
UNIT THREE
AND UNIT ONE...
GRAB
NOW THEY'LL KNOW WE CAME THIS WAY.
WE GOTTA GO!
TMP
THAT HURTS!
SHUT UP!
I NEED YOU TO STAY CLOSE!
OKAY, FINE!
LET GO! YOU'RE BREAK-ING MY WRIST!
TMP
TCH
MAN, THIS IS WHY I HATE SPOILED KIDS.
I'M NOT SOME SPOILED KID!

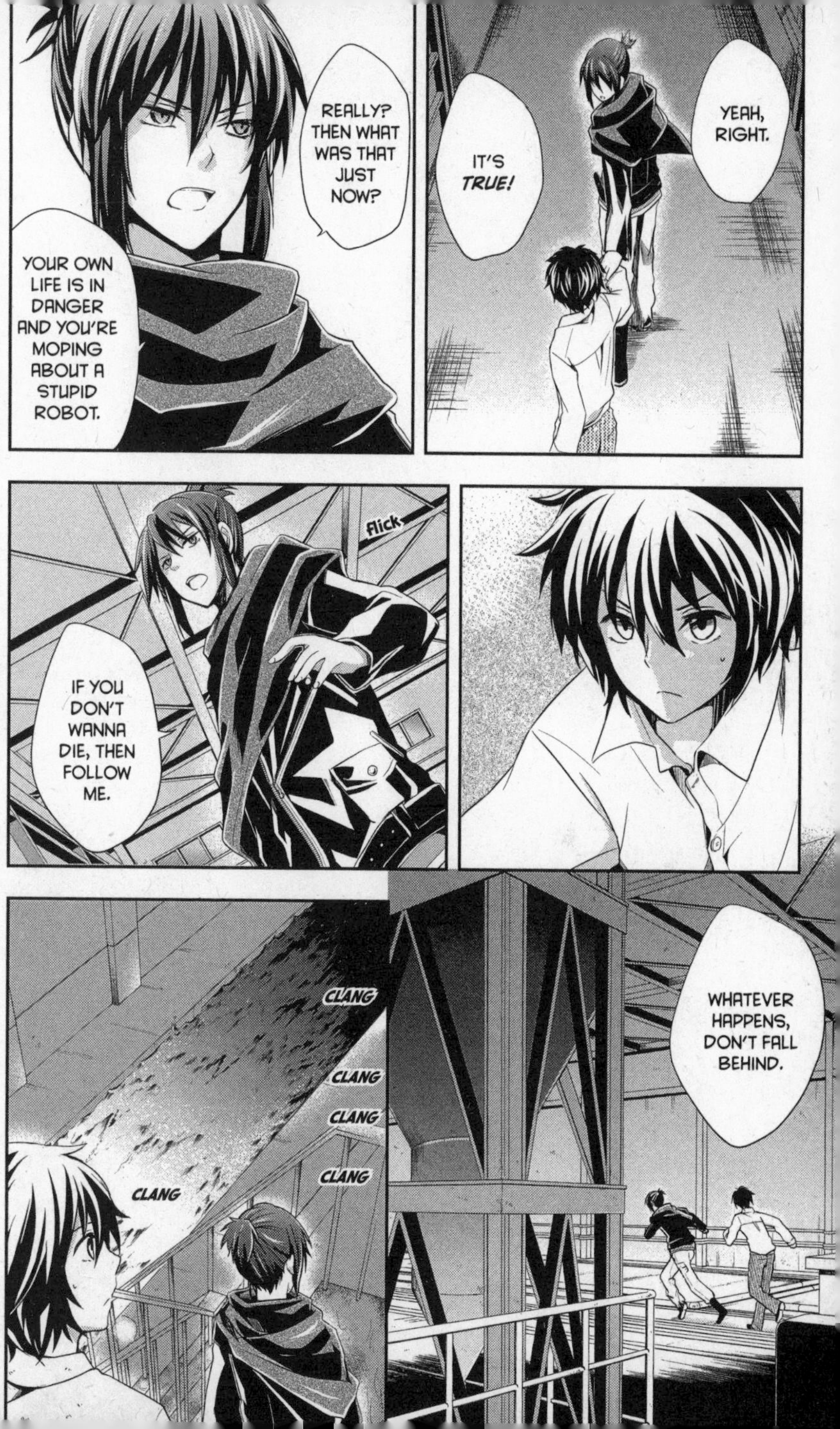
YEAH, RIGHT.
IT'S *TRUE!*
REALLY? THEN WHAT WAS THAT JUST NOW?
YOUR OWN LIFE IS IN DANGER AND YOU'RE MOPING ABOUT A STUPID ROBOT.
flick
IF YOU DON'T WANNA DIE, THEN FOLLOW ME.
WHATEVER HAPPENS, DON'T FALL BEHIND.
CLANG
CLANG
CLANG
CLANG
CLANG

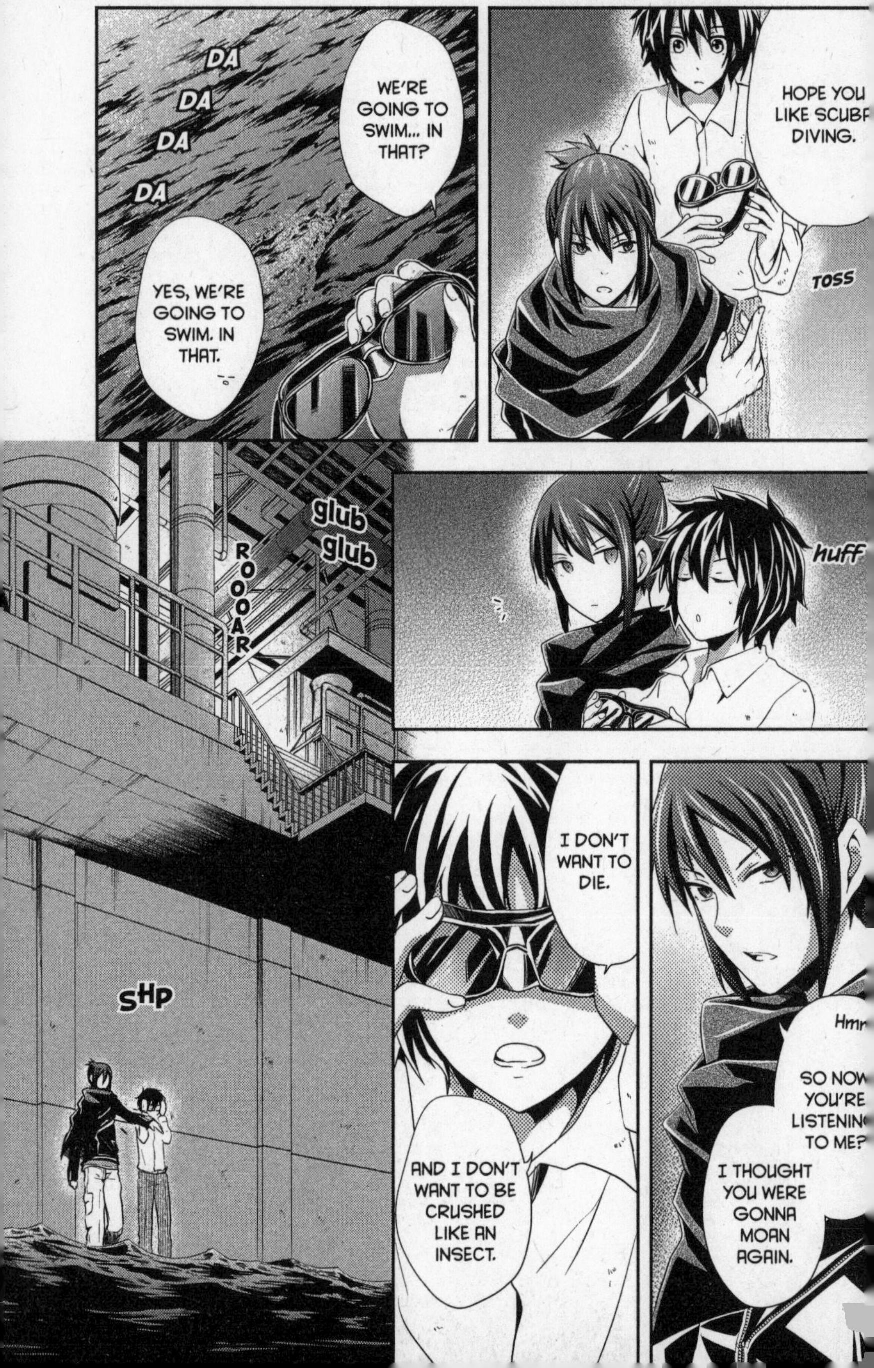
HOPE YOU LIKE SCUB DIVING.
TOSS
WE'RE GOING TO SWIM... IN THAT?
DA
DA
DA
DA
YES, WE'RE GOING TO SWIM. IN THAT.
huff
Hm
SO NO YOU'RE LISTENIN TO ME?
I THOUGHT YOU WERE GONNA MOAN AGAIN.
I DON'T WANT TO DIE.
AND I DON'T WANT TO BE CRUSHED LIKE AN INSECT.
glub
glub
ROOOAR
SHP

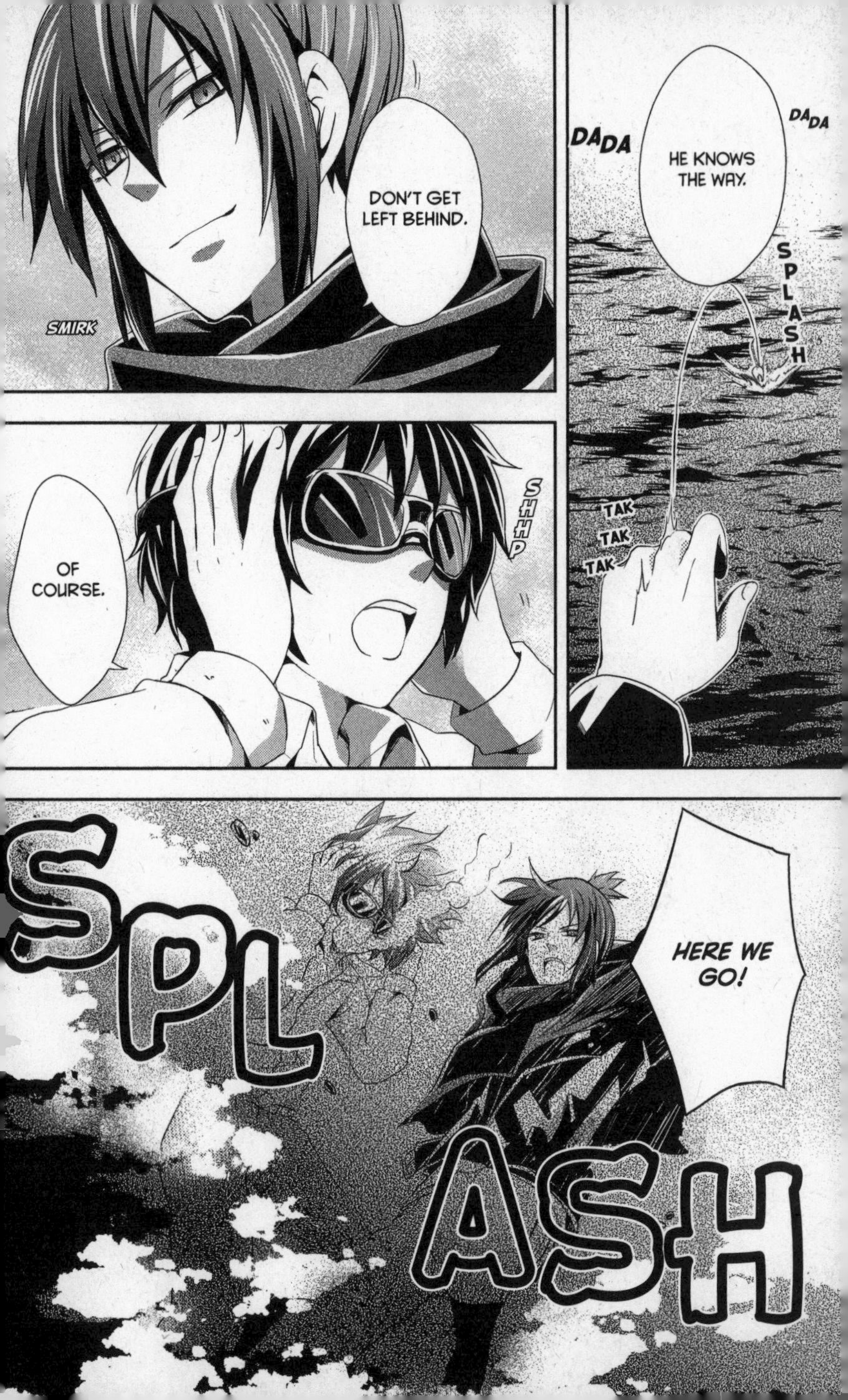
DADA
HE KNOWS THE WAY.
DADA
SPLASH
TAK
TAK
TAK
DON'T GET LEFT BEHIND.
SMIRK
SHHP
OF COURSE.
HERE WE GO!
SPLASH

CHAPTER 3: Of Endless Fear

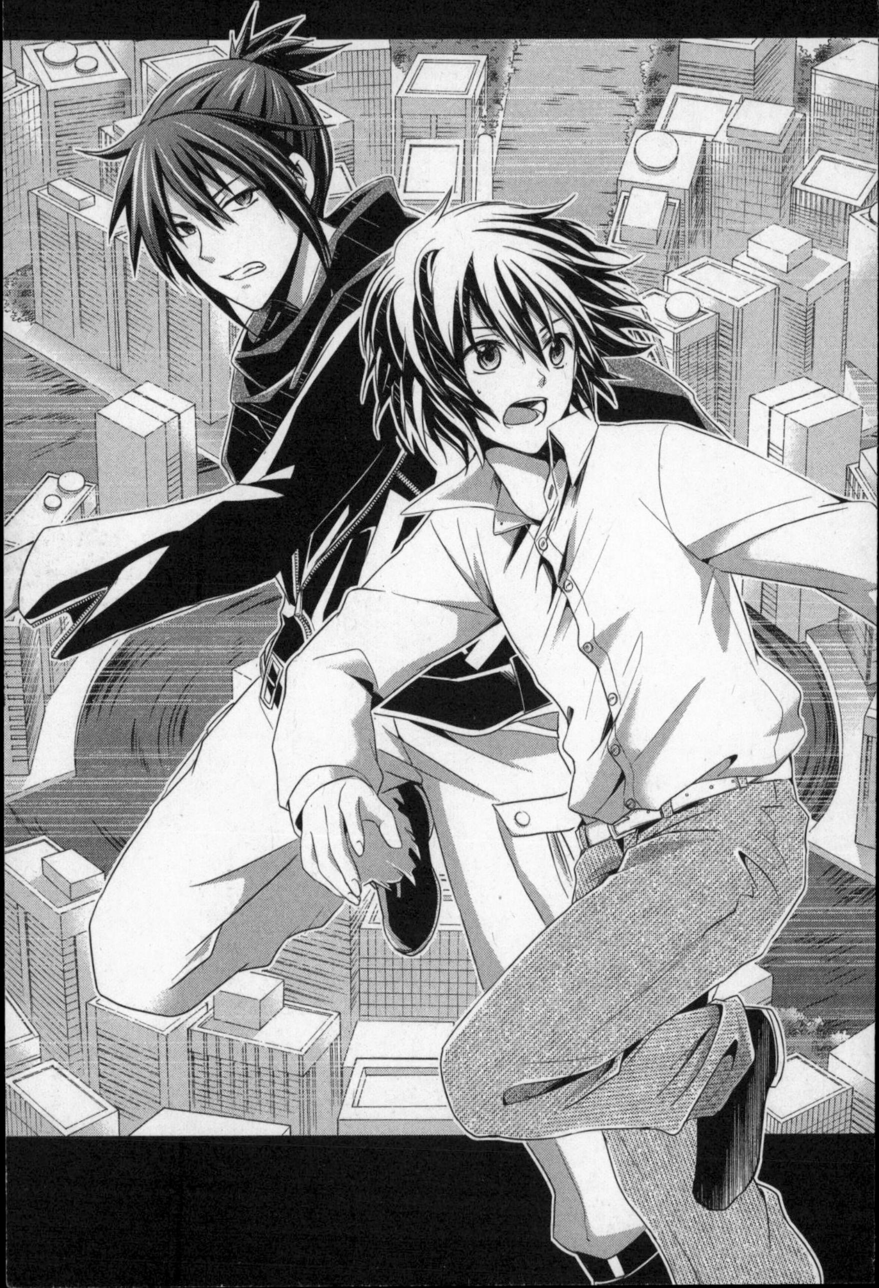

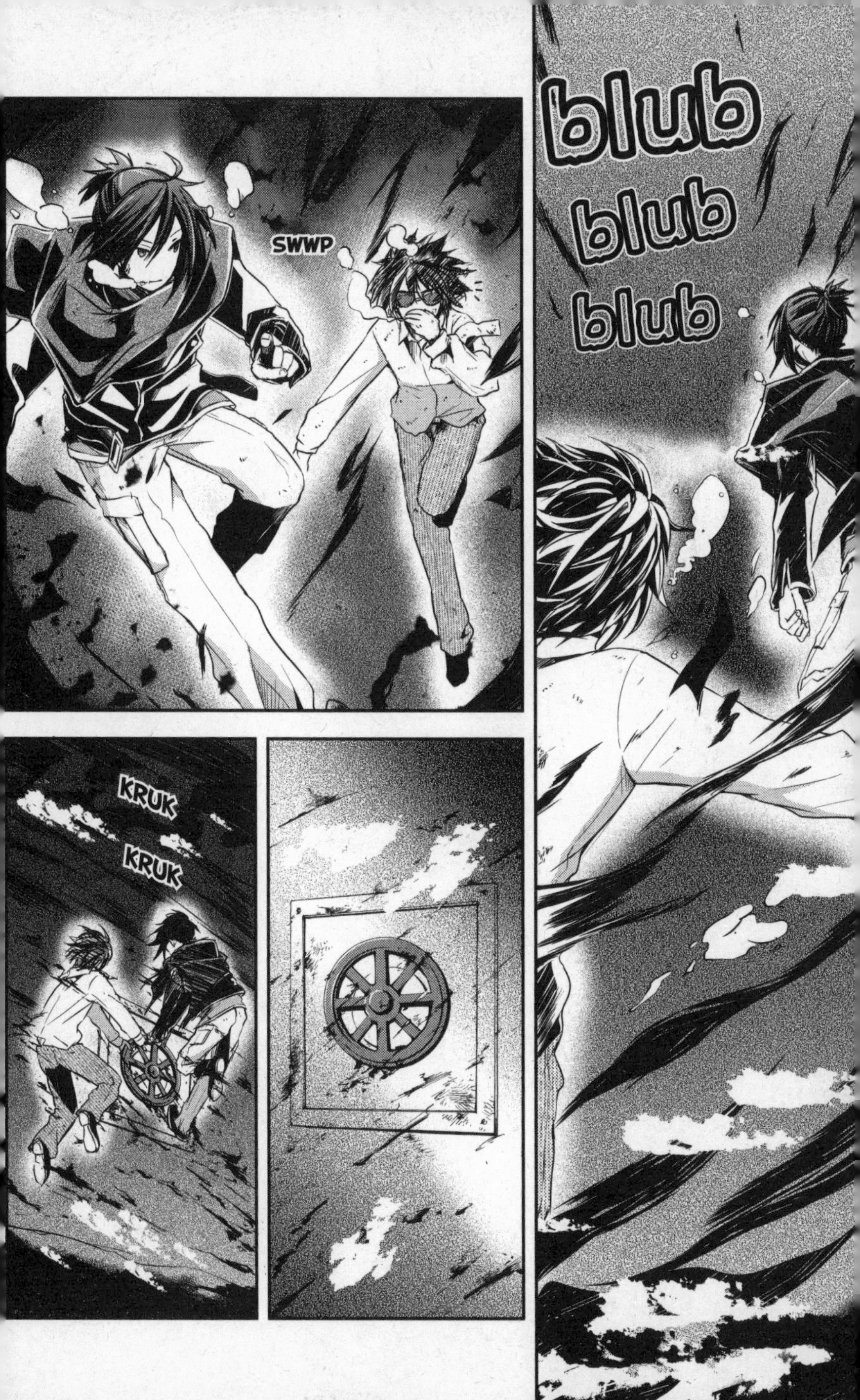
blub
blub
blub
SWWP
KRUK
KRUK

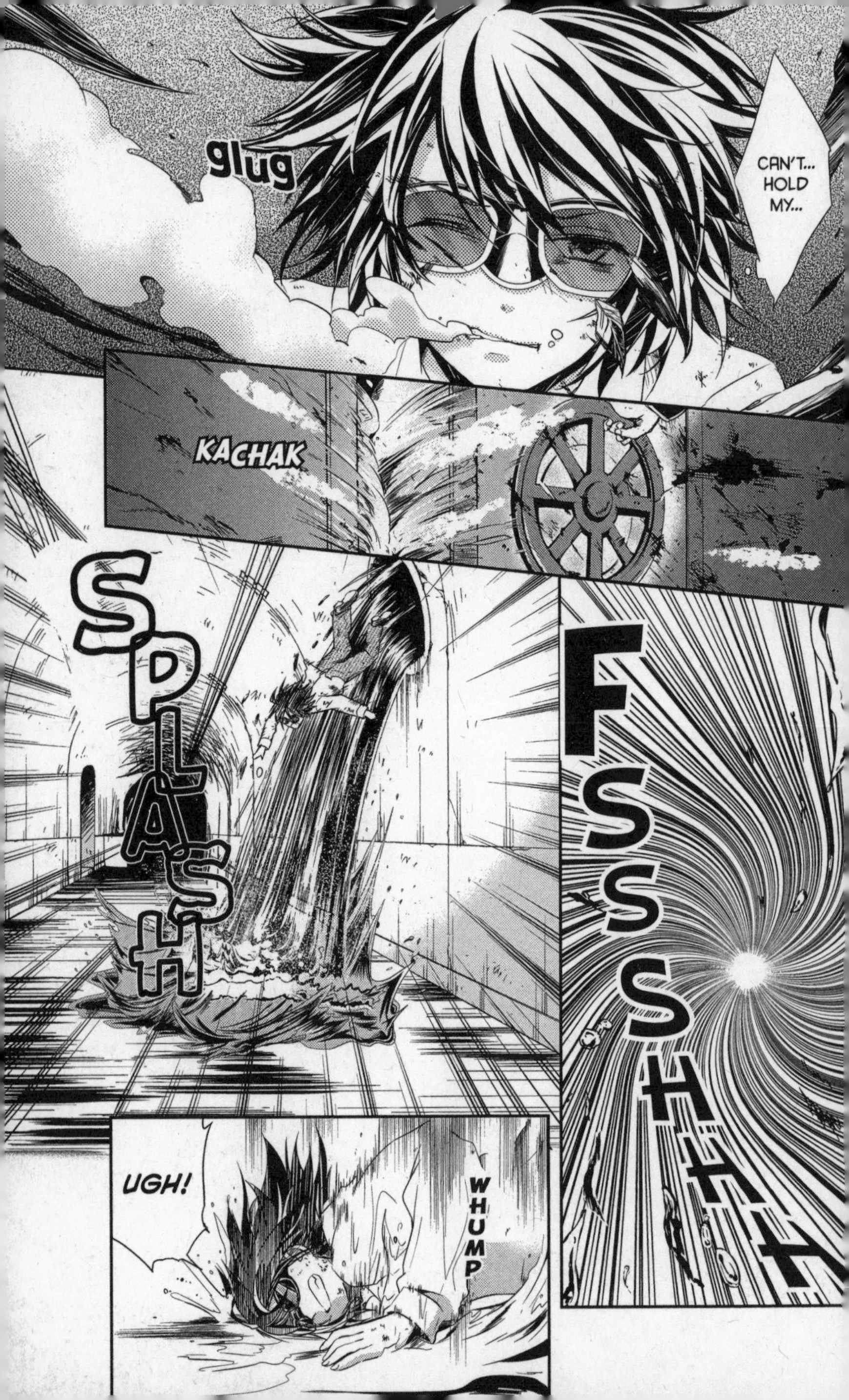
CAN'T... HOLD MY...
glug
KACHAK
FSSSHHHH
SPLASH
UGH!
WHUMP

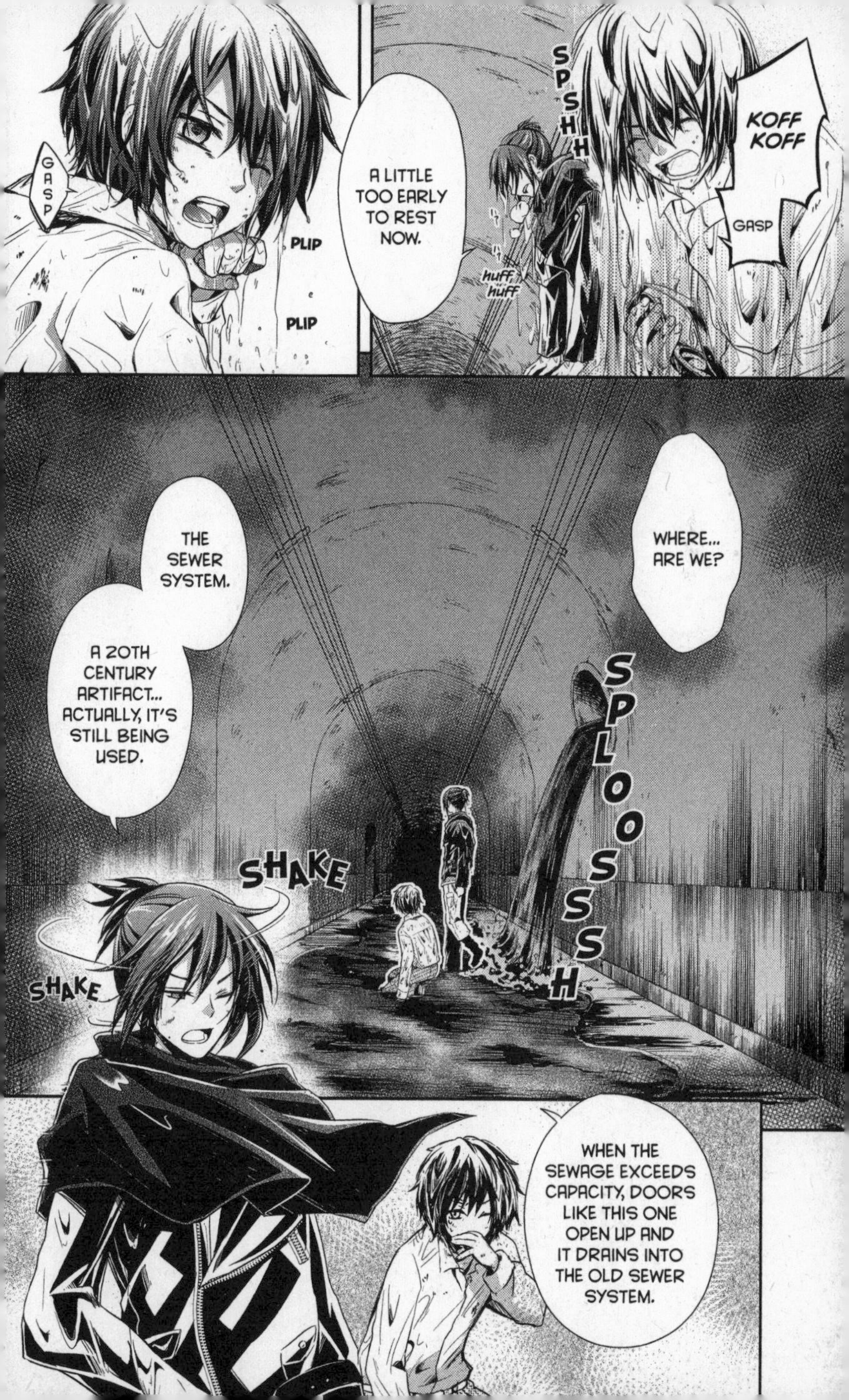
KOFF KOFF
GASP
SPSHH
huff huff
A LITTLE TOO EARLY TO REST NOW.
GASP
PLIP
PLIP
WHERE... ARE WE?
SPLOOSSSH
THE SEWER SYSTEM.
A 20TH CENTURY ARTIFACT... ACTUALLY, IT'S STILL BEING USED.
SHAKE
SHAKE
WHEN THE SEWAGE EXCEEDS CAPACITY, DOORS LIKE THIS ONE OPEN UP AND IT DRAINS INTO THE OLD SEWER SYSTEM.

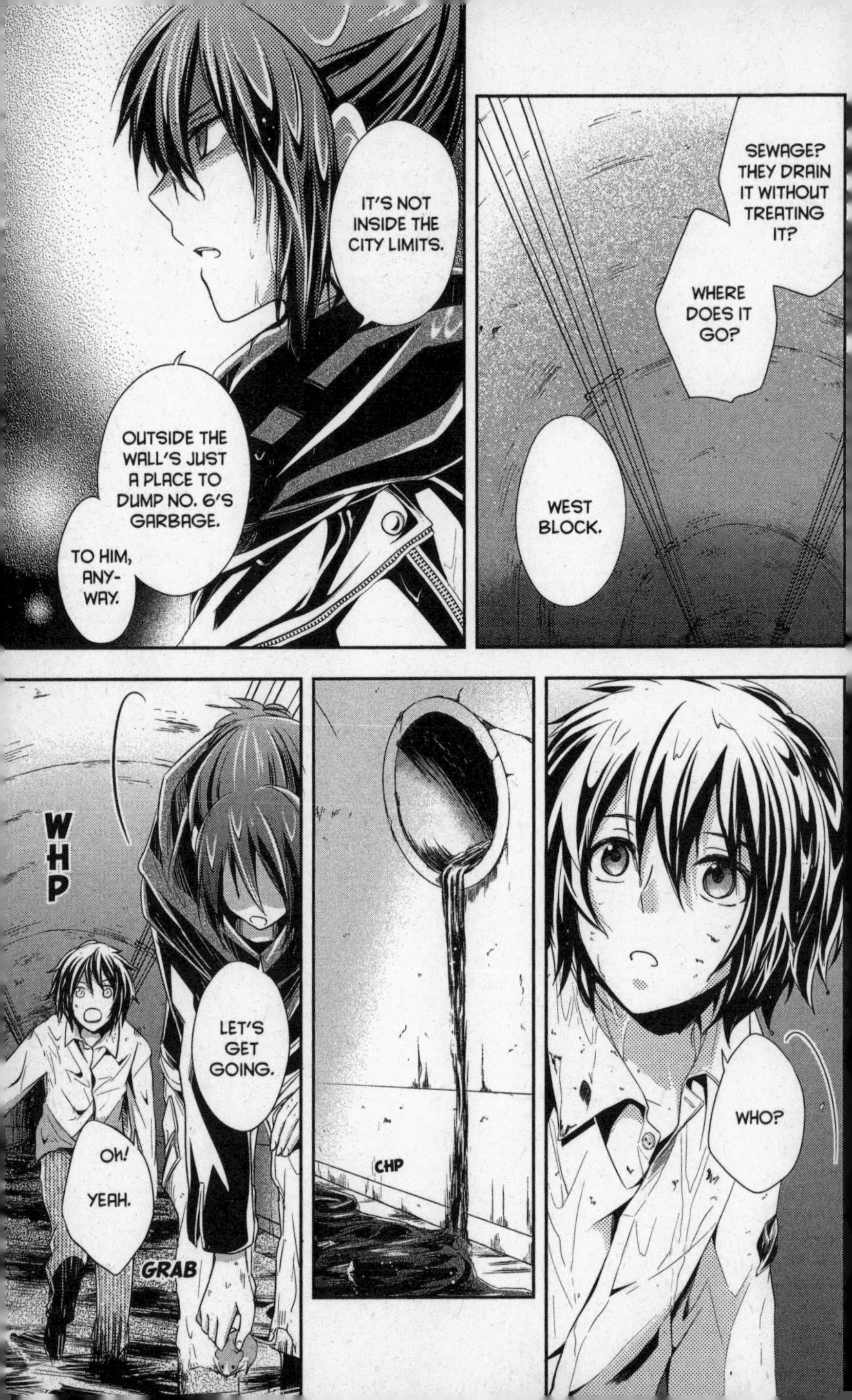
SEWAGE? THEY DRAIN IT WITHOUT TREATING IT?
WHERE DOES IT GO?
WEST BLOCK.
IT'S NOT INSIDE THE CITY LIMITS.
OUTSIDE THE WALL'S JUST A PLACE TO DUMP NO. 6'S GARBAGE.
TO HIM, ANY-WAY.
WHO?
CHP
WHP
LET'S GET GOING.
OH!
YEAH.
GRAB

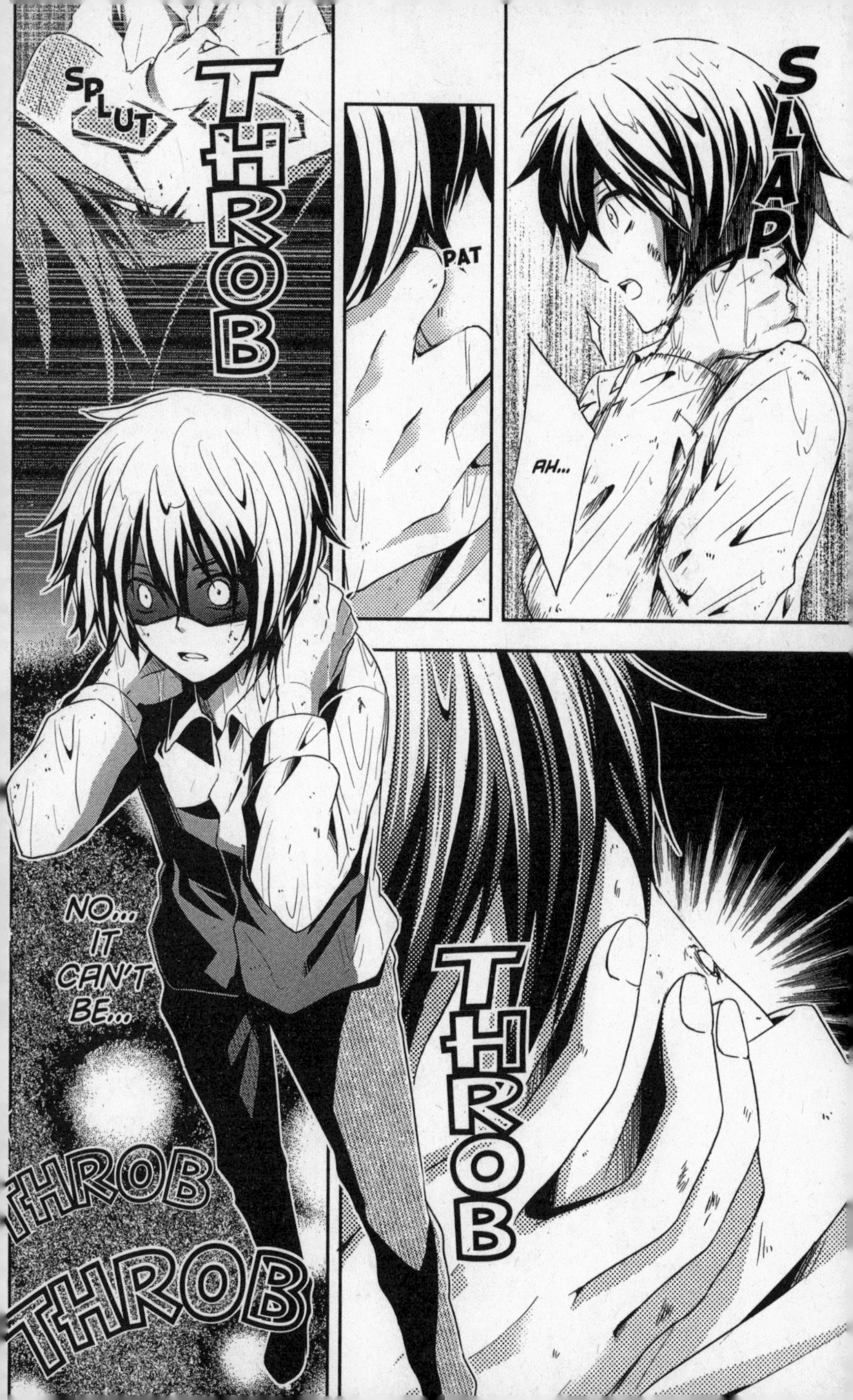
SLAP
AH...
PAT
THROB
SPLUT
THROB
NO... IT CAN'T BE...
THROB
THROB

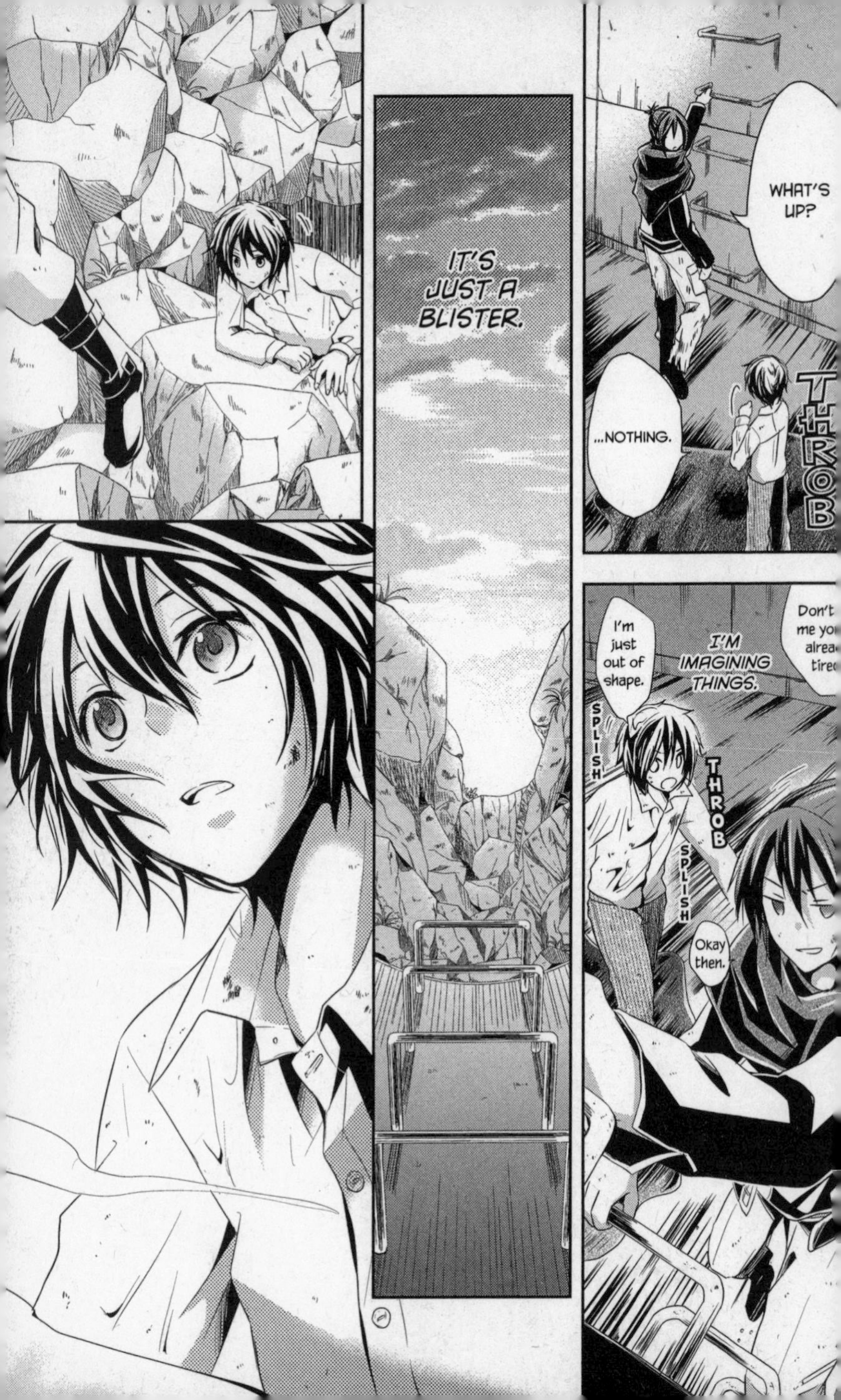
WHAT'S UP?
...NOTHING.
THROB
Don't me yo alrea tire
I'm just out of shape.
I'M IMAGINING THINGS.
SPLISH
THROB
SPLISH
Okay then.
IT'S JUST A BLISTER.

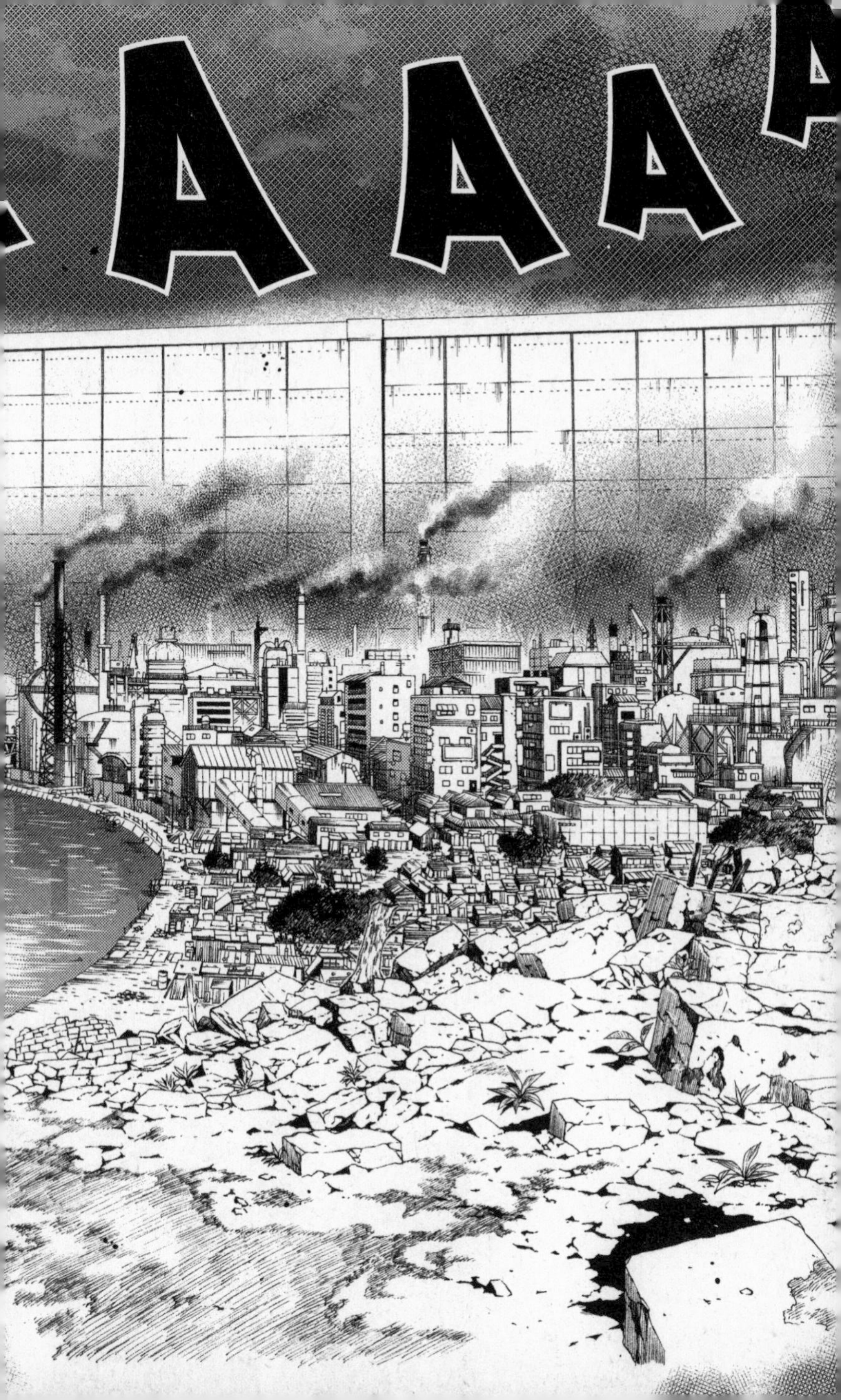
AAAA

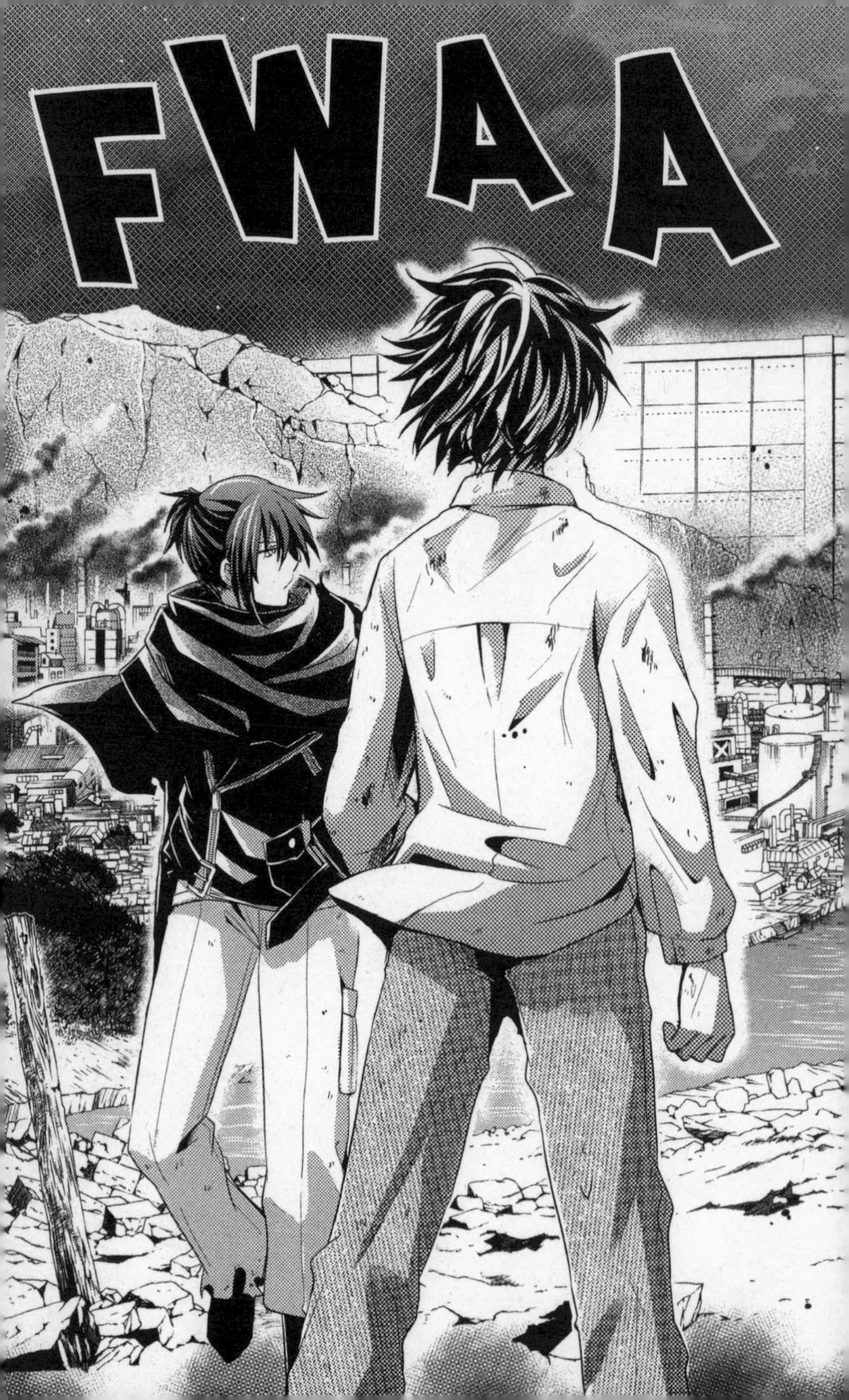
FWAA

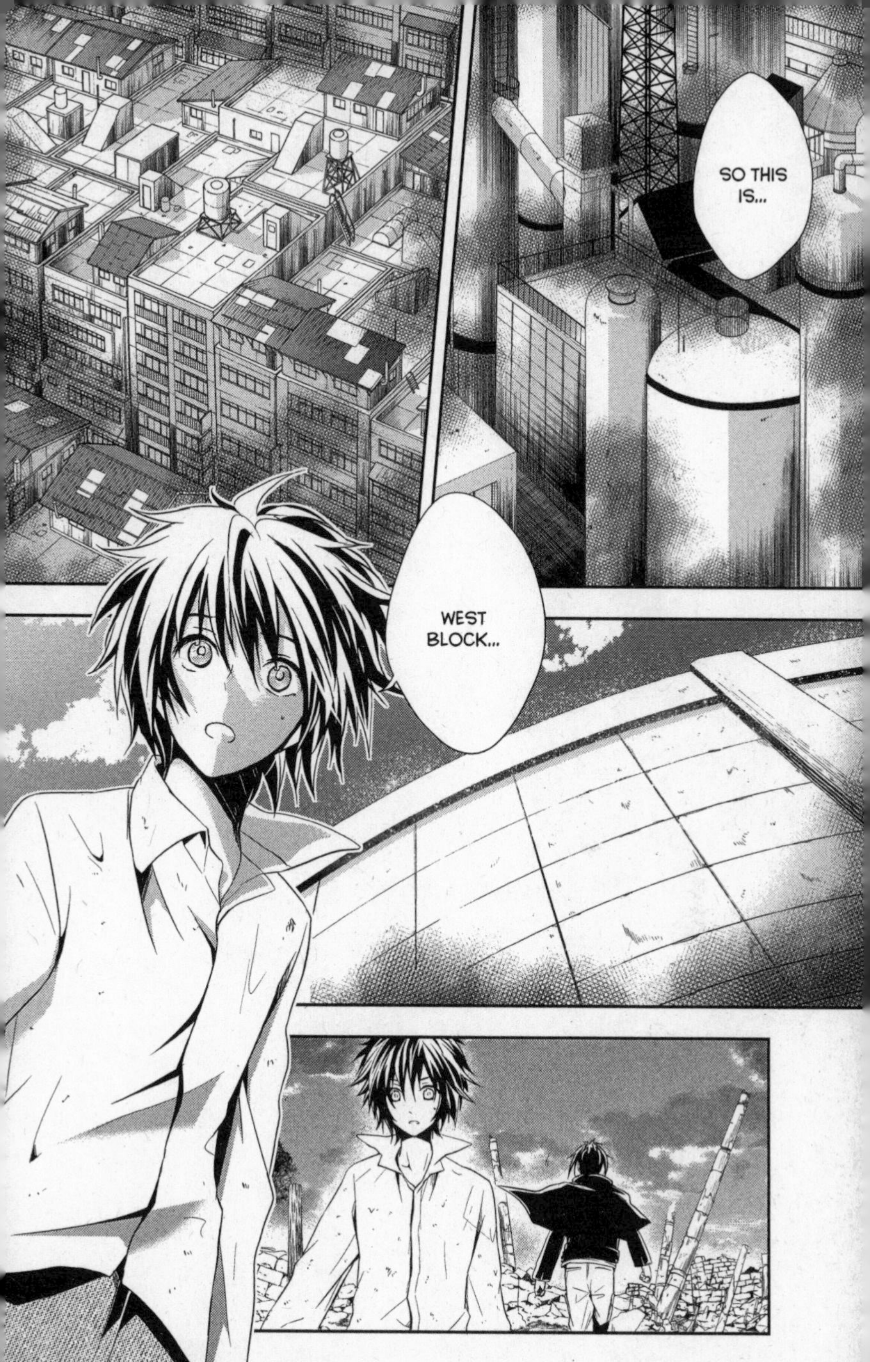
SO THIS IS...
WEST BLOCK...

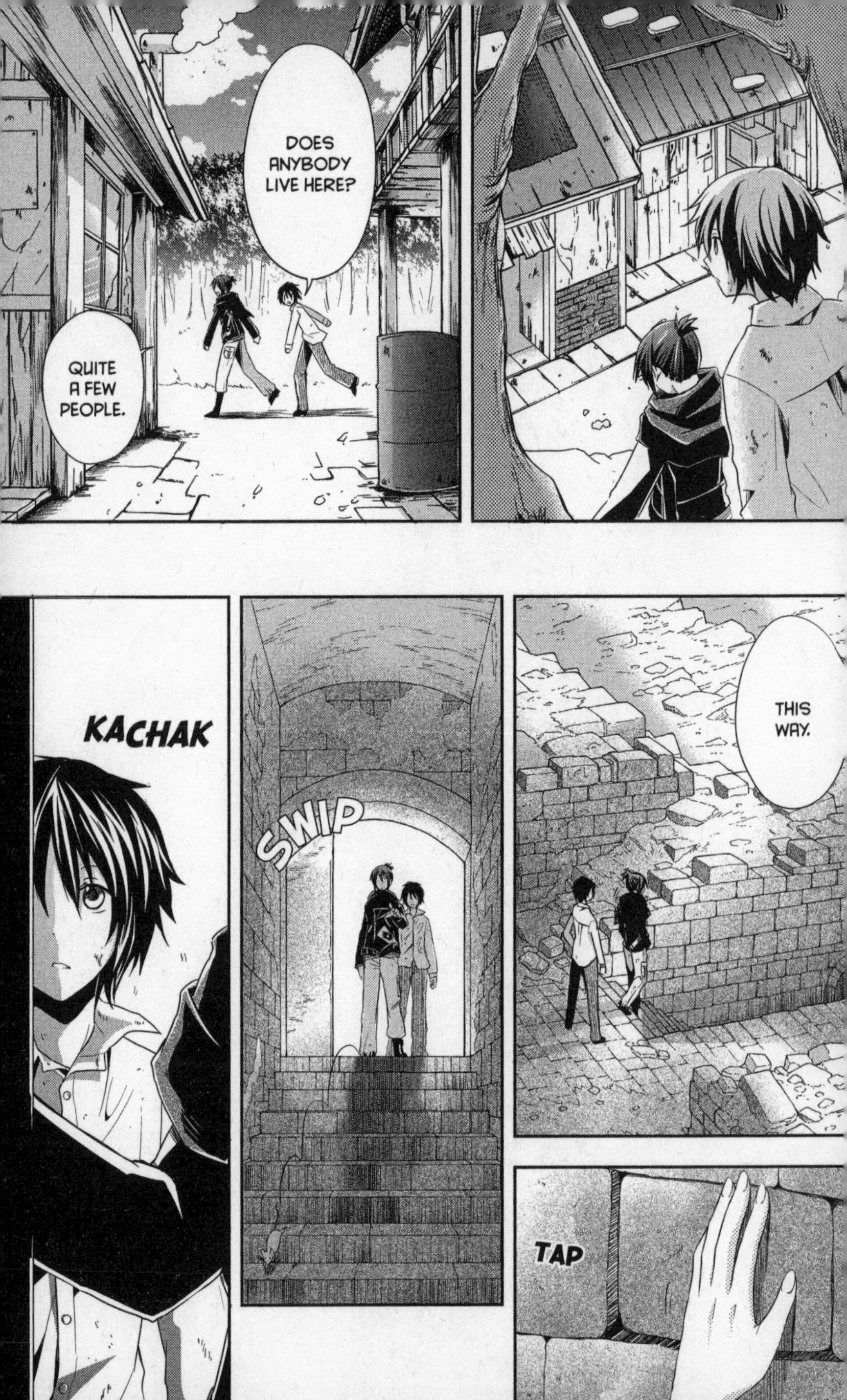
DOES ANYBODY LIVE HERE?
QUITE A FEW PEOPLE.
THIS WAY.
TAP
SWIP
KACHAK

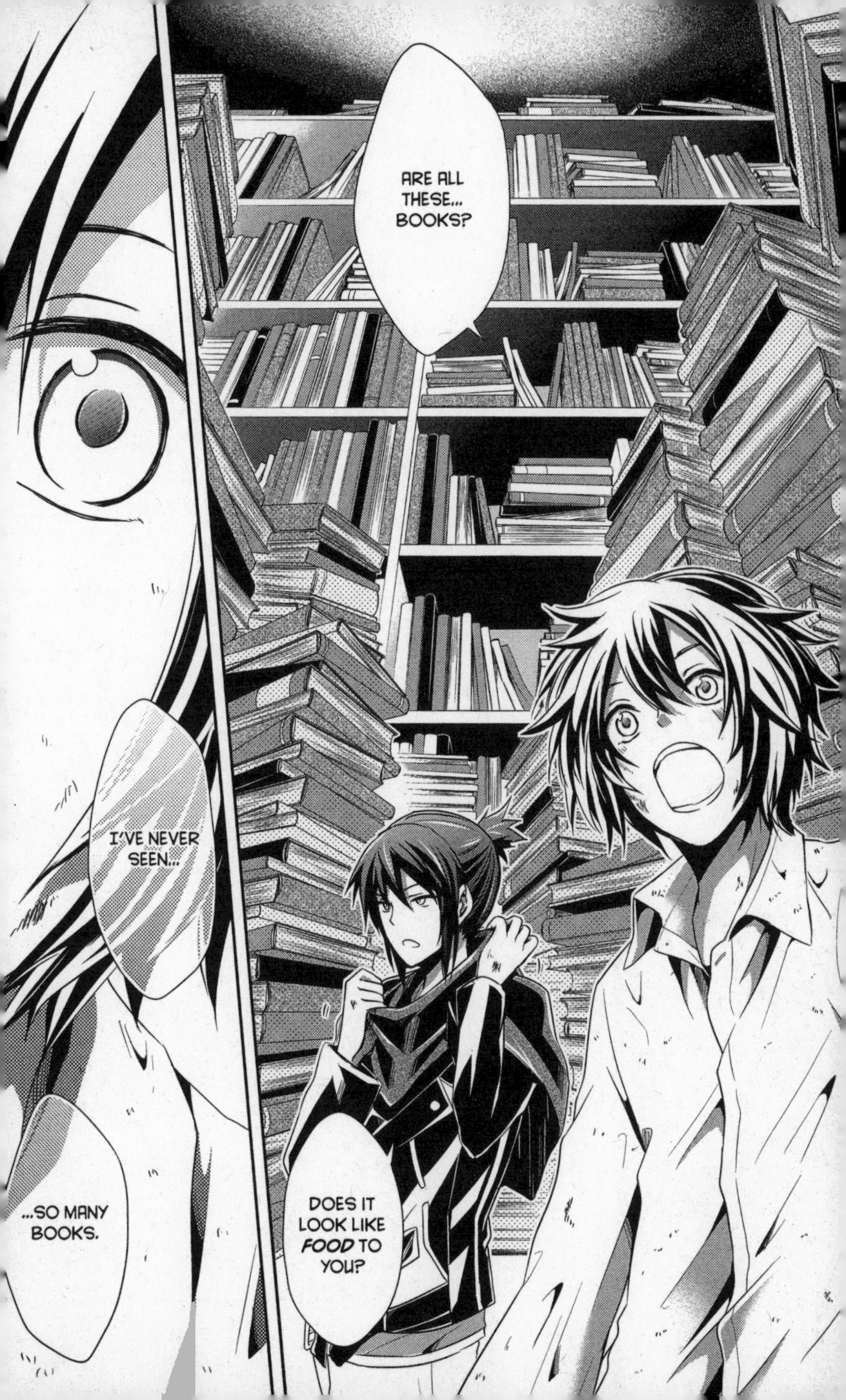
ARE ALL THESE... BOOKS?
DOES IT LOOK LIKE *FOOD* TO YOU?
I'VE NEVER SEEN...
...SO MANY BOOKS.

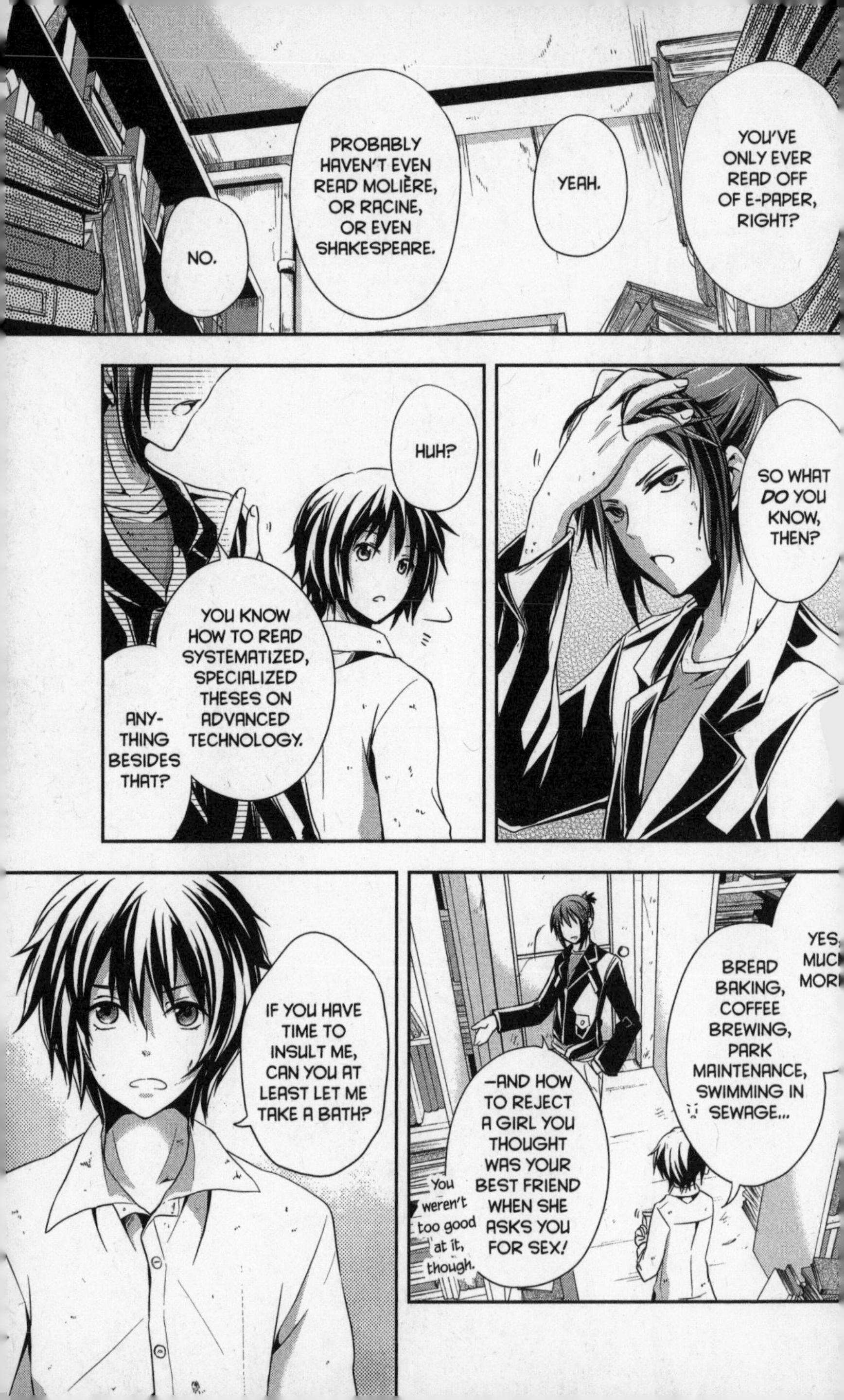
YOU'VE ONLY EVER READ OFF OF E-PAPER, RIGHT?
YEAH.
PROBABLY HAVEN'T EVEN READ MOLIÈRE, OR RACINE, OR EVEN SHAKESPEARE.
NO.
SO WHAT *DO* YOU KNOW, THEN?
HUH?
YOU KNOW HOW TO READ SYSTEMATIZED, SPECIALIZED THESES ON ADVANCED TECHNOLOGY.
ANY-THING BESIDES THAT?
YES, MUC MOR
BREAD BAKING, COFFEE BREWING, PARK MAINTENANCE, SWIMMING IN SEWAGE...
—AND HOW TO REJECT A GIRL YOU THOUGHT WAS YOUR BEST FRIEND WHEN SHE ASKS YOU FOR SEX!
You weren't too good at it, though.
IF YOU HAVE TIME TO INSULT ME, CAN YOU AT LEAST LET ME TAKE A BATH?

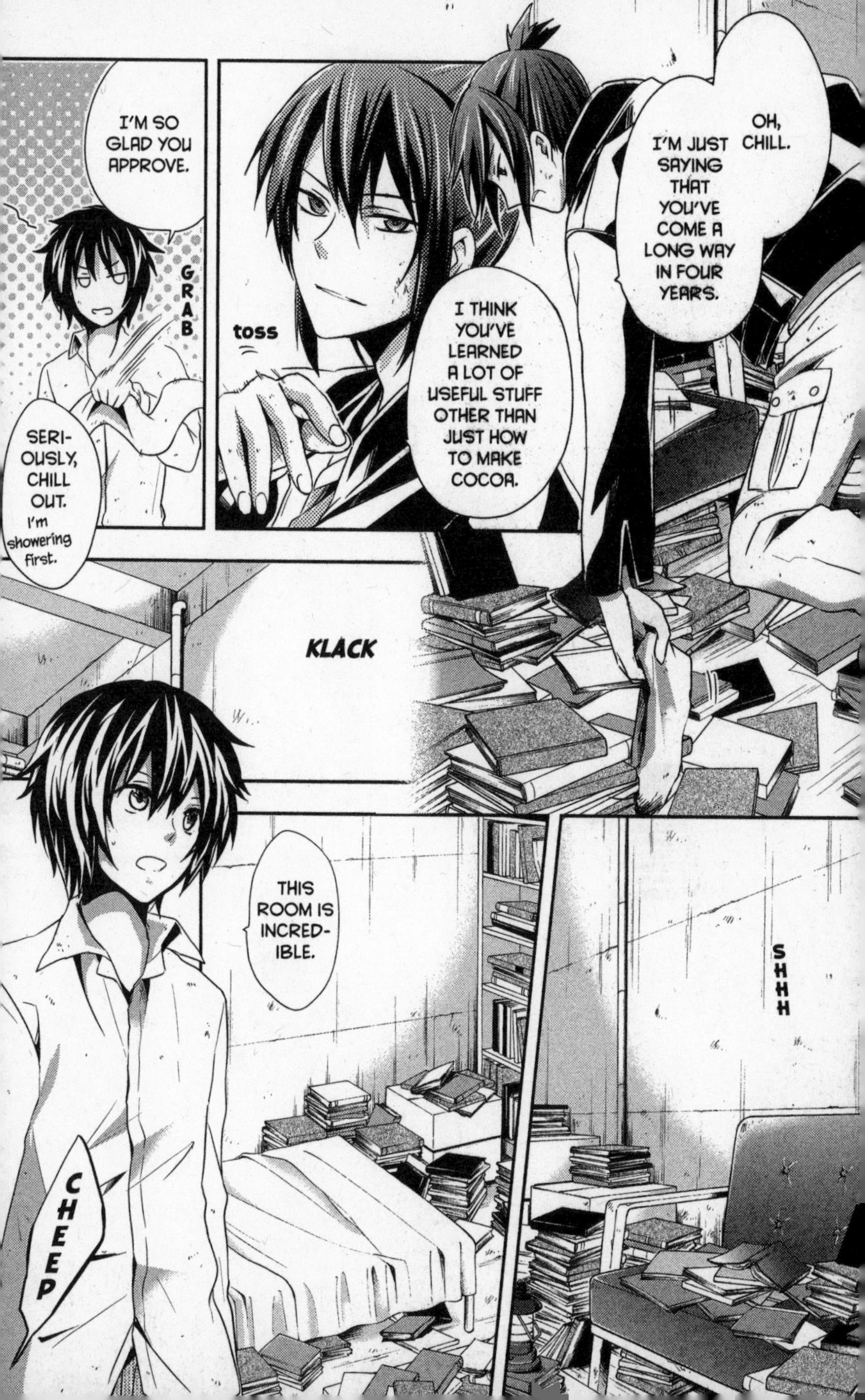
OH, CHILL.
I'M JUST SAYING THAT YOU'VE COME A LONG WAY IN FOUR YEARS.
I THINK YOU'VE LEARNED A LOT OF USEFUL STUFF OTHER THAN JUST HOW TO MAKE COCOA.
toss
I'M SO GLAD YOU APPROVE.
GRAB
SERIOUSLY, CHILL OUT.
I'm showering first.
KLACK
SHHH
THIS ROOM IS INCREDIBLE.
CHEEP

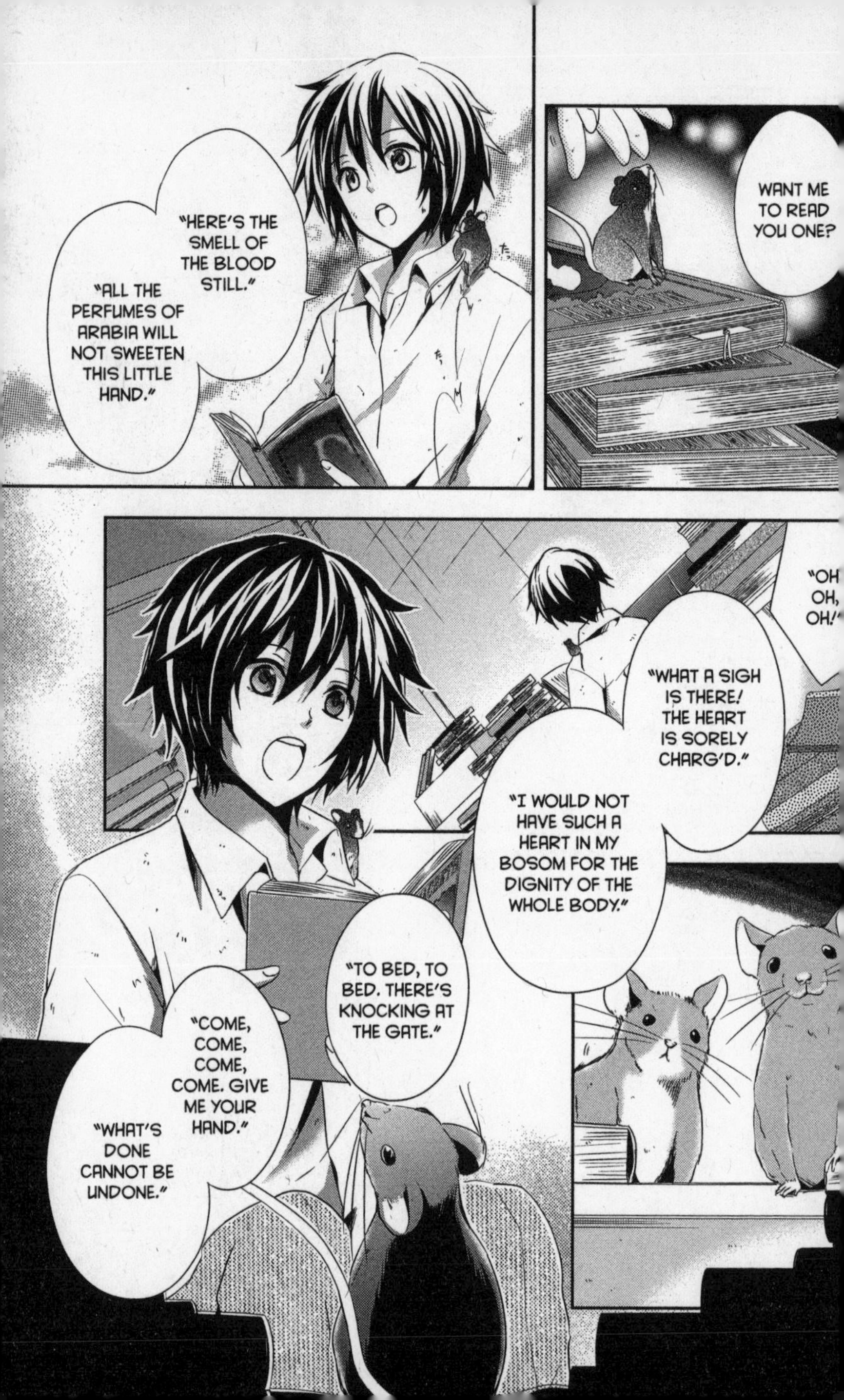
WANT ME TO READ YOU ONE?
"HERE'S THE SMELL OF THE BLOOD STILL."
"ALL THE PERFUMES OF ARABIA WILL NOT SWEETEN THIS LITTLE HAND."
"OH OH, OH!"
"WHAT A SIGH IS THERE! THE HEART IS SORELY CHARG'D."
"I WOULD NOT HAVE SUCH A HEART IN MY BOSOM FOR THE DIGNITY OF THE WHOLE BODY."
"TO BED, TO BED. THERE'S KNOCKING AT THE GATE."
"COME, COME, COME, COME. GIVE ME YOUR HAND."
"WHAT'S DONE CANNOT BE UNDONE."

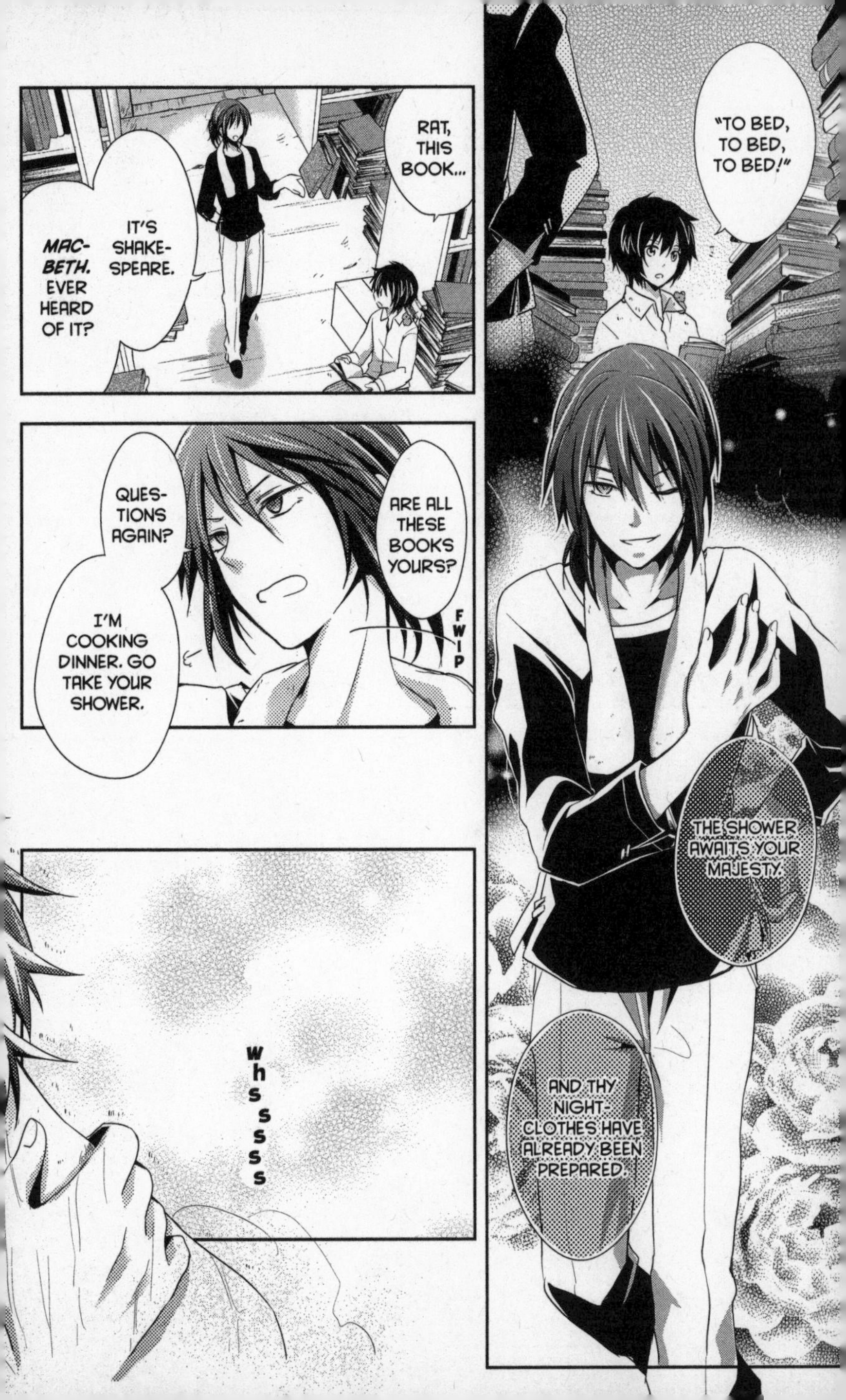
RAT, THIS BOOK...
IT'S SHAKESPEARE.
MACBETH. EVER HEARD OF IT?
ARE ALL THESE BOOKS YOURS?
FWIP
QUESTIONS AGAIN?
I'M COOKING DINNER. GO TAKE YOUR SHOWER.
whssss
"TO BED, TO BED, TO BED!"
THE SHOWER AWAITS YOUR MAJESTY.
AND THY NIGHT-CLOTHES HAVE ALREADY BEEN PREPARED.

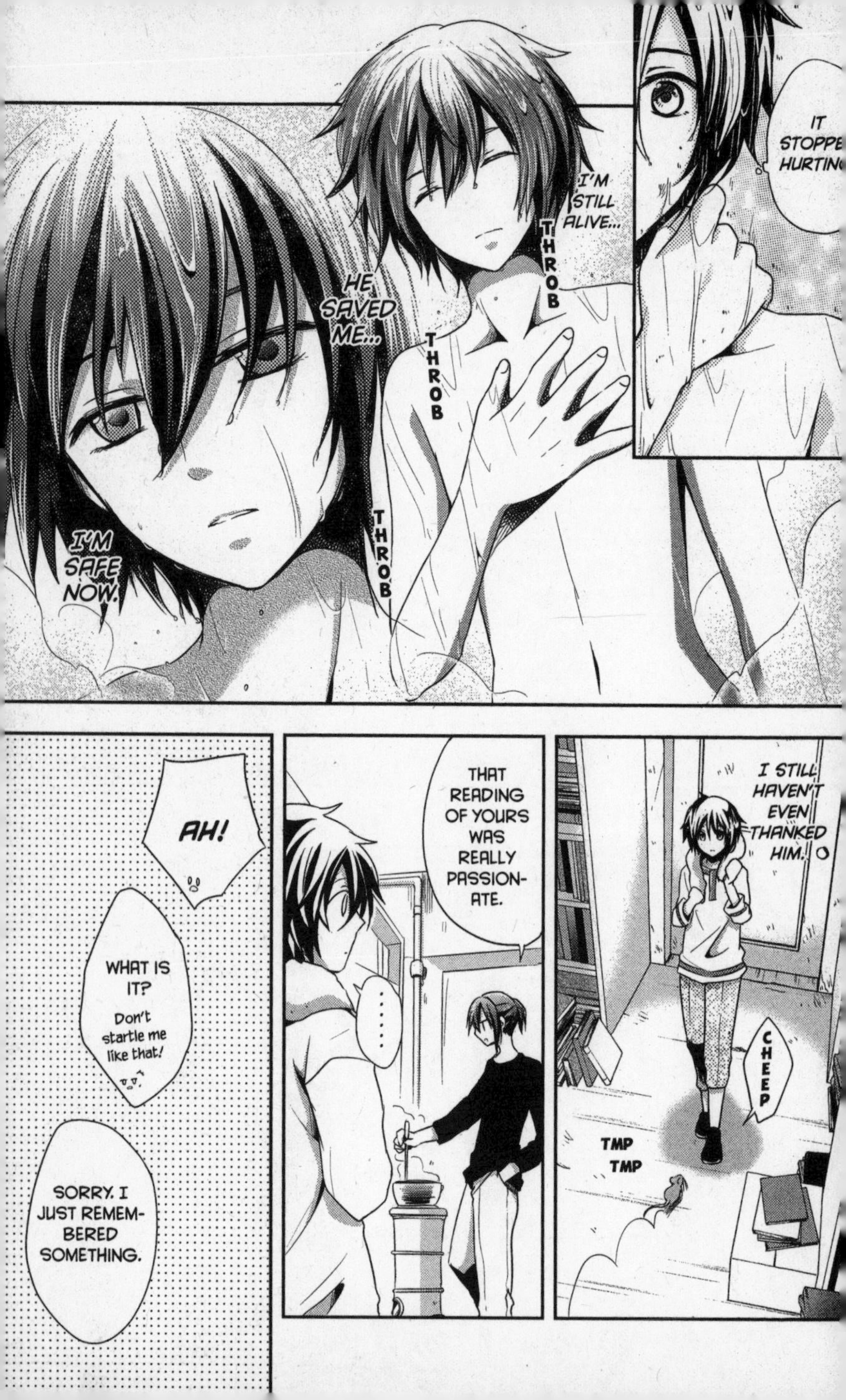
IT STOPPE HURTIN
I'M STILL ALIVE...
THROB
HE SAVED ME...
THROB
THROB
I'M SAFE NOW.
I STILL HAVEN'T EVEN THANKED HIM.
CHEEP
TMP TMP
THAT READING OF YOURS WAS REALLY PASSION-ATE.
......
AH!
WHAT IS IT?
Don't startle me like that!
SORRY. I JUST REMEM-BERED SOMETHING.

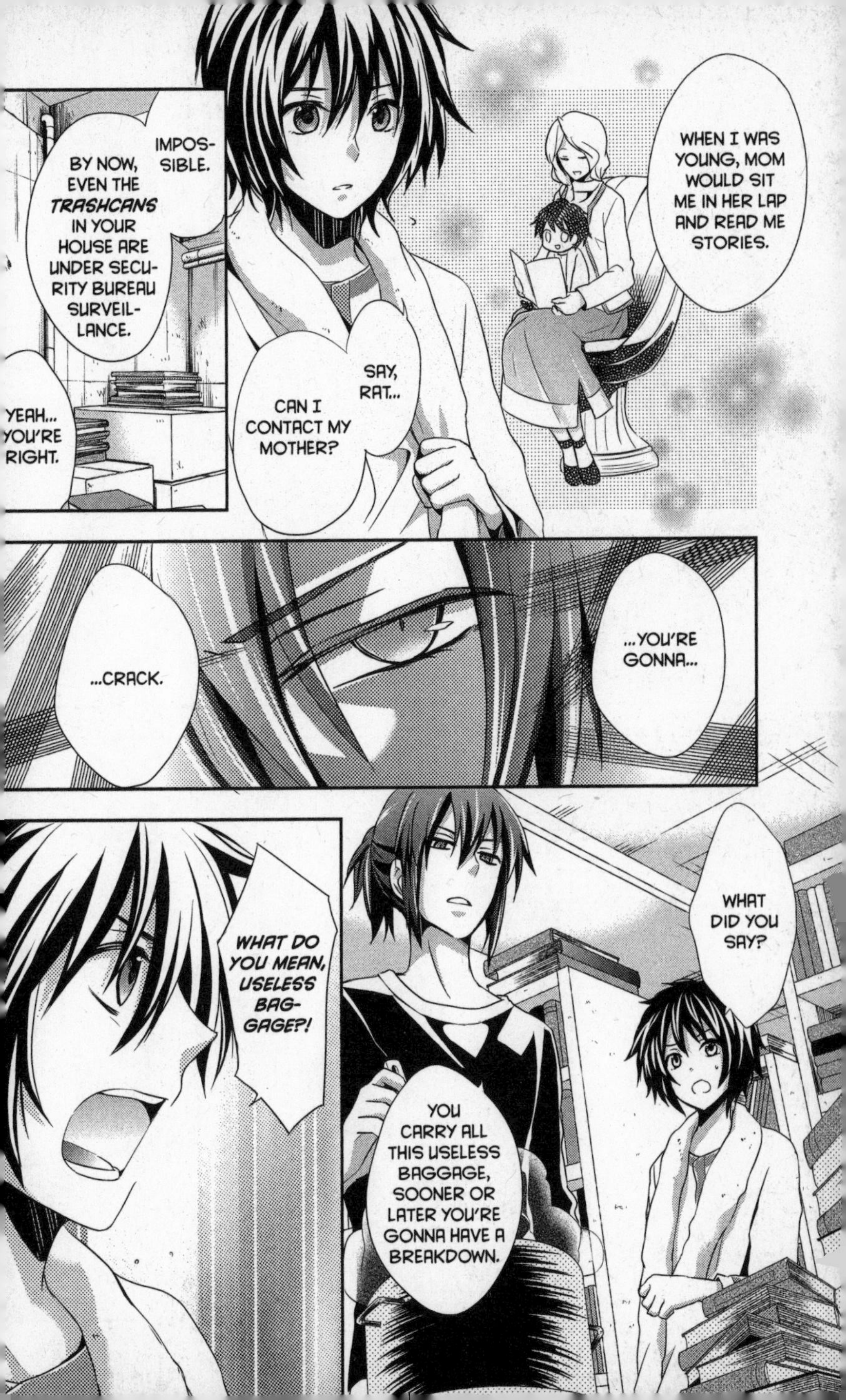
WHEN I WAS YOUNG, MOM WOULD SIT ME IN HER LAP AND READ ME STORIES.
SAY, RAT...
CAN I CONTACT MY MOTHER?
IMPOSSIBLE.
BY NOW, EVEN THE *TRASHCANS* IN YOUR HOUSE ARE UNDER SECURITY BUREAU SURVEILLANCE.
YEAH... YOU'RE RIGHT.
...YOU'RE GONNA...
...CRACK.
WHAT DID YOU SAY?
YOU CARRY ALL THIS USELESS BAGGAGE, SOONER OR LATER YOU'RE GONNA HAVE A BREAKDOWN.
WHAT DO YOU MEAN, USELESS BAGGAGE?!

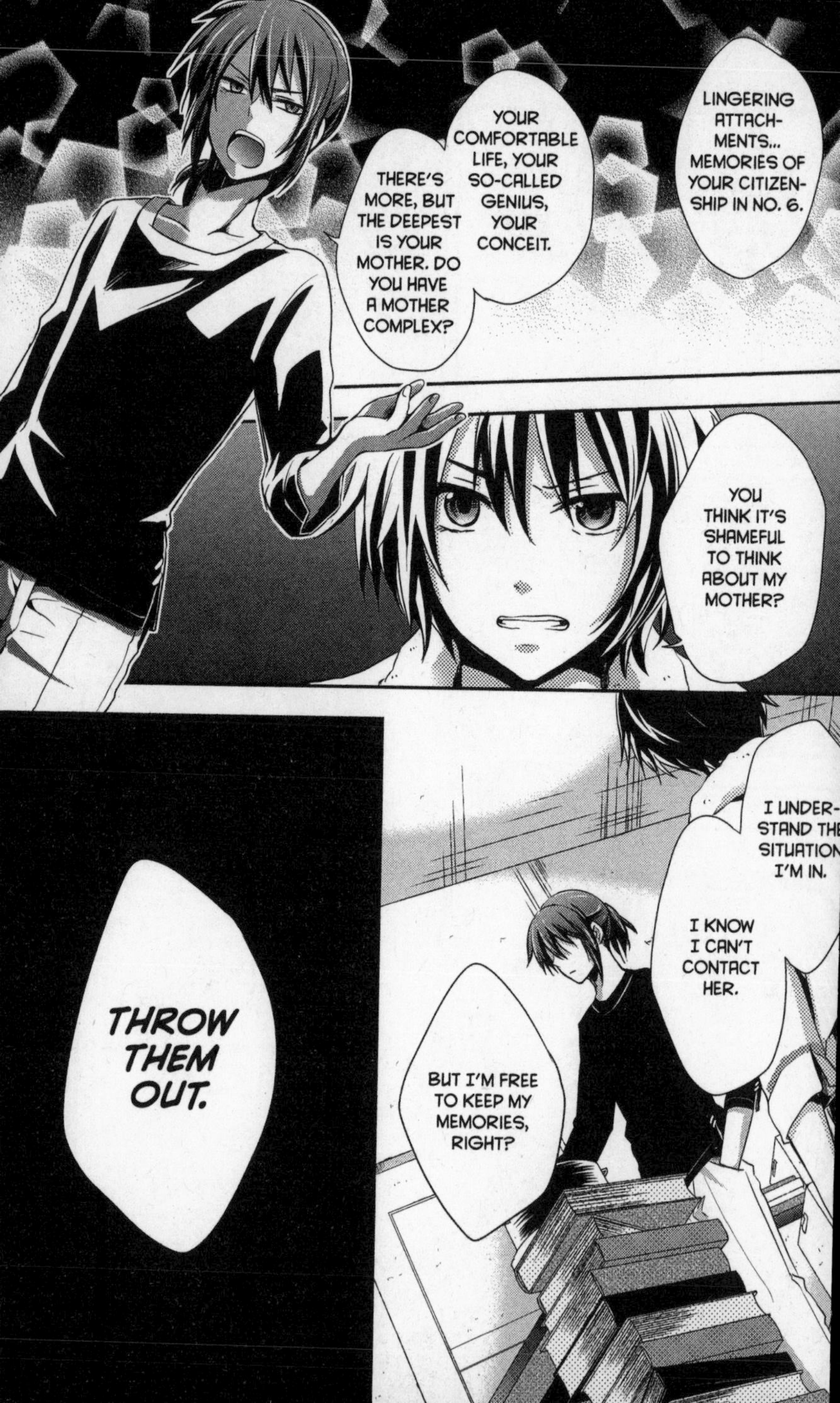
LINGERING ATTACH-MENTS... MEMORIES OF YOUR CITIZEN-SHIP IN NO. 6.
YOUR COMFORTABLE LIFE, YOUR SO-CALLED GENIUS, YOUR CONCEIT.
THERE'S MORE, BUT THE DEEPEST IS YOUR MOTHER. DO YOU HAVE A MOTHER COMPLEX?
YOU THINK IT'S SHAMEFUL TO THINK ABOUT MY MOTHER?
I UNDER-STAND THE SITUATION I'M IN.
I KNOW I CAN'T CONTACT HER.
BUT I'M FREE TO KEEP MY MEMORIES, RIGHT?
THROW THEM OUT.

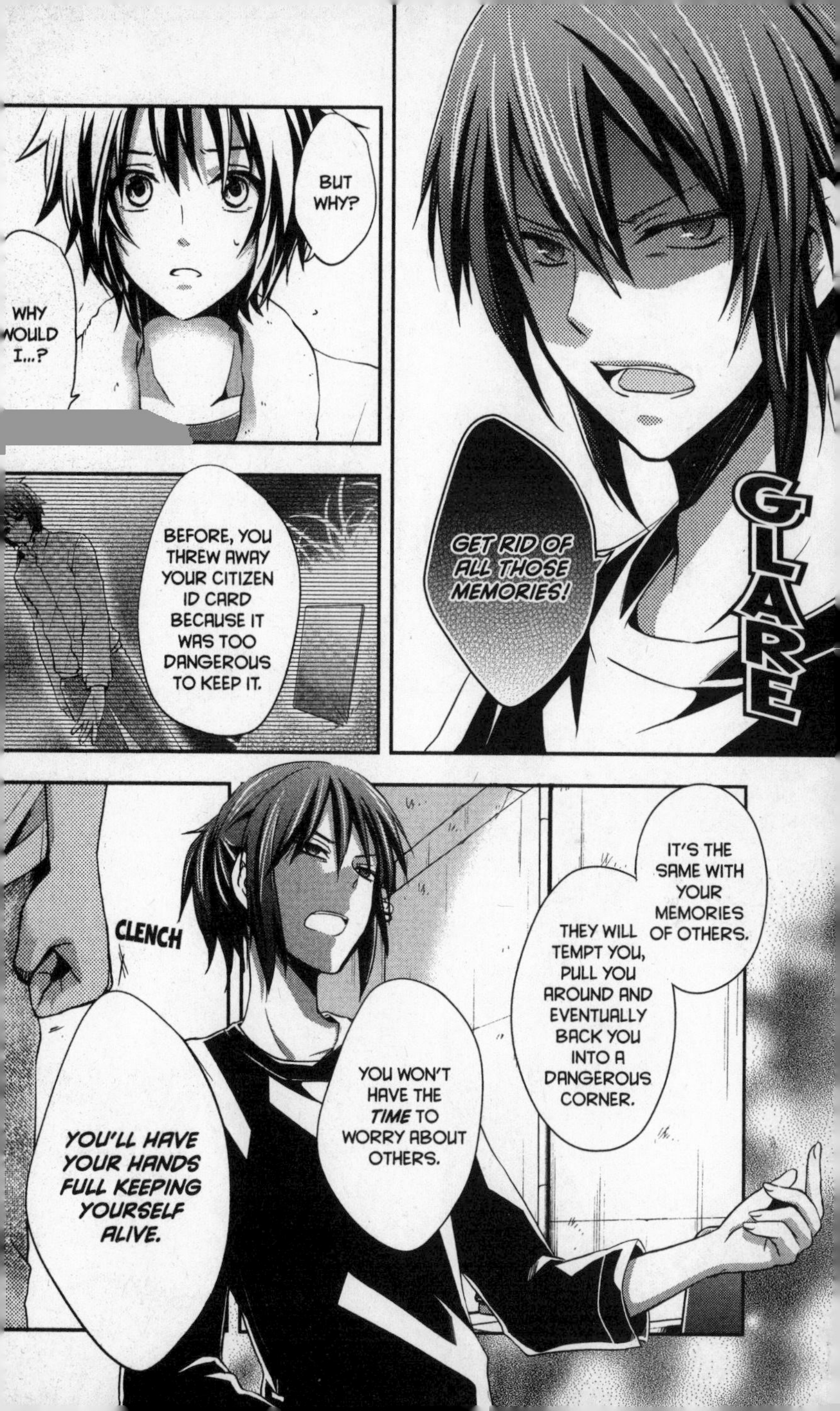
GET RID OF ALL THOSE MEMORIES!
GLARE
BUT WHY?
WHY WOULD I...?
BEFORE, YOU THREW AWAY YOUR CITIZEN ID CARD BECAUSE IT WAS TOO DANGEROUS TO KEEP IT.
IT'S THE SAME WITH YOUR MEMORIES OF OTHERS.
THEY WILL TEMPT YOU, PULL YOU AROUND AND EVENTUALLY BACK YOU INTO A DANGEROUS CORNER.
YOU WON'T HAVE THE *TIME* TO WORRY ABOUT OTHERS.
CLENCH
YOU'LL HAVE YOUR HANDS FULL KEEPING YOURSELF ALIVE.

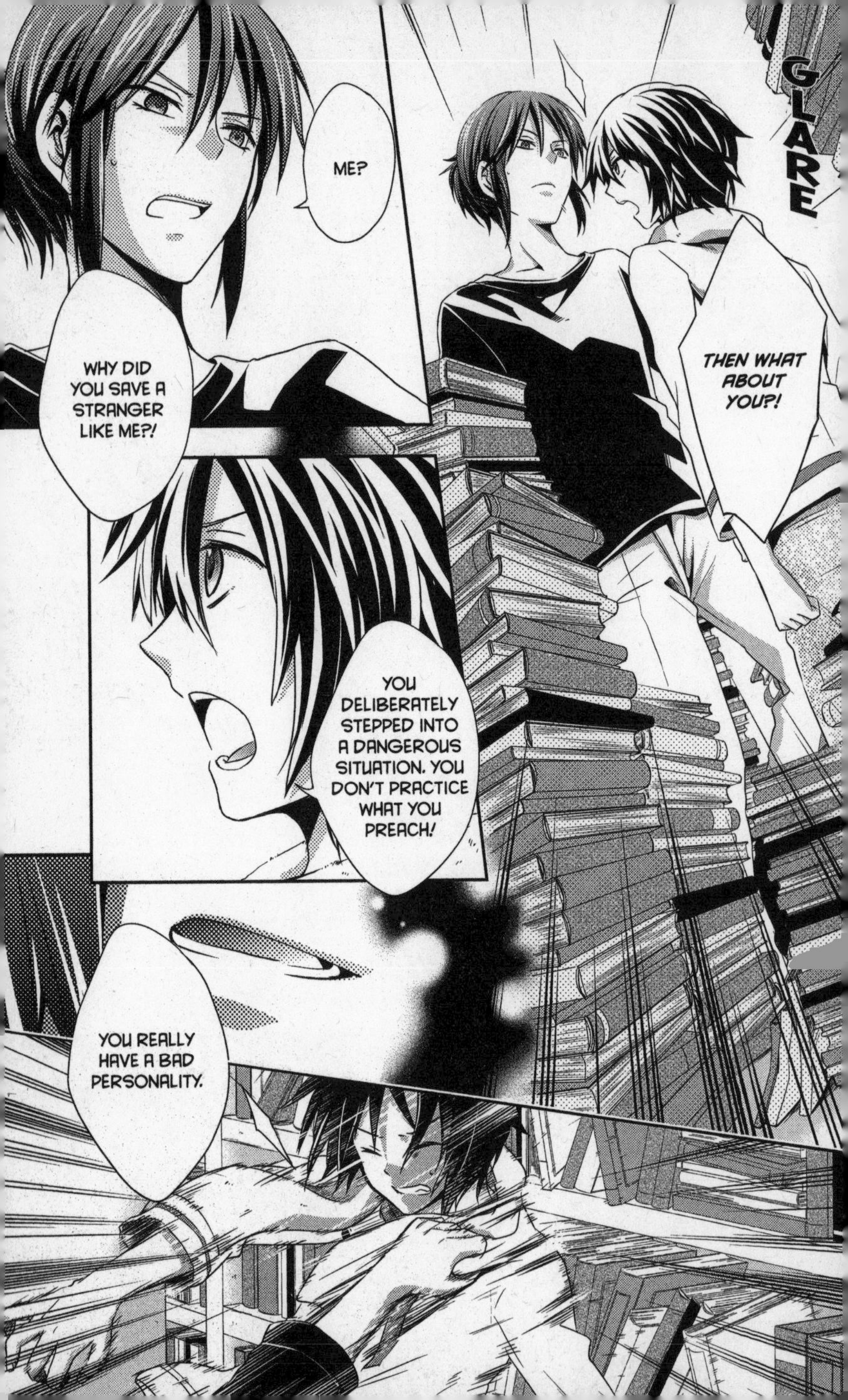
GLARE
THEN WHAT ABOUT YOU?!
ME?
WHY DID YOU SAVE A STRANGER LIKE ME?!
YOU DELIBERATELY STEPPED INTO A DANGEROUS SITUATION. YOU DON'T PRACTICE WHAT YOU PREACH!
YOU REALLY HAVE A BAD PERSONALITY.

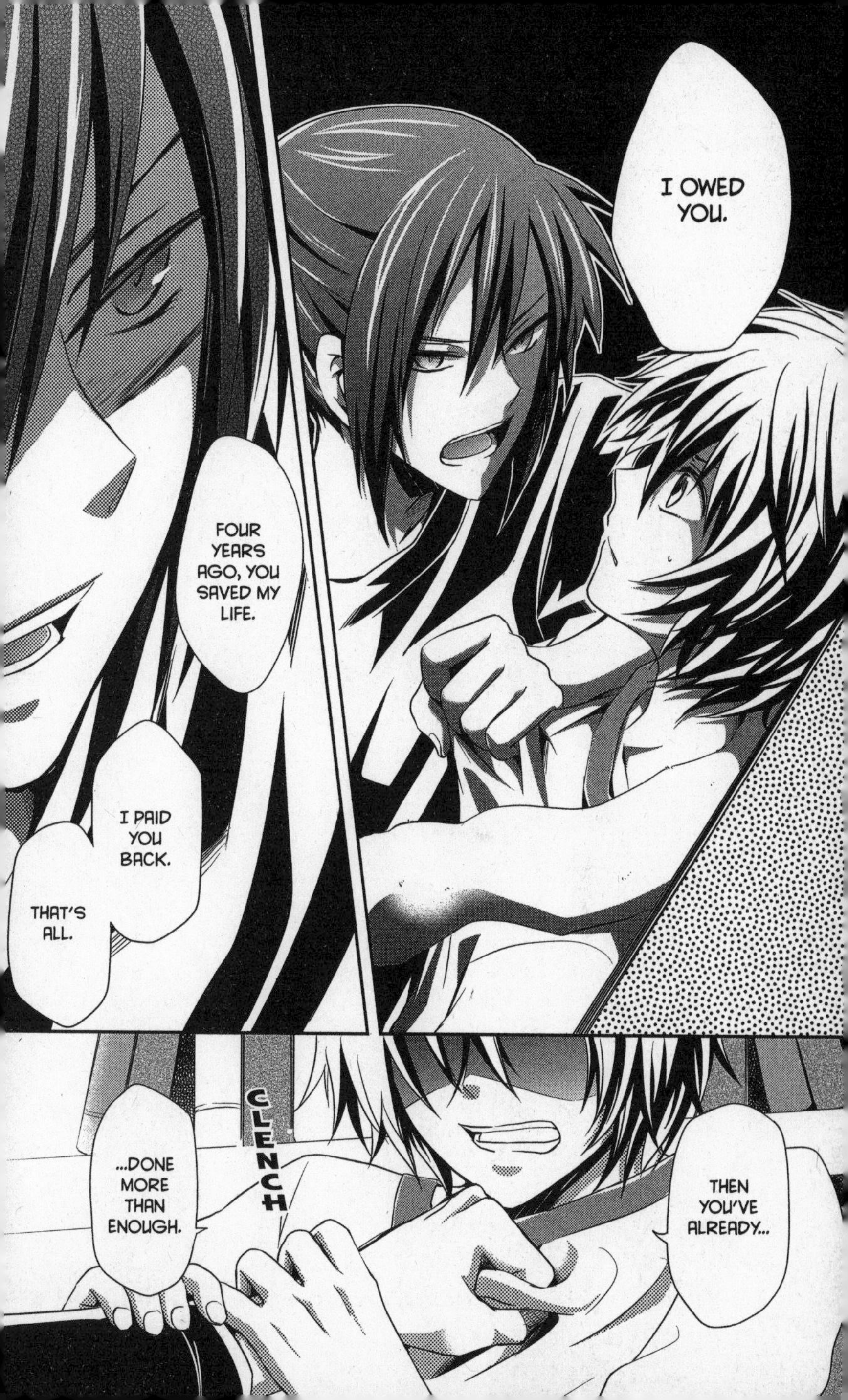
I OWED YOU.
FOUR YEARS AGO, YOU SAVED MY LIFE.
I PAID YOU BACK.
THAT'S ALL.
THEN YOU'VE ALREADY...
CLENCH
...DONE MORE THAN ENOUGH.

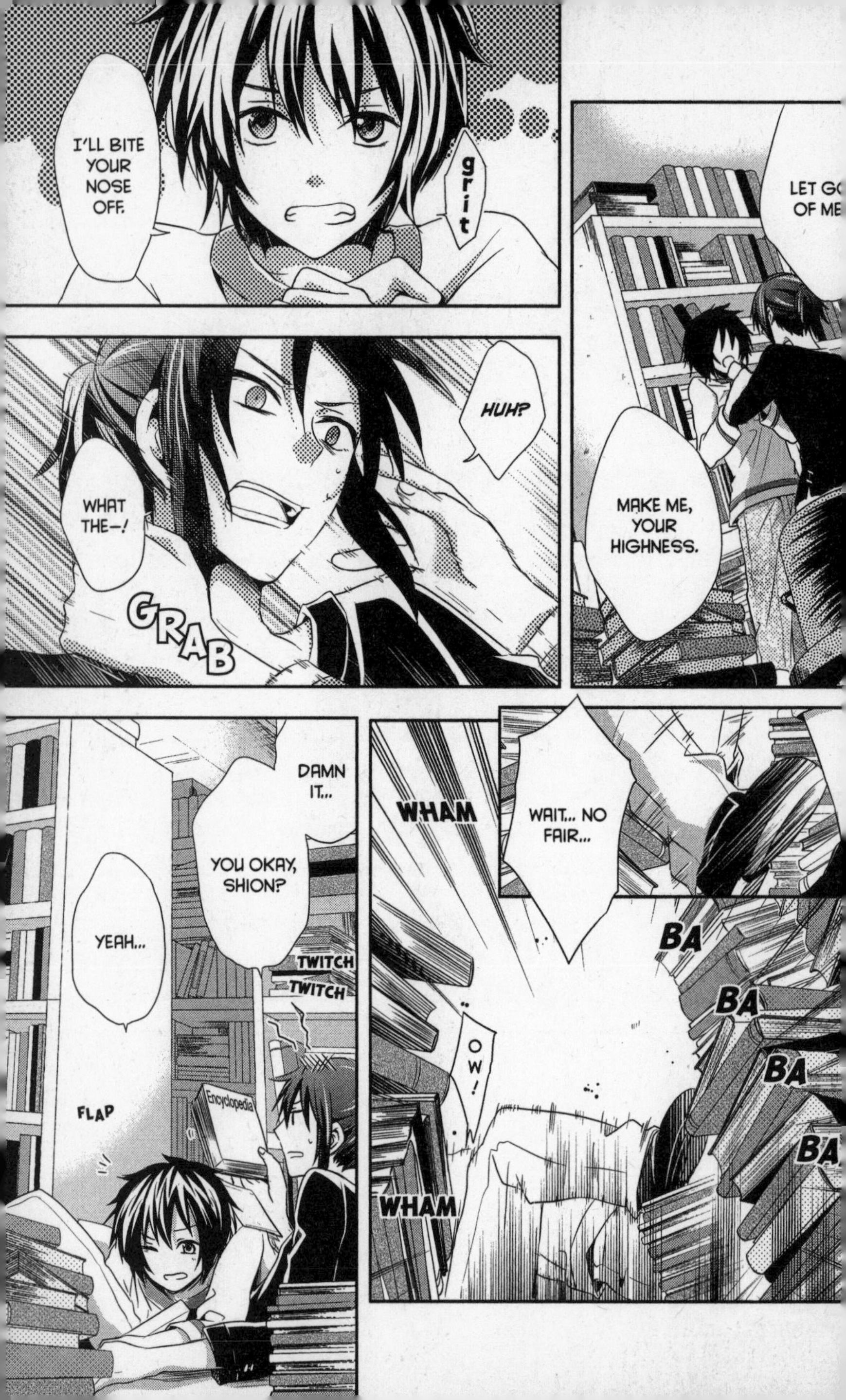
LET GO OF ME
MAKE ME, YOUR HIGHNESS.
I'LL BITE YOUR NOSE OFF.
grit
HUH?
WHAT THE-!
GRAB
WAIT... NO FAIR...
WHAM
BA
BA
BA
BA
OW!
WHAM
DAMN IT...
YOU OKAY, SHION?
YEAH...
TWITCH
TWITCH
Encyclopedia
FLAP

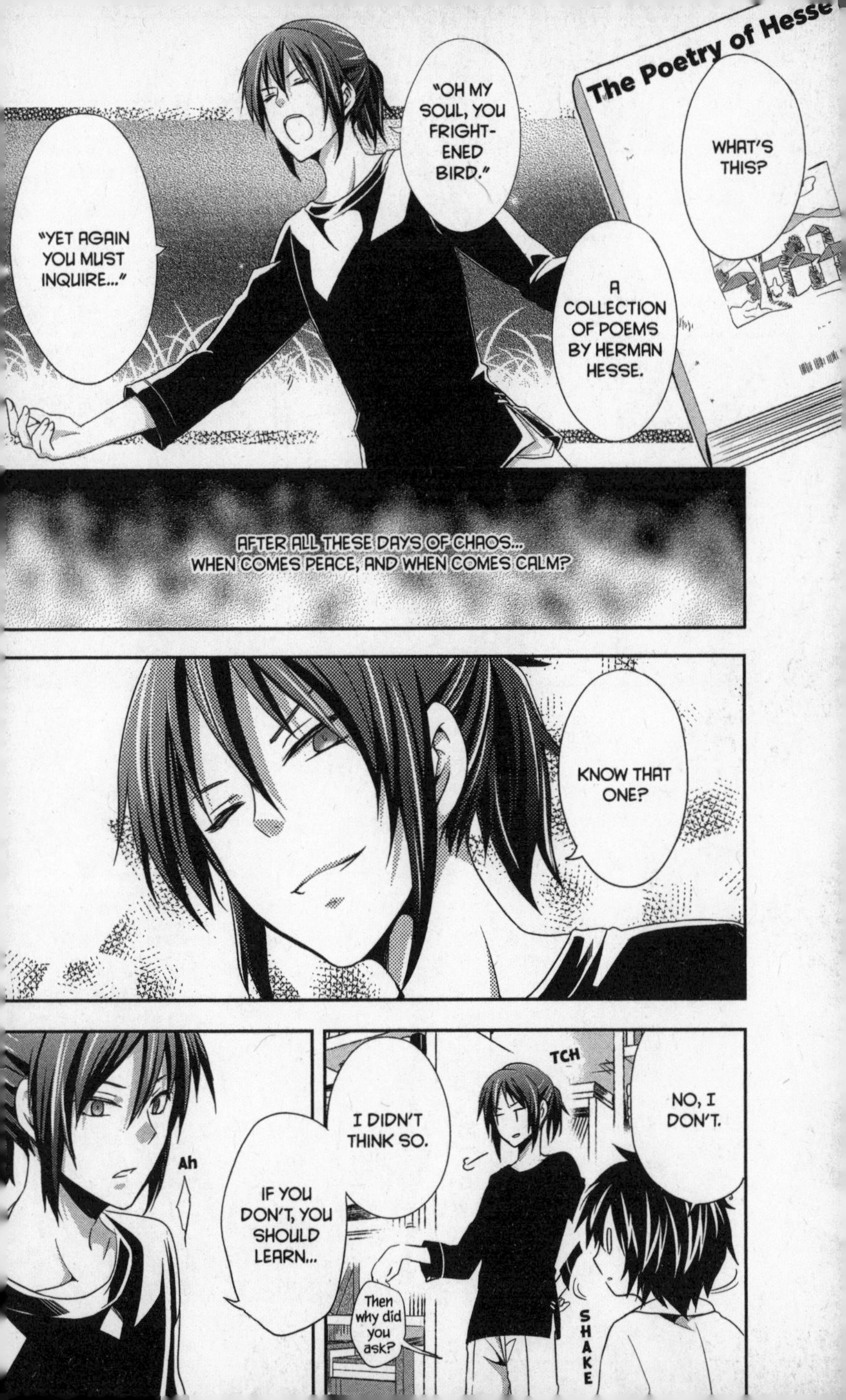
The Poetry of Hesse
WHAT'S THIS?
A COLLECTION OF POEMS BY HERMAN HESSE.
"OH MY SOUL, YOU FRIGHT-ENED BIRD."
"YET AGAIN YOU MUST INQUIRE..."
AFTER ALL THESE DAYS OF CHAOS... WHEN COMES PEACE, AND WHEN COMES CALM?
KNOW THAT ONE?
NO, I DON'T.
SHAKE
TCH
I DIDN'T THINK SO.
Then why did you ask?
IF YOU DON'T, YOU SHOULD LEARN...
Ah

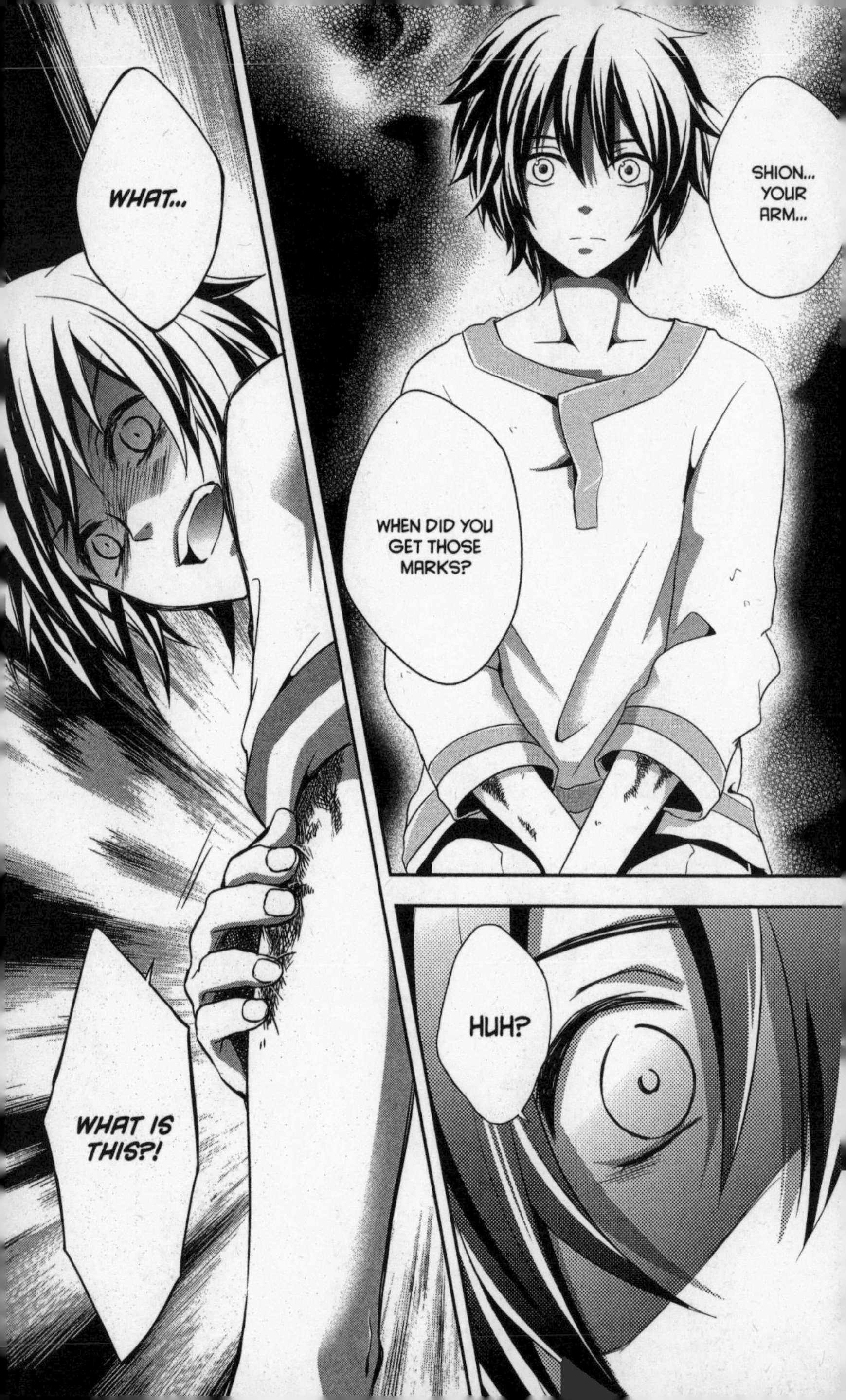
SHION... YOUR ARM...
WHEN DID YOU GET THOSE MARKS?
HUH?
WHAT...
WHAT IS THIS?!

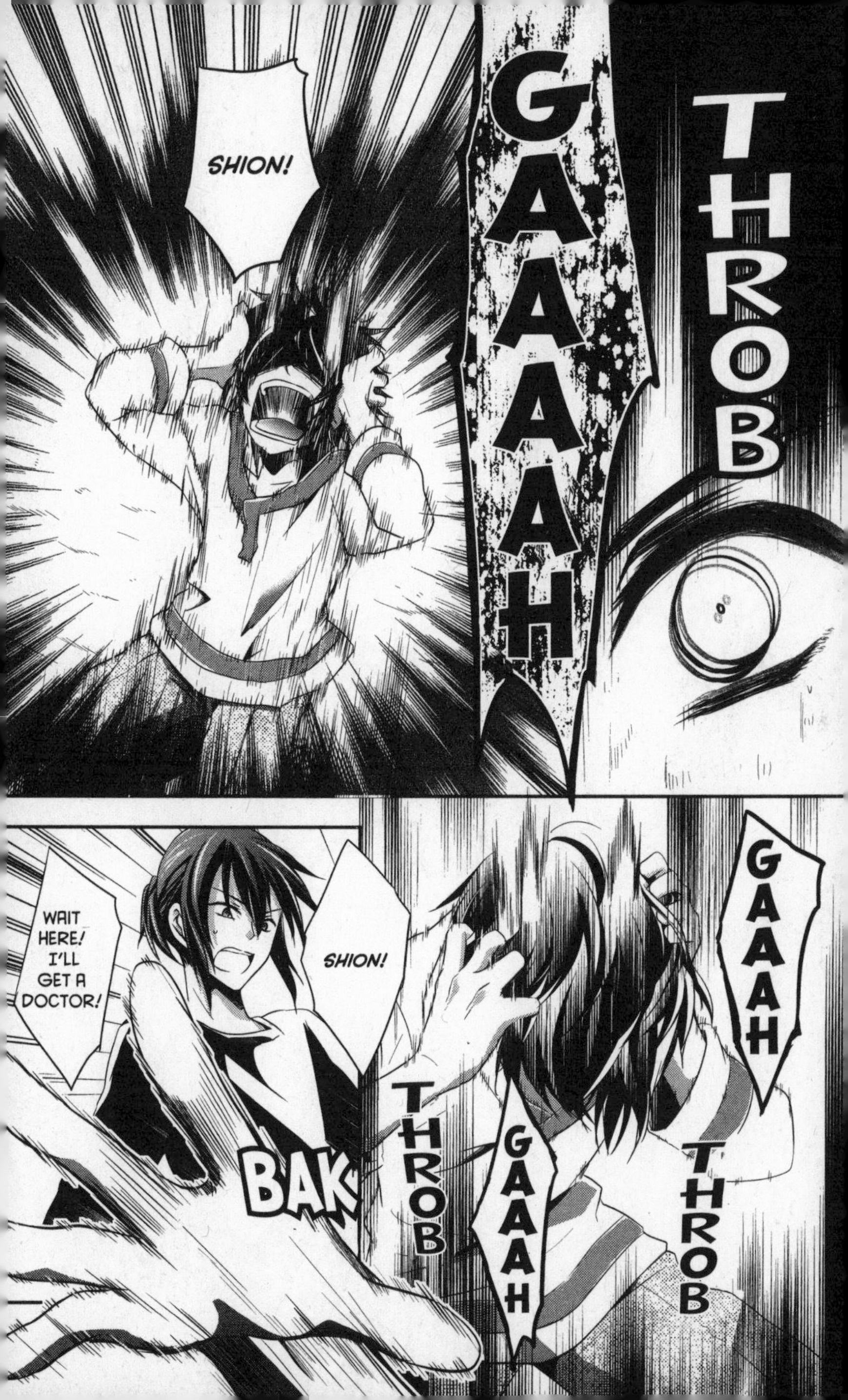
THROB
GAAAH
SHION!
GAAAH
SHION!
WAIT HERE! I'LL GET A DOCTOR!
THROB
GAAAH
THROB
BAK

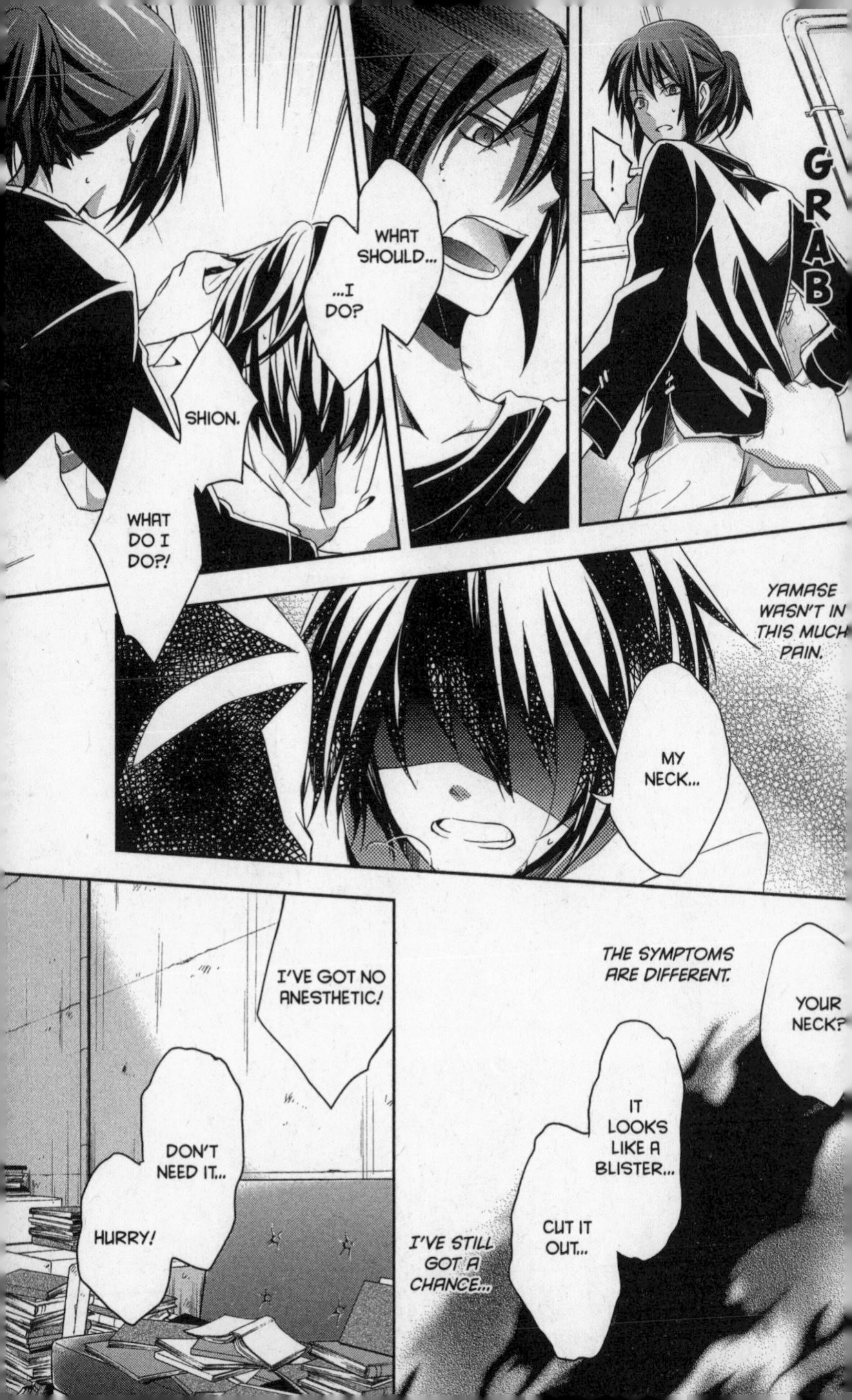
!
GRAB
WHAT SHOULD...
...I DO?
SHION.
WHAT DO I DO?!
YAMASE WASN'T IN THIS MUCH PAIN.
MY NECK...
YOUR NECK?
THE SYMPTOMS ARE DIFFERENT.
IT LOOKS LIKE A BLISTER...
CUT IT OUT...
I'VE STILL GOT A CHANCE...
I'VE GOT NO ANESTHETIC!
DON'T NEED IT...
HURRY!

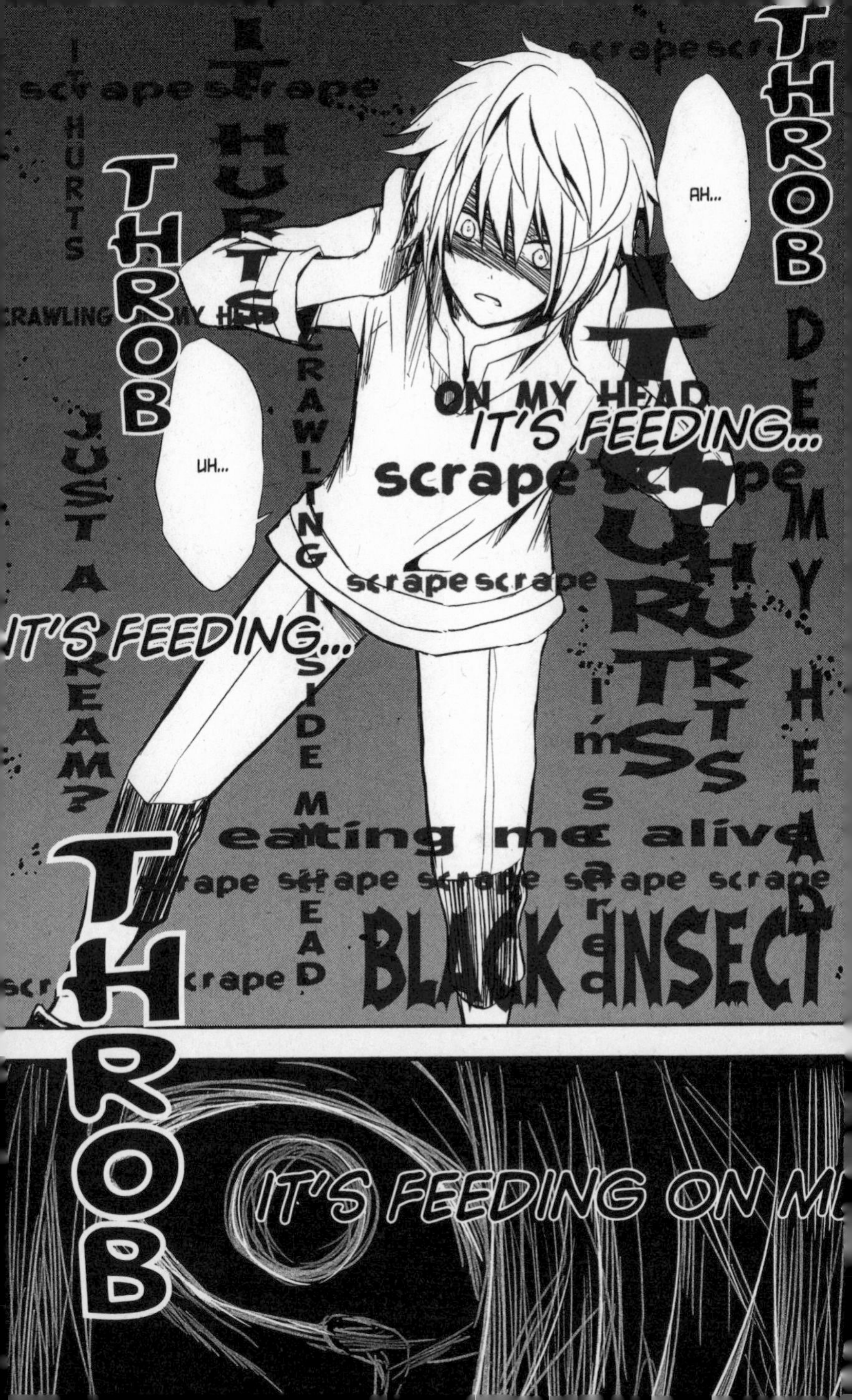

THROB
AH...
IT HURTS
IT'S FEEDING...
ON MY HEAD
scrape scrape
BLACK INSECT
eating me alive
scrape scrape scrape scrape scrape
CRAWLING INSIDE MY HEAD
THROB
IT HURTS
scrape scrape...
I HURTS
UH...
JUST A DREAM?
IT'S FEEDING...
THROB
IT'S FEEDING ON M

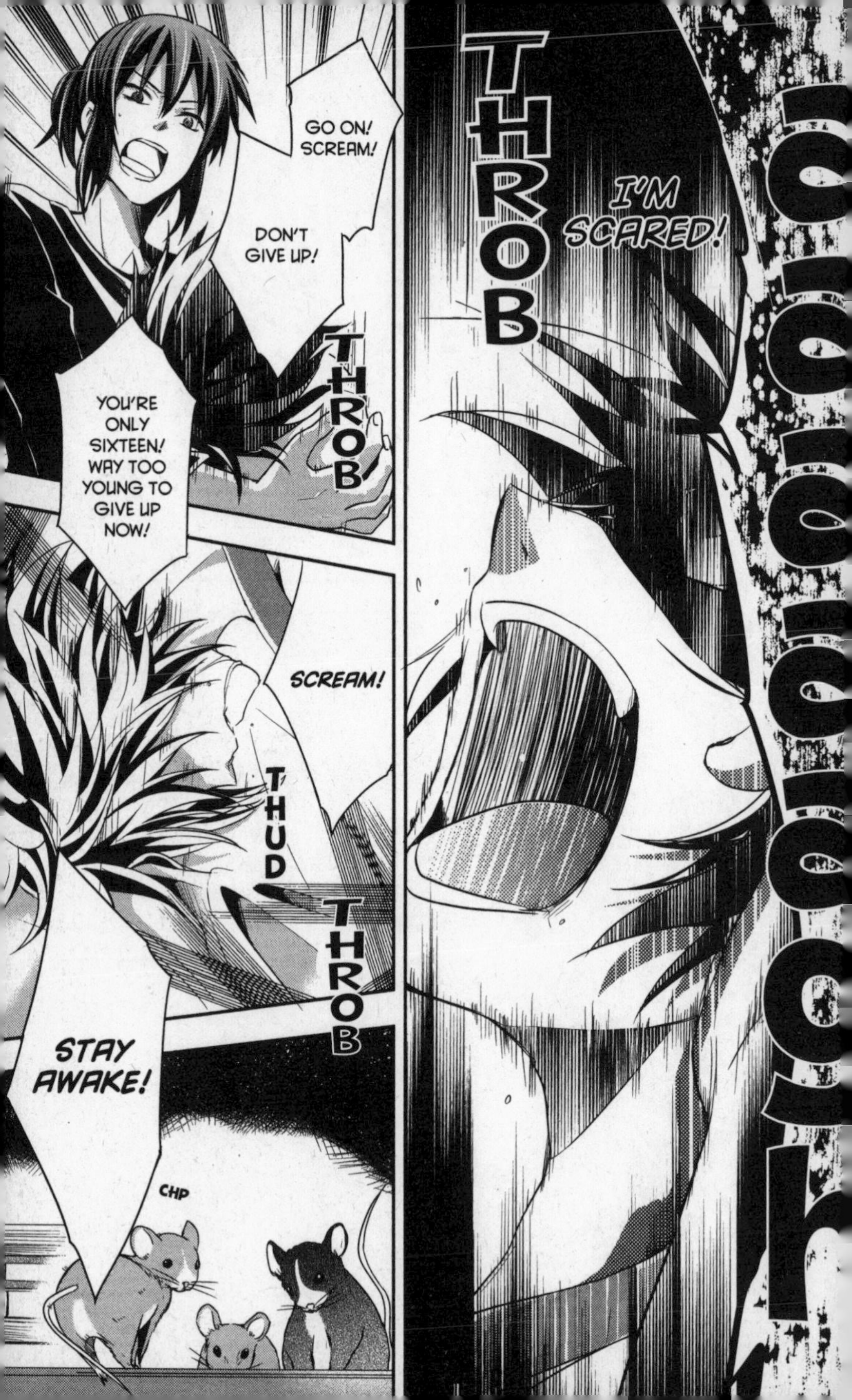
THROB
I'M SCARED!
GO ON! SCREAM!
DON'T GIVE UP!
YOU'RE ONLY SIXTEEN! WAY TOO YOUNG TO GIVE UP NOW!
THROB
SCREAM!
THUD
THROB
STAY AWAKE!
CHP

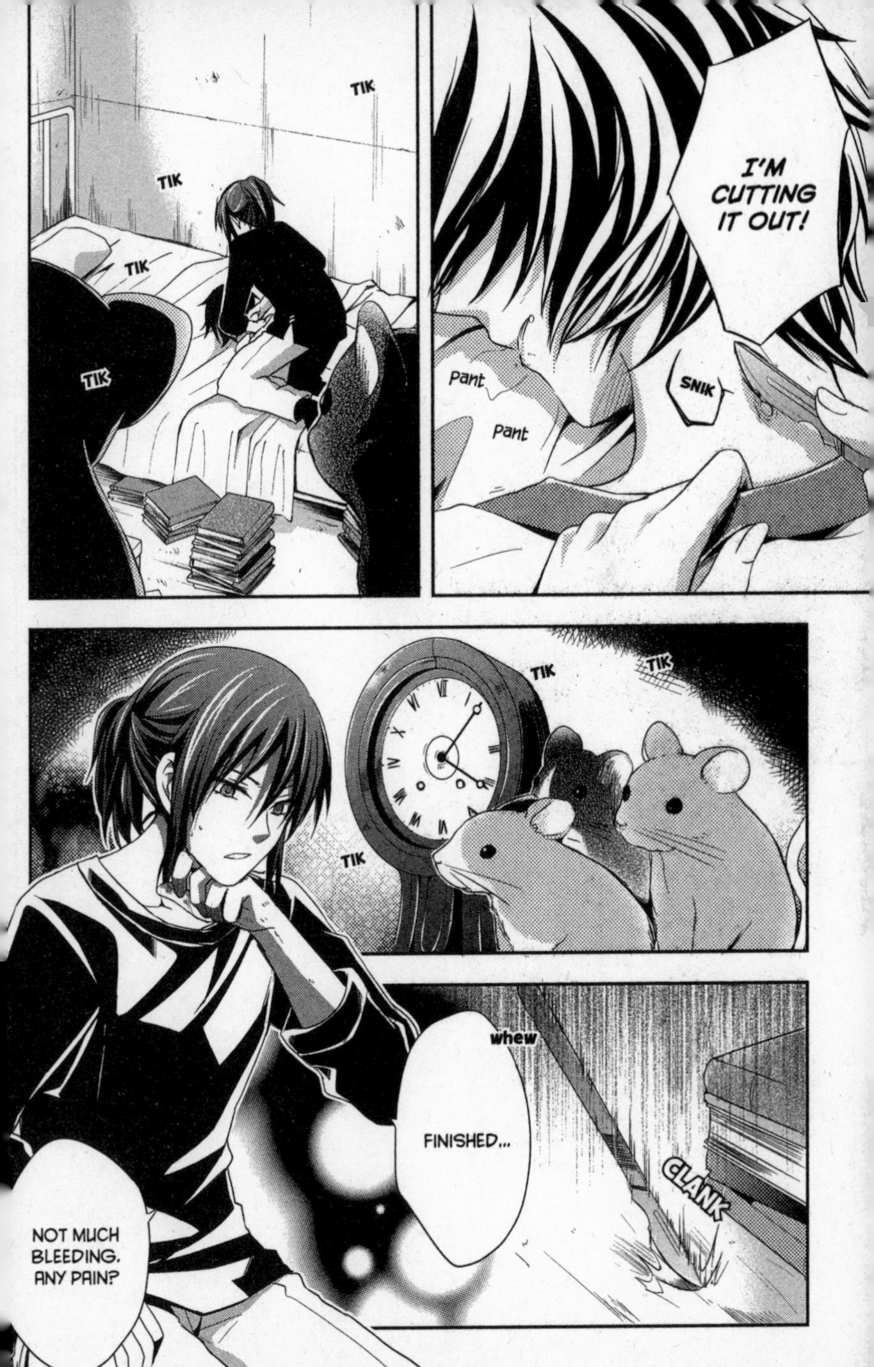
I'M CUTTING IT OUT!
SNIK
pant
pant
TIK
TIK
TIK
TIK
TIK
TIK
TIK
CLANK
whew
FINISHED...
NOT MUCH BLEEDING. ANY PAIN?

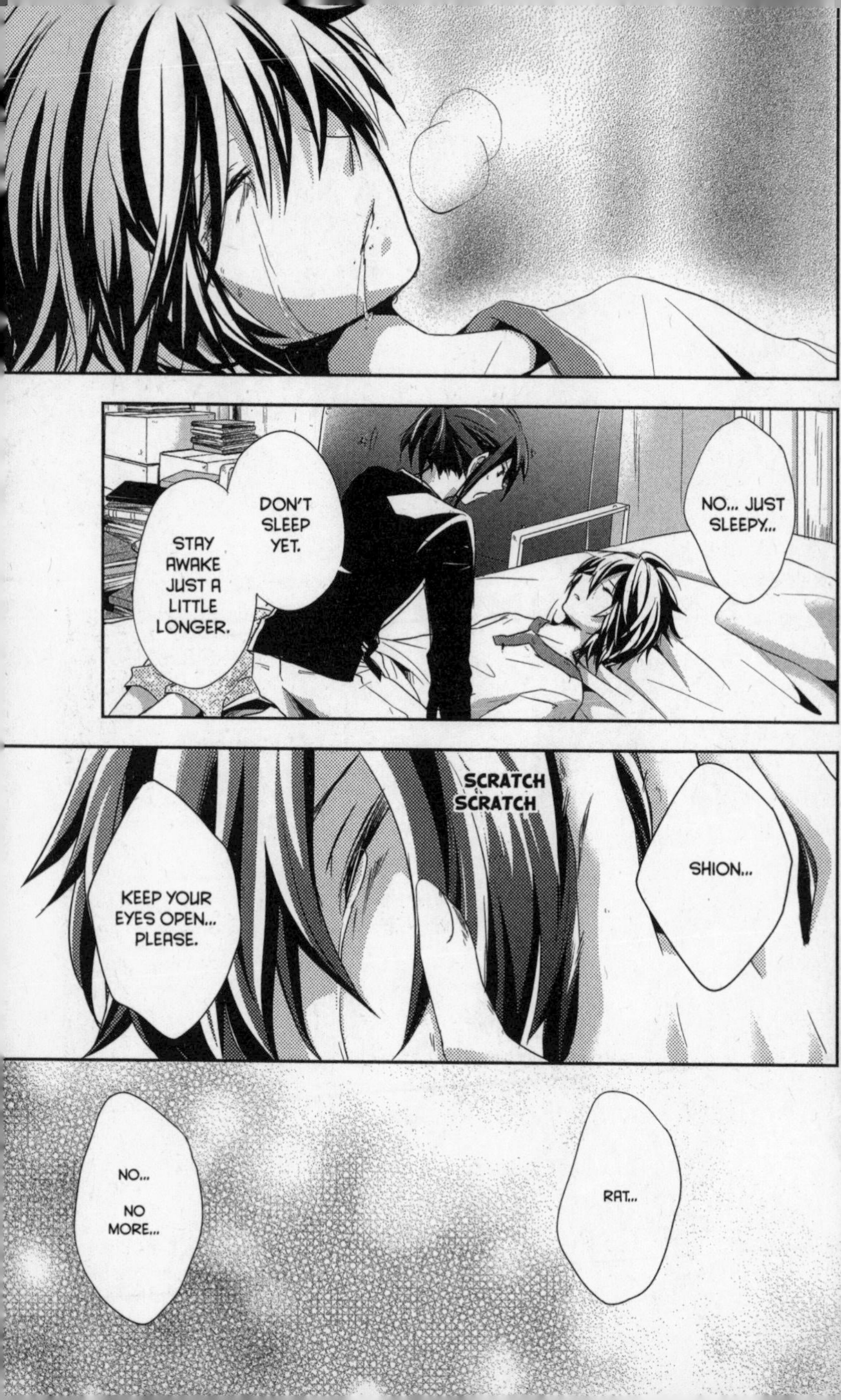
NO... JUST SLEEPY...
DON'T SLEEP YET.
STAY AWAKE JUST A LITTLE LONGER.
SHION...
SCRATCH SCRATCH
KEEP YOUR EYES OPEN... PLEASE.
RAT...
NO... NO MORE...

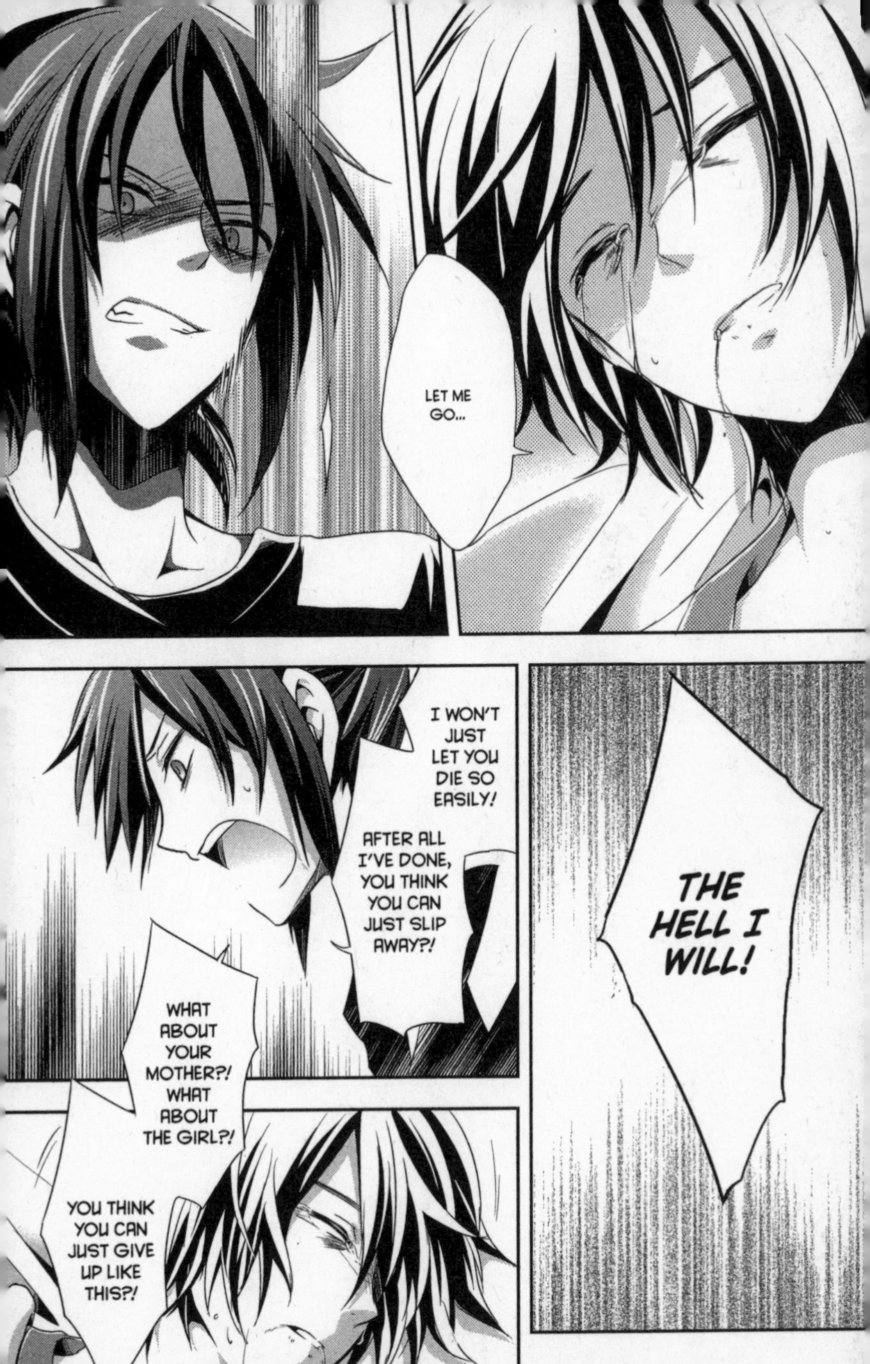
LET ME GO...
THE HELL I WILL!
I WON'T JUST LET YOU DIE SO EASILY!
AFTER ALL I'VE DONE, YOU THINK YOU CAN JUST SLIP AWAY?!
WHAT ABOUT YOUR MOTHER?! WHAT ABOUT THE GIRL?!
YOU THINK YOU CAN JUST GIVE UP LIKE THIS?!

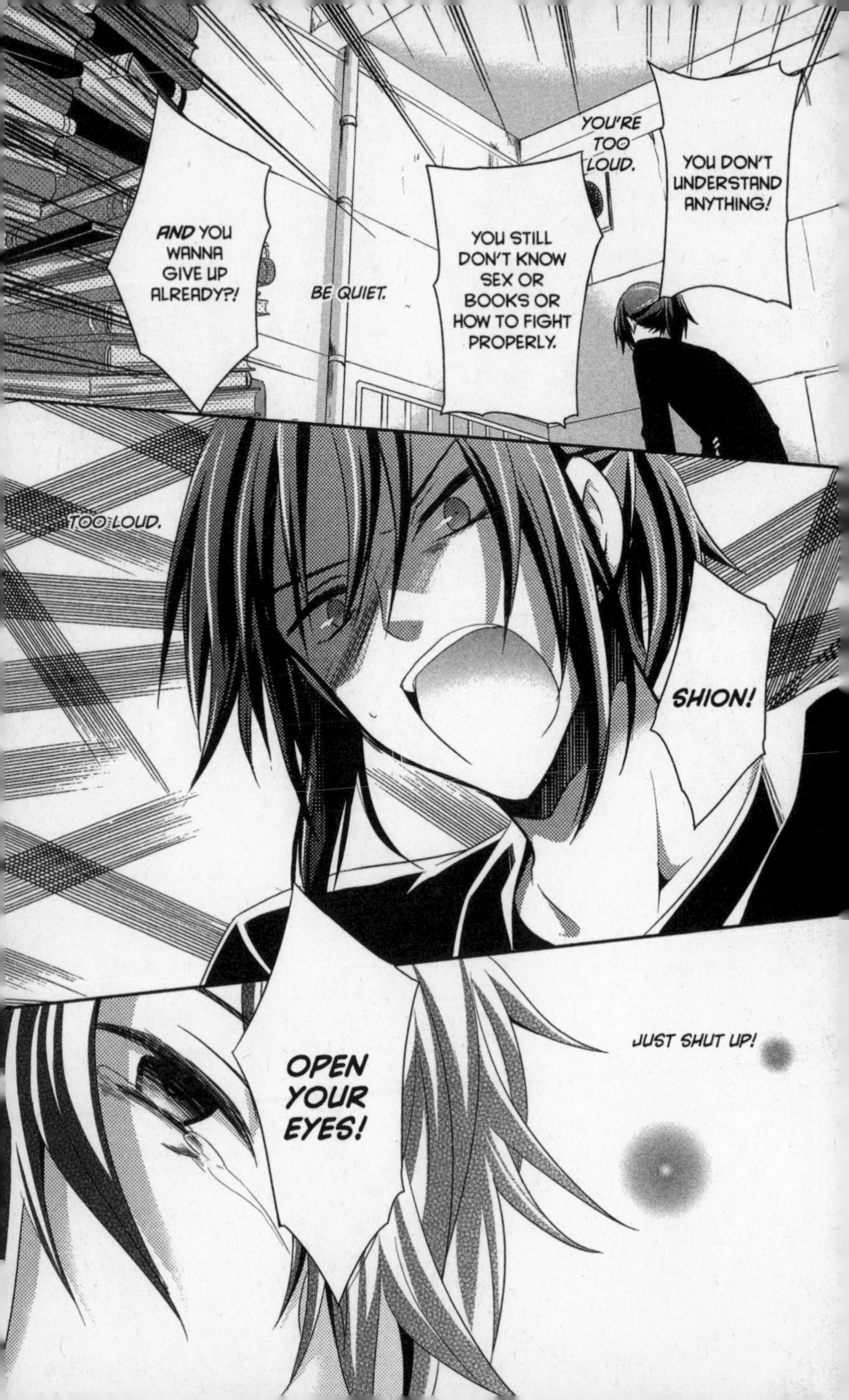
YOU DON'T UNDERSTAND ANYTHING!
YOU'RE TOO LOUD.
YOU STILL DON'T KNOW SEX OR BOOKS OR HOW TO FIGHT PROPERLY.
BE QUIET.
AND YOU WANNA GIVE UP ALREADY?!
SHION!
TOO LOUD.
JUST SHUT UP!
OPEN YOUR EYES!

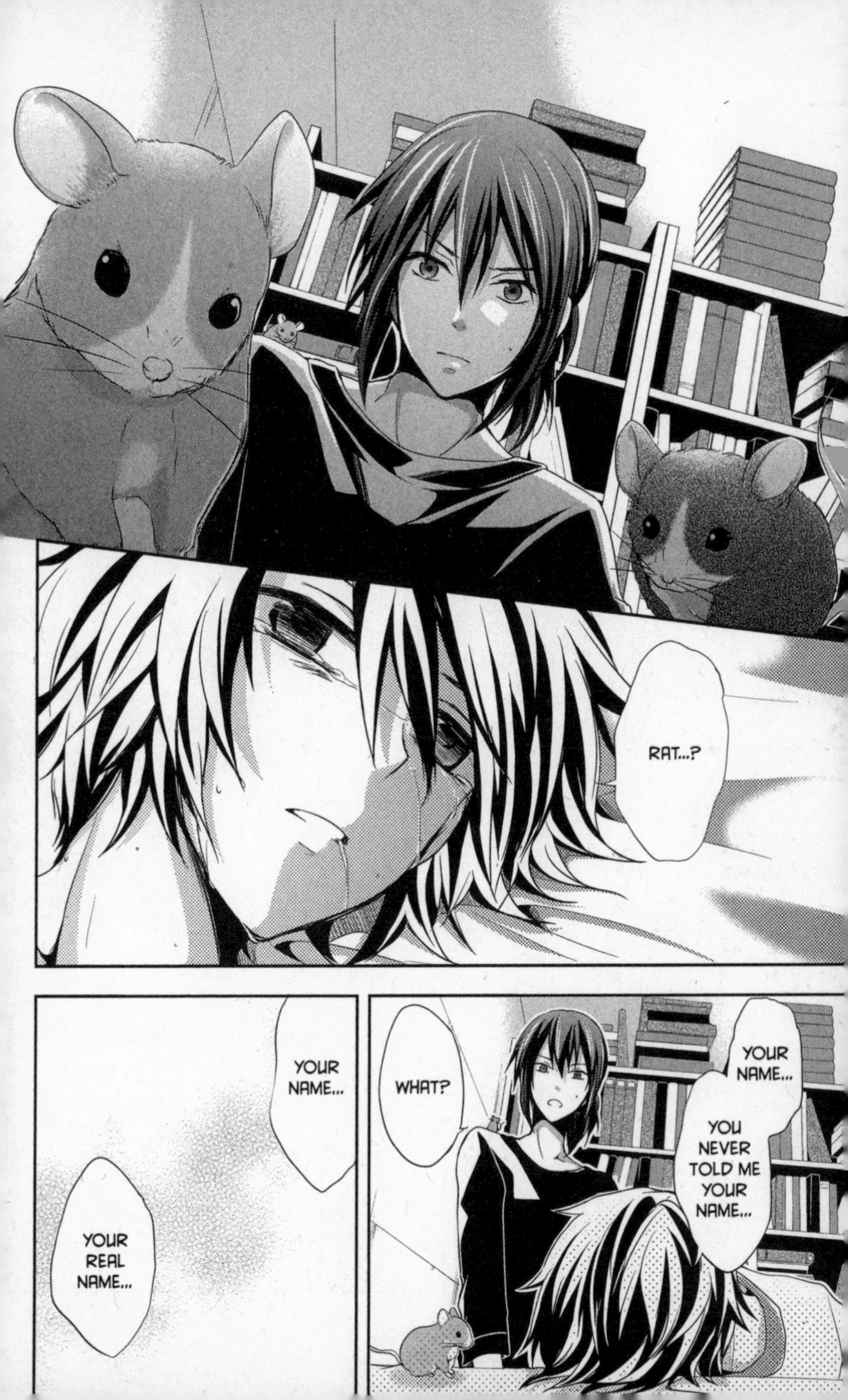

RAT...?
YOUR NAME...
WHAT?
YOU NEVER TOLD ME YOUR NAME...
YOUR NAME...
YOUR REAL NAME...

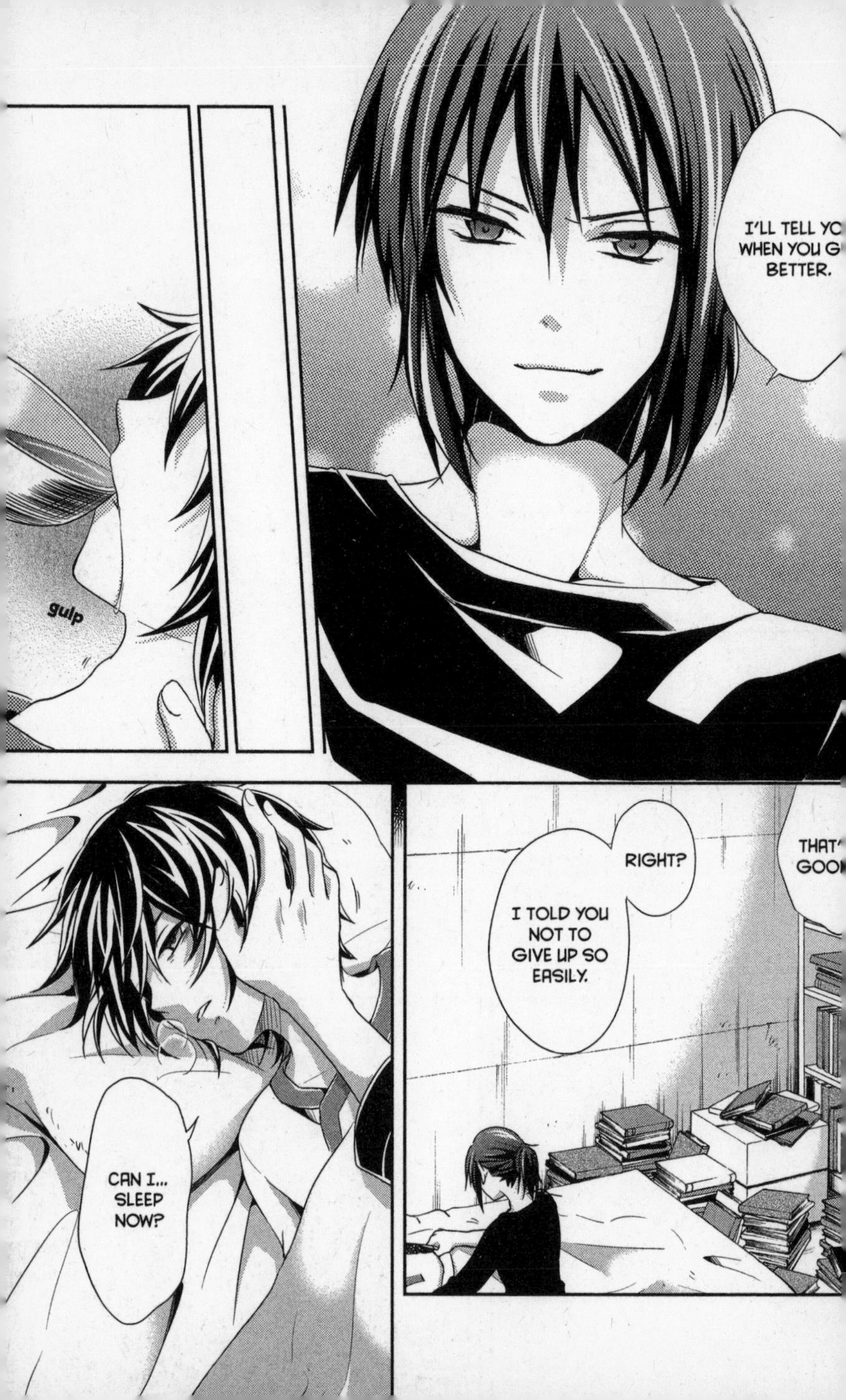
I'LL TELL YO WHEN YOU G BETTER.
gulp
THAT' GOO
RIGHT?
I TOLD YOU NOT TO GIVE UP SO EASILY.
CAN I... SLEEP NOW?

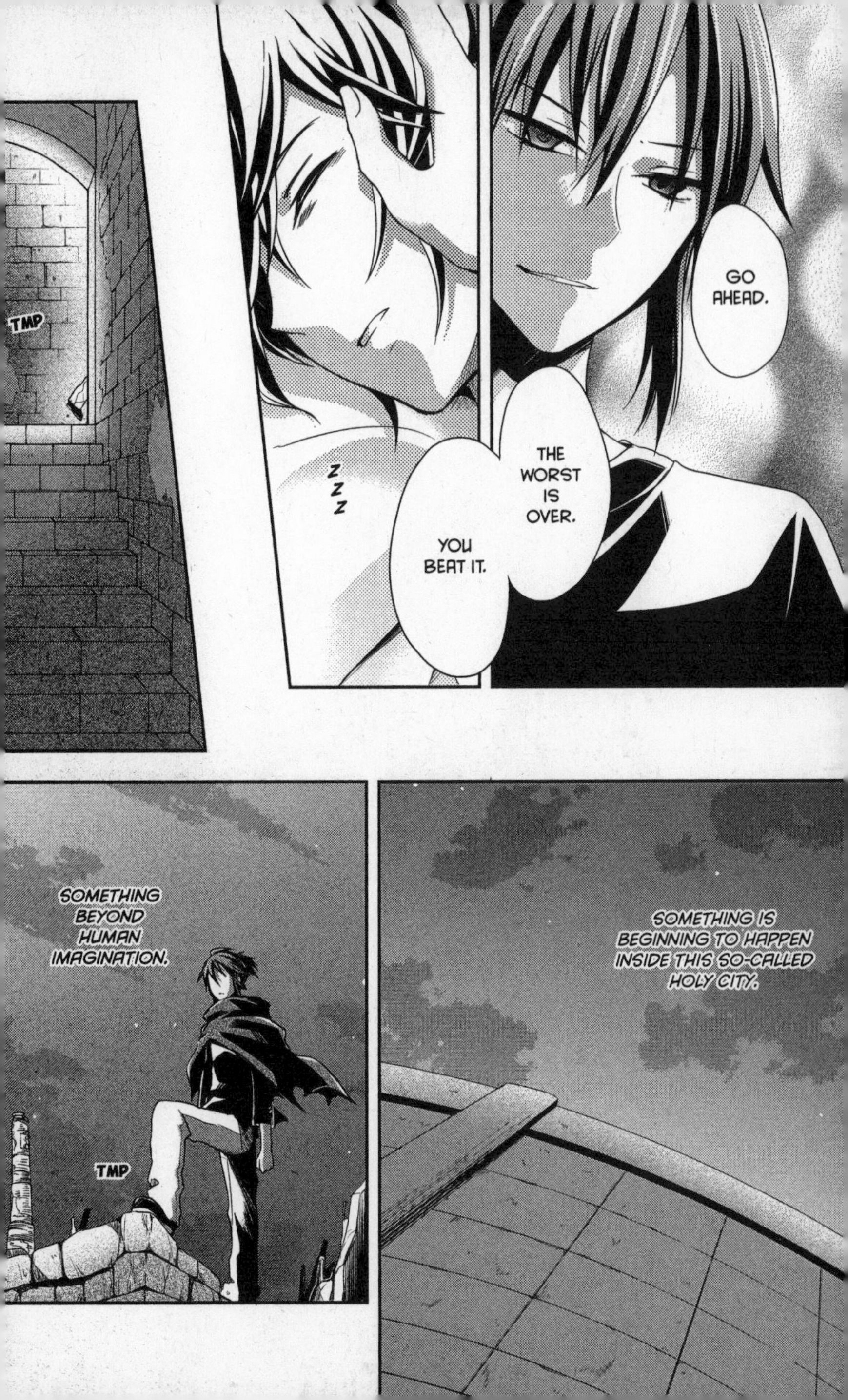
GO AHEAD.
THE WORST IS OVER.
YOU BEAT IT.
Z Z Z
TMP
SOMETHING IS BEGINNING TO HAPPEN INSIDE THIS SO-CALLED HOLY CITY.
SOMETHING BEYOND HUMAN IMAGINATION.
TMP

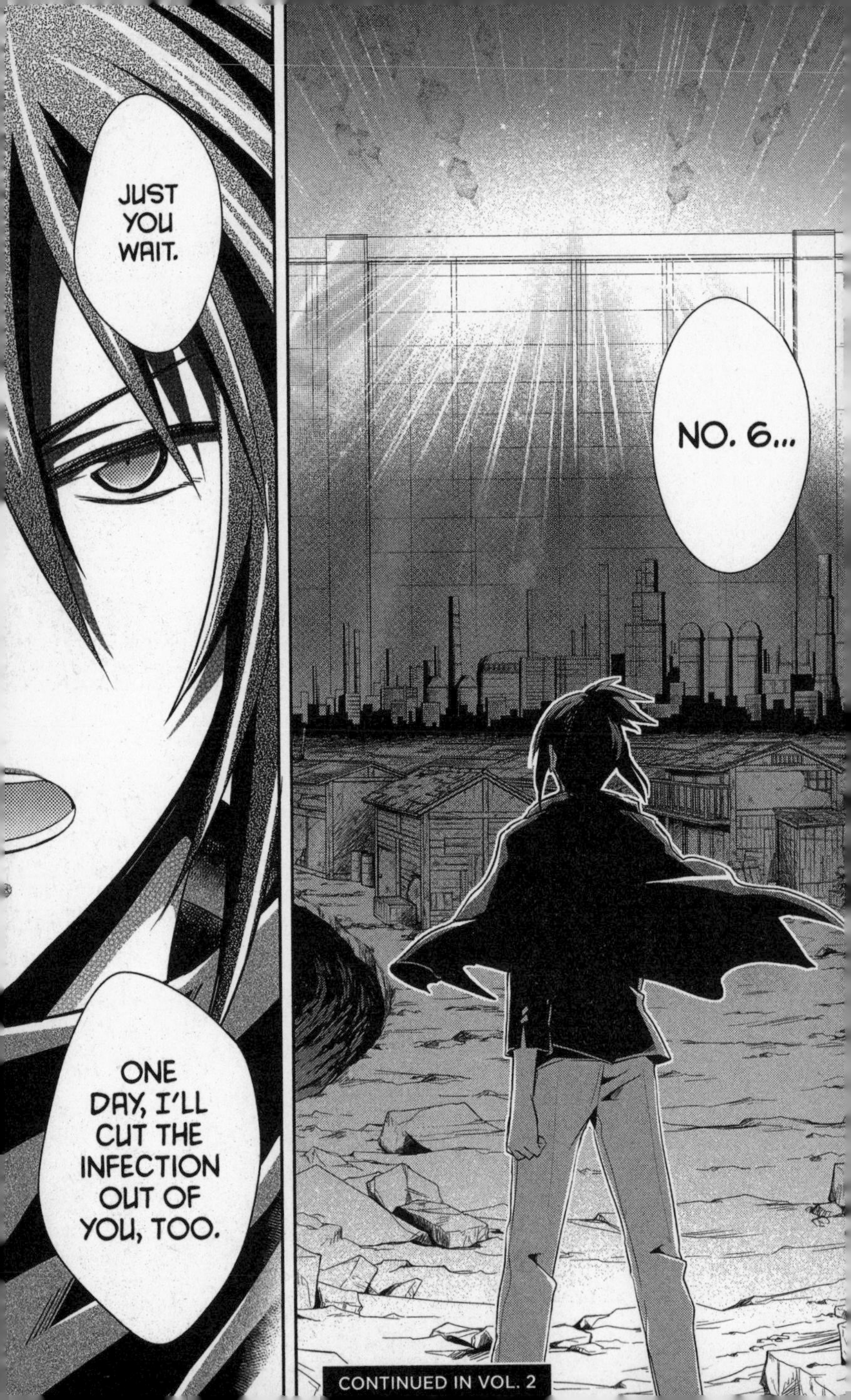
NO. 6...
JUST YOU WAIT.
ONE DAY, I'LL CUT THE INFECTION OUT OF YOU, TOO.
CONTINUED IN VOL. 2

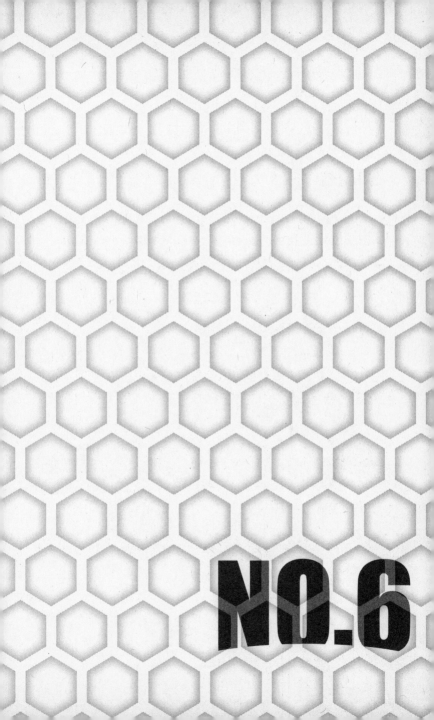

NO.6

Hello, everyone. Asano here.

The Volume 1 comic paperback of "No. 6" is finally on sale. I originally wrote the novels almost ten years ago.

At the time, I couldn't even imagine that this series would become a manga. In the execution, Kino was good enough to draw not only Rat and Shion, but also the entire world of No. 6 in a fresh, beautiful, and cool way.
I am grateful from the bottom of my heart.

To tell the truth, I was curious how someone could ever illustrate this world I created in text, and I was a little nervous.

But Kino composed the world of No. 6 ever so carefully and meticulously, and brought it to life. Now it's a delight for me as a simple reader. That's how I feel.

From here on, I hope you look kindly upon this project of ours.

Atsuko Asano

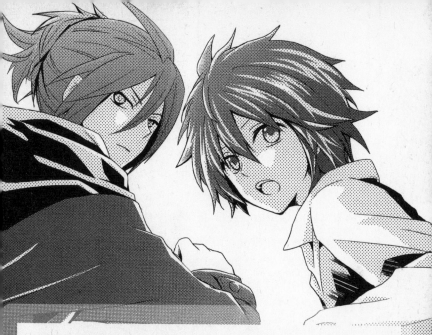

Hello. I am Hinoki Kino, the artist who had the privilege of drawing No. 6. First of all, I would like to extend my deepest thanks to Ms. Atsuko Asano, the mother and creator of not only Shion and Rat, but also the entire world of "No. 6"; to everyone in the editorial department at Kondansha's ARIA for providing this wonderful chance to a young, inexperienced artist like myself; and to everyone else who worked on this project.

To the editorial staff, the anime staff, and everyone else who supported from the shadows: I know I caused a lot of trouble, but I was only able to draw because you shared your help and wisdom with me.

I was so happy to have the chance to work on a series I love by an author I love. From the moment I first started to read it, I couldn't stop. I was sucked into the world of No. 6 and could not escape! As I composed the rough drafts, I thought, "I've got to put this scene in! And that scene!" When I was finally finished, I had overrun my page allotment by thirty pages! Many times over, my editor and I wept as we trimmed down the resulting pages. It's a memory that pains my heart. Those of you who are starting with the comics version of No. 6, go back to the original novels and compare.

I am sure some of you will say I drew the world of No. 6 wrong, or that my interpretation of the story was all wrong, but I still hope you enjoy it as a different version of the same story.

The character designs by toi8 were so cute, so cool, that I wish I could make them move in a more animated way!

I'm still unseasoned, but I'm putting everything I've got into it, and I'm grateful to have you all watching over me.

In the next volume, we enter West Block! Lots of new characters appear in vol. 2, so keep an eye out for it.

Hinoki Kino

SPECIAL THANKS!

Atsuko Asano

Everyone on the editorial staff
at Kodansha's Aria
My editor K-gata
toi8
Everyone on the anime staff
Everyone at NARTI;S

*Drawing help
Honma
Tsunocchi
Parko
Sayuri Noguchi

*3D
Lin Wankui
*Color background help
dominori
*Comics
Megi

Suzuka Oda
Minezawa
Ten Nakamura
H Iwata
K Fuji
I Hikaru
K-n
My family
Everyone else who helped out

And all of the readers!

Thank you very much!

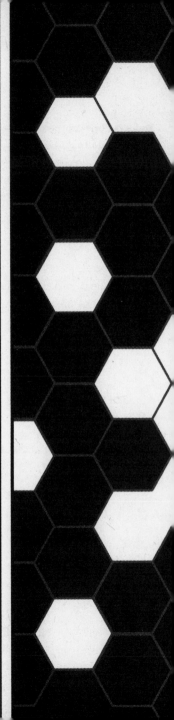

lansha Comics Trade Paperback Original.

shed in the United States by Kodansha Comics, an imprint of Kodansha
Publishing, LLC, New York.

cation rights for this English edition arranged through Kodansha Ltd.,
).

published in Japan in 2011 by Kodansha Ltd., Tokyo
978-1-61262-355-9

ed in the United States of America.

.kodanshacomics.com

5 5 4 3 2

slator: Jonathan Tarbox & Kazuko Shimizu
ring: Christy Sawyer
ng: Ben Applegate